LIVED IT WRONG

Gerard Menuhin

LIVED IT WRONG

An autobiography

Reconquista Press

Front cover: Gerard Menuhin, *Missing Spokes* (detail)

© 2020 Reconquista Press
www.reconquistapress.com

ISBN: 978-1-912853-16-8

FOR MYSELF

I wish I loved the Human Race;
I wish I loved its silly face;
I wish I liked the way it walks;
I wish I liked the way it talks;
And when I'm introduced to one,
I wish I thought "What Jolly Fun!"

Sir Walter Alexander Raleigh

CONTENTS

Foreword		13
I	Join the Dots	15
II	Light to Dark	31
III	A Life of Duty or You Can Have Your Cake and Eat It Too	51
IV	Prep School and Cramming	67
V	Eton	81
VI	Mykonos, Mothers	89
VII	More Eton	103
VIII	Paris and Roland	119
IX	Film and Frustration	127
X	Progress	147
XI	Stanford	155
XII	Paris Again, New York, Los Angeles	173
XIII	Be Careful What You Wish For, You Might Get It	185
XIV	Mykonos Again	187
XV	Gstaad, an Overview and Retrospective	193
XVI	Misguided Novel, Misguided Proposal	201
XVII	Marriage	209
XVIII	Albania	215
XIX	My Mother Again	221
XX	Dallying	229
XXI	Brussels	235
XXII	Training in Architectural Restoration	245
XXIII	Divorce, New Interests, Old Resentments and a Minor Achievement	249
XXIV	Switzerland, Overview and Retrospective	257
XXV	Zurich	265
XXVI	My Father	273
XXVII	Foundations and Substructures	279
XXVIII	Musings	289
XXIX	Ending Up	293

FOREWORD

You know when you buy a new product or appliance there's usually a greeting in the manual like 'Congratulations on buying the etc., etc.'? Well, I can't congratulate you for buying this book. You probably bought it because you expected to read an intimate assessment of Yehudi Menuhin, by one of his own sons. YM was a great man, one of the outstanding figures of the 20th century. That is also my opinion. However, the instances in which his greatness was apparent to me do not belong in the present record. This book is about me and my experiences. So, if you don't want to read about me — admittedly a far less compelling subject than YM — I suggest you ask for a refund.

Chapter I

JOIN THE DOTS

Christening, with Nurse Craigie, September 1948.

Playing with sprinkler on the lawn at Alma, 1950.

These are photographs, rather than an account, because I can't remember how it was. A photograph may lie, but it's hard enough getting a child of two to stand still, let alone to pose, and there is also something absolutely natural about these snaps. This is just a child. His world is natural, as it should be.

Inherent in every child are the seeds of its eventual development and potential success. The child only needs guidance, in how to evacuate its bowels, how to tie its laces, how to cross the street, how not to offend people, how to stay out of trouble. In fact, in all the rules that boil down to one simple dictum: do it because it works. These rules are therefore civic conventions; they help the child to join society, which is in most cases essential.

Unfortunately, over and above these essentials, nearly all children receive instruction in how to please their parents, instruction which inevitably supersedes the more valuable, long term, general training. In the old days, a moral tone was added to this: the child who succeeded in pleasing its parents, for instance by being seen and not heard, was 'good'. (My generation was the intermediate one, between 'seen and not heard' and today's 'everywhere too loud and opinionated'.) All children wish to please their parents because they love them, to start with at least. So they all cooperate unwittingly in their own undoing and are all, in their respective degrees, lost.

In this sense parents have it made. The progenitors, the gods from whom all goodness flows, the wisest, best looking, tallest, strongest folk in their child's universe — they really shouldn't be able to go wrong. But they nearly always do, because they seek to impose rules that make their own lives easier, or, with the best will in the world, that no longer apply to the next generation.

In fact, parents have very little to teach their children. Their chief duties consist in being guides and sounding boards only. They should be constantly alert and aware, attentive and concerned; never intrusive or redundant. This alone is a tall order. These qualities are already sufficiently difficult to achieve, without seeking to provide the Wisdom of Solomon and the pedagogical precision of a Regius professor. Most parents do not seek to be such, but only to be always right and to control the tiny world immediate to them because they have so little effect on the larger world around them. Besides, they created their children, didn't they? And what they created they own and should manage. Instead of taking joy in their children's progress, their aptitudes and successes, many parents view these as challenges to their authority and competition to their own abilities. In short, 'They fuck you up, your mum and dad, they may not mean to, but they do', as Philip Larkin famously wrote.

It is not an original observation to say that one cannot distinguish one's earliest recollections from a photograph or from an older acquaintance's account of it. All I know is that the baby in the nurse's arms looks normal, and that the little boy playing with water, judging from his smile, seems to be getting the pleasure one would expect a two-year-old to derive from this pastime. For contrast, a film maker or image-shuffler might juxtapose these pictures with one of the frowning twelve-year-old.

Not best pleased, with my tutor, Gstaad, 1960.

Besides possessing the spur to their own advancement, all children are naturally curious. So was I. However, repeated and powerful doses of repression, reprimand, embarrassment and humiliation, and their result: inhibition, stifled my curiosity, until there really wasn't any left. If there was something I wanted to do, I analysed it until I discovered that there were as many reasons for not doing it as for doing it, so that it had no special value after all.

People need a quest to drive them. I came up with a few, not terribly invigorating, quests; they faded with time and failure. Now I don't care about anything very much, except perhaps about aesthetics and superficial courtesy. That is, I am easily offended by ugliness, in sight as in sound, and I am intolerant of discourtesy, while taking insincerity for granted.

With my maternal grandmother at the door of her home, Mulberry House.

LIVED IT WRONG

Summer 1954, Los Gatos, California

Alma, California.

The scent of hot brush, of juniper, pervades the air. The smell of juniper will be in my nostrils from then on, a sense memory which brings back those happy days at once. Hansel or Gretel, one of the rather miserable Siamese cats has got lost again. I pedal my yellow metal bulldozer in the large circular sandpit and then along the brick path to the garage. Carl, the caretaker, is mowing the lawn. Schwester Marie, our Swiss nanny known as Ma, has found a rattlesnake and Carl chops its head off with a spade. It continues to wriggle for quite a while. He slits it open to show the eggs inside — or is this from National Geographic or even from the first film I remember seeing: *The Living Desert*? *The Living Desert* (playing at the Saratoga cinema) contained scenes of cruelty among insects and animals. Possibly this was my first or one of my first insights into the unfairness of life. In the film, a tarantula behaved as a tarantula behaves, as did a scorpion.

Carl drives me, in his Ford 150 truck, to 'The Boys' next door for painting lessons. Next door involves driving down the mile-long driveway, along the dam at the base of the valley, and up the next driveway to Cathedral Oaks, so named for the magnificent old trees which shade the house. Frank and George are a homosexual couple. Their acquaintance with my mother goes back to the 1930s, when they attended concerts at my maternal grandmother's house (Mulberry House) in Chelsea. In their over-decorated home, filled with volumes of collected but probably never read classics, The Boys labour in a variety of disciplines, in oil, in gesso, illustrating books, ornamenting furniture, boxes and other objects, like 18th century craftsmen. They also have an orchard of persimmons, which I learn to eat only when they are ripe, so as not to make my mouth pucker up.

Carl drives me to school where I attend first grade. During my first days at school, I am mocked because I wear shorts; thereafter, I am allowed to wear long trousers. The school in Los Gatos is a typical American single-storey block, set in a couple of acres of grounds. Education, if one could call it that, is hardly arduous. In fact, my teacher begs my mother to persuade me to do my homework. We eat lunch out of our lunchboxes, lined up on the concrete, under the shelter of the roof. Every morning, we face the flag in the corner of the room and recite the Pledge of Allegiance. I sit several rows back, behind a girl I am infatuated with called Judy, who has long black hair. One afternoon, Carl drives me to Judy's house. She lives in a rundown neighbourhood. It is my only visit of its kind. Judy's brother has hit another boy with an airgun pellet and so we don't play much.

I also take French lessons with a monk at a local monastery, but — to forestall the expected inquiry — I don't think he 'interfered' (quaint expression) with me.

In those days, my grandparents occupied an elegant property in Monte Sereno, on the other side of Los Gatos, with gates and an oval drive. Here, I remember becoming aware of them for the first time. I sat in my high chair and my grandfather fed me with the encouraging words: "Open the garage door so the car can drive in." Christmas, we celebrated first at my grandparents, where a friend of theirs would dress up as Santa Claus and pretend to have come down the chimney, and a second time at home.

23 July 1954

Virtually my whole class has been invited to my sixth birthday, which, because it is organized by Carl and Ma, is a splendid affair in every sense, although Carl shows films in the music room of me when I was younger and without my clothes on, which is amusing for the parents, but less for me. We also play hide and seek, and I hide in the culvert under the drive. Among my presents is a fire engine with a long retractable ladder. I am proud when a classmate describes this present in school on the next day. (What happened to this vehicle? Wasn't I attached to it? Why didn't it accompany us to Europe? Doctor, can my problematic development be traced to the loss of this toy?)

Lorraine and I are exploring around the pool houses. Lorraine suddenly shouts that she sees Tinker Bell. I try so hard to see her too that I'm almost sure I do, flying among the irises. Lorraine is my grandmother-approved girlfriend. Nonnina approves of her because she's intelligent. Lorraine is vivacious and has lots of red-blond hair. Her parents are old friends of Nonnina & Nonnetto. Nonnina is my father's opinionated mother. True, she has travelled and has iron self-discipline (I discovered recently, in a cedar chest I inherited, the girdle of fabric with which she ensured that her waist did not exceed 22 inches or 56 centimetres), but she awards herself far too much sagacity, and therefore, authority. She has got away with this attitude throughout the upbringing of her own children and to their cost. Fostered by my father's meteoric career, for which my grandmother no doubt takes credit, her unbending character, so admired by those who don't know her, is really nothing more than a severe personality disorder. Lorraine's mother, because she defers to my grandmother, has almost attained the status of a confidant. Nonnina has already half-seriously determined that I will marry Lorraine. My mother and father don't seem concerned one way or the other. Lorraine is allowed to sleep over in my bedroom because it's my birthday. After Ma puts the lights out, Lorraine volunteers to show me hers if I show her mine. She's eleven and already has hair. This is quite a thrill.

My grandparents with their dogs.

I am in bed for my nap and my sixteen-year-old half-sister, Zamira, comes in. All of a sudden, she pulls the sheet over my head and sits on the end of it. She is a very fat girl and her weight pins the sheet down so that I cannot move. I have the feeling of being trapped, smothered. I panic and begin to shout. Ma hears me and runs in. Zamira pretends that we were just playing a game. I wake up dazed from my nap and run into the corner of a cupboard. Carl drives Ma and me down to Dr. Jones, on Santa Cruz Avenue, who puts stitches in my right eyebrow.

Following my father's divorce, Zamira chooses to stay with him, while her brother, Krov, stays with their mother. Zamira, as first-born and moreover female, shares with all other women in my father's eyes a special position. Zamira knows she's 'speshull' and profits from this preference over her lifetime.

My half-sister Zamira with my mother.

My half-brother Krov.

I don't know what gives this house its distinctive atmosphere. Perhaps it's the furnishings, which impart a solemn, tranquil silence: the grass cloth walls, the thick dark brown stair carpet, the huge, dim living room and the bright, multi-windowed dining room with its glass and green wrought iron furniture. The grownups sit at a central table, while we children and the nanny sit at a smaller glass and bamboo table. (I kept the smaller table later and moved it from apartment to apartment and then to the house in Oregon, where I left it along with all my other inherited furniture.) There is some activity in the nursery, playroom and kitchen, but in the communal rooms, the elegant furnishings — most of them chosen and purchased from Gumps in San Francisco by my father's first wife — slumber expectantly but in vain; my parents very rarely entertain.

May, 1954

This morning my father comes into the room Ma shares with my younger brother and cuffs me. It doesn't hurt much, as it's only a smack on my bottom. But the fact that this gentle, distant man hits me at all is momentous, as he never intervenes in our upbringing or even enters Ma's room. It is also just about the only conscious physical contact I have recently had with him. He hits me because I have been disrespectful to my mother. I have called her some name and then made it worse by trying to explain, using the word 'she' to describe my mother. On top of my original sin, this incenses him. "Don't call your mother 'she'," he explodes, and adds for good measure the canon my brother and I are to hear innumerable times: "Your mother is wonderful." Naturally, there is no recourse against a wonder, so we are helpless. My mother, on the other hand, is often openly critical of my father, as this suits her scheme of being a misused wife.

Now and then, I have piano lessons with Sylvia Nordby, who sits next to me on a second stool. If she were not so pretty, I doubt that she would be able to teach me anything at all.

Charlie is my tutor. He has a weasel face. He teaches me to count with matchsticks. Charlie is strange; he tries to train a racoon he has caught, dragging it along on walks by a string. Much later my grandmother tells me that Charlie had to leave after he was discovered taking photographs of a naked boy (not myself, at least I don't think so). Charlie is from England because English tutors are better, as everyone knows, and also because my mother is uncomfortable in California. Although she has gone through the war years in Europe and comes from a country still in the throes of rationing, she's unable to relax and enjoy the advantages of abundance and simplicity; of uneducated but uncomplicated, if occasionally pretentious, folk.

This is mainly because my mother's objective in life is to make herself pitied, she's a professional martyr. Even under normal circumstances, in her beloved London, it would be hard to commiserate with her, but in the paradise of plenty that is California, in this beautiful, spacious house, married to this phenomenally successful, good-looking, solicitous and generous man, her attitude is simply ridiculous. She misses the English voice, perhaps someone to whom to relate her ballet experiences. She is out of her depth and unwilling to adapt. She brings over the driver, Leach, so she has at least two comforting English confederates. Although they cannot discuss ballet with her, they know enough to listen to her when she drones on about it. Another thorn in her side is Carl's wife Ruth, who is red-headed, and therefore, according to my mother, notoriously over-sexed, and has designs on every man. She also contradicts my mother's Latin gardening lore. My mother's life is made even more onerous by Ma's spinsterish nature. Ma (dour), unmarried and almost forty, following my brother's birth, replaces Hedy (cheerful), who, in turn, is replaced by Juliana (harmless). In the absence of my parents, my world revolves around these Swiss nannies. Faced with the choice of staying with her children in her fully staffed and luxurious house, or travelling with her husband all over the world and sharing his acclaim, she chooses the latter. She writes weekly postcards to me, with Beatrix Potter motifs, explaining how fraught her life is, what with the packing and unpacking. Ma's letters to her (of which I found a few recently) report on our progress and health.

Winter 1954

A trip to London. As usual, on the way to the airport, I admire the Wonderloaf next to the Bayshore Freeway, endlessly being sliced on its elevated stand. Another Constellation flight, during which the engine vibrations make me vomit. We stay at Claridges, where my mother has known the doorman 'since the war'. Sometimes we stay here, and sometimes at Lady Crosfield's immense mansion, 'Witanhurst', in Highgate. I accompanied my parents so often during my earliest years that my mother used to say that I had crossed the Atlantic four times before I was two years old. Lady Crosfield ('Aunt Domini', to us) is Greek. She married the late Sir Arthur Crosfield, a soap magnate and, between the wars, used to hold famous tennis parties in her grounds which form the largest private estate in London, after Buckingham Palace. Lady Crosfield is mean. Her house is under-heated, and her notoriously underpaid staff consists only of 'chef' and his wife, who are also Greek. Ma, Jeremy and I always stay in a large apartment at the top of the house, and my parents have a suite on the first floor. The property is fun to explore and there are some enticing rhododendron thickets. Exceptionally, I can play with chef's son, who is about my age.

I catch chickenpox and pass it on to my father, who is quite ill.

25 December 1954

I am compelled by my parents and by good manners to accede to Lady Crosfield's request to sing 'We Three Kings of Orient Are', a Christmas carol, by the tree in the hall. I can't remember what kind of a present I receive in return, but only that it is inadequate compensation for the embarrassment of having to sing.

My father's colleague, Nathan Milstein, has praised the qualities of the Swiss village of Gstaad. Accordingly, my parents rent Chalet Les Frênes, across from the Palace Hotel. It's oldish and rather dark. One day, I am introduced to what will become my new home, Chalet Flora, a boarding school.

31 November, 1955
Los Gatos

My memories of school include being disguised as a pirate for Halloween; my brother Jeremy, as a pixie. On another occasion, we are shown a B&W cartoon about tooth care. Bad tooth care results in guerrillas attacking the teeth with plaque, which must then be scoured off by fighter planes. It's a fun film.

My grandparents' house, their third home in Los Gatos, is on a hillside at 191 Kimble Avenue. It's a sort of Caucasian retreat, possibly the closest my grandmother could get to the life she would lead, if she lived in her native Crimean habitat. There are hints, in parts, of a kind of caravanserai, or perhaps the interior of an Arabian tent, in which all horizontal and many vertical surfaces are covered by rugs, interspersed on the walls by ancient black and white photos and bookcases, and on the floors, by colourfully covered mattresses and cushions. The scent of cloves permeates the house, emanating from a bowl in the living room. When my grandfather isn't writing his virulent diatribes against the Zionists, he's cultivating his citrus and avocado trees. My grandmother is writing to her friends, cooking sometimes rather peculiar dishes, or entertaining neighbours and their children. She loves children and nothing more than to organize Easter egg hunts or other traditional pastimes for them.

Near the hilltop is the Sacred Heart Novitiate which produces really terrible wines and brandy, the only alcohol my grandparents keep, although they don't drink it themselves. (My grandfather very occasionally treats himself to a Pabst beer, a typically watery American brew, when he makes himself scrambled eggs with matzos crumbled into them.) The brandy comes in handy for the Italian cleaning woman, who sometimes whines: *"Posso farmi una piccola bevita?"* However, if one gets to the grapes before the novices have fooled with them, as we boys do with Ma, they can be hung on clothes racks to ripen outdoors. Ma grows watermelons and squash in her vegetable garden, behind one of the cottages above the pool. On a trip to Yosemite, where brown bears come up to our cabin to rummage in the garbage cans, she digs up a tree she claims is rare and we take it home, despite Carl's disapproval.

A day at the beach. Nonnina, Nonetto and I drive to Santa Cruz in their black Buick Special. Nonetto is a very slow driver, cautious at the wheel, as he is in all things, except of course in his political opinions. We have provisions in case we should break down during the half-hour journey. However, we crest the mountains on Highway 17 without incident, roll down to the ocean, and park on the pier. Above the beach looms a roller coaster, but I barely notice it, and although Nonnina might be spirited enough to give it a go, Nonetto would get a heart attack just considering it.

I do not venture into the sea, as I can hardly swim, despite the beautiful pool at home. This quintessential Californian accessory forms an irregular kidney-configuration, with a long shallow end, into which all manner of sea life is painted, separated by a rope with large orange plastic lozenges from a very deep end, over which hangs the diving board. My father has asked Vera Magidoff, his biographer's wife, to teach me to swim. She may be doing her best, but her personal charm does not match Sylvia's, so my progress in the water is even slower than at the keyboard. In return for at least imitating a passable breaststroke-cum-dog-paddle, I receive an inflatable canoe.

At the beach, the sand is clean and there are few people, I'm quite happy with my bucket and spade. At noon, we return to the pier for clam chowder, passing the thriving fish market with its piles of exotic and colourful fish on ice, where Nonnina buys her fish and exchanges banalities in Italian with the proprietor.

My grandparents were perfect in their roles and it must have come as a great disappointment to them when their son and their grandchildren moved permanently to Europe. Life under the dependable Californian sun, in a property of 300 acres, without the slightest inhibiting factor, was not the most helpful preparation for the kind of European school to which my parents in their infinite wisdom and total ignorance had condemned me.

Chapter II

LIGHT TO DARK

Early Education: Chalet Flora, Gstaad, Switzerland

It would be an exaggeration to say, when, in 1956, I heard that the liner *Andrea Doria* had collided with the *Stockholm*, and had sunk with great loss of life, that I fervently wished I had been among the drowned. But I was not happy.

This news reached me on the balcony of the school in Gstaad which I shared with about twenty other unfortunate children who had been disposed of here by absent or uncaring parents. I had just turned eight and had originally been consigned to the school at about six and a half, in improvisatory fashion, as a temporary expedient while my parents made up their minds about moving to Europe. This neo-Gothic excuse for an educational establishment was camouflaged in a large chalet, from the balconies of which hung boxes of red geraniums in deceptive cheer, like a backdrop to *The Sound of Music*. For the few parents who ever bothered to visit their children, the geraniums probably had a reassuring effect ("so typically Swiss, isn't it, dear?"). But for their children, life behind the window boxes was grim. 'Tante' Flora, the owner, headmistress and public face of the school, was a sort of human counterpart to the geraniums. She was a grey-haired biddy, in her fifties I imagine, who radiated the grandmotherly aura with which baking companies like to promote 'Home Baked Cookies'. She received parents and prospective victims in her corner office, a cosy boudoir furnished with antiques and chintz-covered armchairs. If she did not actually offer to knit them a little grey cardigan like hers, it was only because the role she played must have been sufficiently convincing without such embellishments. Only her pupils ever met the rest of the gang, as fine a collection of perverts and third rate pedagogues as ever graced a Swiss version of the school in *Decline and Fall*. In fact, they all gave the impression of being bad-tempered and miserable.

This sad and embittered crew consisted of three women and a forlorn man, a personality so erased that I cannot remember his name. Probably long accustomed to being commanded by the women, he was the least offensive of the bunch, wearing a perpetually hangdog expression and teaching geography in a defeated manner. Mlle Schwam was a grey and white, bun-haired, absorbent figure who was rumoured to have some medical qualifications. Prim little Mlle Coin, a particularly nasty example of French-Swiss spinsterish schoolmarmery, had a mouth pursed as tight as an anal sphincter. She liked to pick on one of the children and shame him in front of the others. The power behind the throne and the most sinister of all was Mlle Crop. Tall and wiry, a leather-faced chain smoker with a crew cut, she had a gold skiing medal and a fondness for corporal punishment. She was also Auntie Flora's lover. Flora and Crop were ideally set up to play good cop/bad cop; when one failed to get the desired results, or the infraction was considered too serious, the other administered the correction. (Names altered to protect the guilty.)

Presumably, parents were shown the swimming pool and tennis court as evidence of physical exercise in the school's curriculum, but the pool was never filled and no child ever set foot on the decaying tennis court. While we learnt to ski in the winters, in the summers only desultory attempts at calisthenics attested to this undertaking. However, the fees could not have been too paltry, as Crop, probably a partner in the racket, built herself a chalet on the proceeds after retirement.

From the instant the front door closed with finality behind me and I became aware of the pervasively rank smell of the aging black and white checked linoleum which paved the ground floor, despair seized me. Everything about this school was new and unpleasant. For one thing it was a boarding school. For another, everyone except me spoke French, even the English brother and sister and the Brazilian boy and the twin Venezuelan girls. As the only monolingual child in the school, it behoved me to learn French quickly in order to make myself understood. Perhaps it was my musical ear, or just desperation and fear of the teachers, but with Mlle Coin's menacing encouragement, I succeeded in doing this in record time.

We children slept in four dormitories, segregated by sex but not by age. I shared a room with six other boys. My bed-neighbour, Serge, the son of a Brazilian diplomat, at thirteen, was the biggest boy in the school and liked to prove his physical superiority by challenging the others to box him. He would not accept a refusal. When Serge was not demonstrating his version of the Queensberry rules on a smaller boy, he would invite one into his bed to be farted at. I preferred the olfactory to the physical assault.

I was totally unprepared for the rigours of a European boarding school. It would be hard to think of an educational experience that differed more radically from the carefree air of First Grade in sunny California, alternating with the voluptuous house, than this sinister boarding establishment, with its band of disreputable educators.

At first the shock of the change just confused me, but as the routine set in, I became stupefied by misery. I had always been a spirited, outgoing child, but I felt so lonely and homesick — despite having never experienced the warmth of a normal home — that I thought I would never smile again.

I dreaded the classroom where the letters of the alphabet had to be written in French, just so, between three sets of lines, two lower ones close together for the lower-case letters and a higher line for the capitals; I dreaded the bathroom surveillance by the lean headmistress; I dreaded the dormitory where Serge waited to ambush me; I dreaded the dining room where, seated on the bench at one of two long tables, I had to finish everything on my plate, no matter how much I hated it. I still remember the night they served chestnuts with cream, perhaps a downmarket version of Mont Blanc. Chestnuts are one of the few things I cannot eat; their musty odour induces in me immediate nausea. Naturally, this weakness was impossible to explain to whichever of the harridans was presiding over the table that night. I toyed with the chestnuts until everyone else had left the room and then, putting them into my pockets, I stole down the gloomy, linoleum-infested corridor to the fetid loo off the changing room, locked myself in, opened the window, and threw them far out into the snowy night. I think I feared that flushing them down the toilet might block the system and give me away.

The kaleidoscope of memory exposes various unhappy incidents: queuing in the first floor communal bathroom to have my hair brushed vigorously and powder applied to my scalp, after an outbreak of lice; a girl from the dormitory down the corridor catching me naked on my way back from the bathroom and an older boy rebuking me: it was wrong for a boy to show himself naked to a girl. This had never occurred to me. Or a Belgian boy and I, confined to a dormitory for an hour during the afternoon, for talking in class (years later, I received a letter from him, suggesting a reunion for therapeutic reasons of all those who had suffered at Chalet Flora). Or the compulsory afternoon communal nap, when we had to lie perfectly still, with our eyes closed on a row of mattresses in a sheltered area under the schoolhouse. According to French-Swiss belief, children of six and seven must nap after lunch.

Soon after my induction into this school, my mother came to visit. I clung to her legs. "Please don't make me stay," I begged her. My mother soon set me straight. "If you knew what my life was like, you wouldn't ask me that. Your childhood is the best time of your life. Imagine what it's like for me to have to worry about you all the time." I had not considered this. It did seem unfair of me to add my own little worries to my mother's already enormous burdens. My mother had often told me how she had to spend all her time looking after my father, who tended to lose his hats and gloves, and how she had to remind him of just about everything.

My mother sent me a weekly postcard from wherever she happened to be, with pictures of pussycats or exotic views, always explaining how tedious and disagreeable her life was with all the people she was forced to meet and all the hats and gloves she had to pick up for my father, and helpfully correcting my spelling. Much later, I came to realize that these dolorous postcards were a standard item she sent to everyone, including her staff, perhaps as a way of trying to dispel the impression that her life was congenial. She set such store by this futile dissimulation that she probably came to believe it herself and, indeed, enjoyed none of the extraordinary advantages of an existence replete with pleasure and new experiences.

Although they were rarely there, my parents had rented Chalet Wasserngrat, above the village (more cheerful than the first), so I was allowed to go home on weekends. Ma would accompany me there and back on foot, which took about twenty minutes. I liked the change, but my unhappiness increased almost to desperation when the time came to return to school. A typical Bernese, Ma was a great walker and outdoors person, and here, she was back in her element. She was a taciturn woman, but she nevertheless took seriously her duty to look after our health. My brother's presence during this period has faded from memory, but he must have participated in this exercise. Come rain or shine, there was bound to be at least one three-hour walk during the weekend. These trudges could be compared favourably to Sławomir Rawicz's *The Long Walk*, a fascinatingly horrific account of a Polish prisoner of war's escape from a Siberian labour camp, which did not lighten my mood. When I was not reading in my room, I used to listen to my father's recording of the Mendelssohn or Bruch concertos, which were on the same record, or to the Beethoven violin concerto. I can still recall clearly the position of the fireplace, the record player, and the bookcase close by. These sentimental strains, echoing through the nearly empty house, marked my

Sunday afternoons, until Ma called me to put on my shoes and go back to the nightmare. Invariably, a terrible anguish seized me. For many years, I preferred not to hear these magnificent pieces, for fear of being overcome by that familiar stupor of dejection and forsakenness.

My own instruction at the pianoforte hung by a thread, consisting of attempts to learn a minuet by Couperin, with the help of a musical martinet of the traditional francophone variety.

My birthdays fell during the summer vacation and my mother organized these just as she always did, ceremoniously. On my eighth birthday, she told me that I could invite whomever I wanted among my friends from school. When I informed her that there was no one I wanted to invite, my mother insisted that I must know someone. So I invited the Venezuelan twins, with their matching shocks of sheer black hair, who were harmless and whom I pitied because they had to learn their Catholic catechism, and they sat decorously at table and opened their presents when they were told to and carefully ate a piece of cake each and exclaimed politely when the table fireworks blew paper hats and party favours all over the place, as though they didn't probably have bigger and better parties at home, or maybe they didn't. At six, as arranged, they were picked up by a driver. They both said thank-you to my mother as they left. "What nice, well-behaved little girls," my mother said, "I'm glad you know how to pick your friends."

When I was older, I sometimes walked back to school by myself. I remember once being caught in a storm near a sawmill, into which I naturally ran. The Italians who worked at the mill were sitting on logs and eating their lunch. One of them called me over and shared his sandwiches with me while I waited for the rain to stop. I had had little or no experience of strangers and the man's generosity, compared to the imperious and callous treatment I was accustomed to at school and at home, touched me.

So I tried not to cry too much. If this was the best time of my life, I dreaded to think what I had to look forward to. When the school crocodile walked around the village and passed in front of my parents' house, I averted my eyes and forced myself not to wonder if they were there. I learned to ski and to speak French, and to keep my thoughts to myself, for whom was I to share them with? At lights out, I crawled thankfully into my bed, which had no pillows because, according to the French-Swiss, pillows were unhealthy to sleep on, and tried to obliterate my existence in sleep.

No child should ever have to feel so unhappy; no child of mine ever will. What is particularly regrettable about this kind of conditioning is not only the temporary unhappiness through which the child is compelled unnecessarily to pass, but the ineradicable impression of a grim, hostile world such an experience makes on it. It is in the most basic sense impractical for both parents and children, for the inhibitions imposed on an open, inquisitive mind are irreversible, and lead to a lifetime of anxiety. To kill the natural enthusiasm and curiosity which every young person possesses and which will provide the adult with essential aid and information, in order for the teacher conveniently to instil rote-learning, is not only cruel, it is a senseless waste of natural resources.

Until recently, I had explained to myself my parents' decision to keep me at this school by assuming their ignorance of its true nature. We would have been afraid to include grievances in our supervised Sunday letters home because Tante Flora checked them, allegedly for grammatical errors, before they were sent. I supposed that I had hardly protested to my parents about the school, because they seemed so inaccessible. Whatever I may have confided to Ma must either never have been passed on, or was ignored by them. Yet, in 1994, my mother, whose age and mental infirmity had caused her to drop her guard, confessed the incident when I had implored her not to send me back to this school and mentioned that Ma had added her weight, but that she "had felt that she had to be strong for both of us". She thus sought compassion from me for the suffering she had allegedly endured by refusing to remove me from the school, managing — in her own eyes at least — to attach this load too to the great weight she had been obliged to carry.

Although I have scant respect for such practices, about forty years later, on a trip to Portland (the only American city I really like), I visited a hypnotist a friend had mentioned, in order to see if I could recall these experiences, more precisely, to see if I had been abused. As I could have predicted, with the best will in the world, I could not succumb to hypnosis.

A sort of envoi to this chapter in my life was my last meeting with Tante Flora and Crop, who happened to be sitting in the row behind me during some event in the Seventies, at the local town hall. During the intermission, I turned around and spotted them, and, without hesitation, embraced them both. (What do you make of that, Doctor? The 'Stockholm Syndrome'?)

Apart from French and skiing, the only thing I learnt at that school was knitting. I am not sure whether this subject figured officially in the boys' curriculum, but, when Tante Flora read to some of us in a would-be cosy Sunday get-together, we were issued with needles and yarn, in order I fancy to keep us from fidgeting. I rather enjoyed this. Two years later, this bad habit of knitting was to get me into trouble on the beach in Santander, when my concentration on the multicoloured bookmark I was knitting for my mother caused me to overlook a berserk mutt which ran at me and bit me in the shoulder. It was while we were staying at the same hotel that I attempted to befriend the collie of one of the other guests and was rewarded with a nick between the eyes. These incidents may account for my fondness for dogs. Apropos animals attacking people, but in this case more deservedly, a matador who was also staying at the hotel was gored, not I am afraid at the bull-fight we were taken to see. We watched out of a window as he was returned to the hotel on a litter.

Chalet Flora, cheerless interlude.

I learnt to ski on wooden skies with a laminated plastic finish, standard for the Fifties. We wore comfortable ankle-high leather boots, fastened with laces. Over the years, these gave way, first to an elasticised band, then to metal clips. These boots looked quite elegant and one could walk in them almost as easily as in shoes. I finally exchanged them for a pair of wax or foam filled red plastic horrors at Alpine Meadows, Tahoe, in 1972. Skiing in Gstaad was very different sixty years ago. There were fewer runs of course, but there were also far fewer people. Those one saw were decent, quiet, conservatively dressed and unpretentious. The best among them skied beautifully, keeping their skis always close together. One winter we were all very impressed by the accomplishments of a one-legged Norwegian. Today, he would be run over immediately by some drunken snowboarder wearing plugged-in music, or would be encouraged to participate in the 'special' Olympics.

But I remember only courtesy then. People did not ski in order to show off their clothes or wacky fashions. Getting high at lunch and colliding with other skiers was not considered to be part of the fun. There were no lines, nor was one admitted to the slopes by automated turnstiles, but by local people, deferential and friendly. The unfortunate fact these days that they should be neither anymore is due to the trashy type of tourist or parvenu homeowner they have to deal with now, as much as to their own yokelism. In the Fifties, there was not a scrap of litter to be seen anywhere, nor a note of blaring music to be heard. The skier could stop without having to glance fearfully over their shoulder, and listen to the sound of snow falling off the trees in the perfect silence. No gigantic snow-clearing machines would appear suddenly, lights flashing, exhaust spewing darkly, out of the mist, leaving behind them tank tracks of ridged snow.

In those days, skis lasted for several years, their elasticity maintained by inserting small chocks of wood at mid-point between them. Their length was determined by aligning the ski-tip with the wrist (arm extended), and poles were armpit height. It is true that it took much longer to learn to control these skis and turning them required a considerable effort, but that was how one derived some exercise from downhill skiing. Most Swiss resorts were not on the crowd's maps then, if there was even a crowd. On the contrary: I count myself among the last of the truly privileged to have been able to experience this beautiful sport at the height of its individual appeal; before it became just another mass recreation, its every facet exploited for financial gain.

In retrospect, those years represent for me the last decades of individual expression. The foreigner who could not afford to visit a Swiss alpine resort could probably find equal if different diversion in his own country. Quite a few Europeans, in Britain as in Switzerland, still belonged to a caste and a generation which understood that it would not be judged nor should it judge by appearances. Novelty was not an attraction for its own sake; no single person, unknown a month previously and promoted to international attention by costly advertising campaigns but not necessarily through any intrinsic merit, could have revolutionized art, food or fashion. In Europe, the concept of marketing was not yet acknowledged as a profession. Clothes did not literally make a statement about the wearer: it would have been unthinkable then for anyone to give themselves credit for parading in attire or accessories which exposed and advertised the manufacturer's name. As customers, they would have rejected the label of 'consumer' as unacceptably demeaning. This is one definition of individuality: that a person be impervious to the blandishments of advertising but choose only with an eye to quality, based on personal experience. But you try to explain that to the apps-people *'made from plastic in a mould'* (Iron Butterfly, 1968), brimming with instant Facebooking, or gleaned from a new generation of dedicated idlers called 'influencers'.

August 1956

My parents, brother, half-sister and I, and Ma, are staying at a beach house in Lerici, on the Adriatic. The house has been found for us by Iris Origo, née Cutting, the American wife of the Marchese Origo. Iris and my parents met originally in 1949. My mother is so struck by Iris's praise of 'Schwester Marie', her daughters' Swiss nanny, in her book, *War in Val d'Orcia*, that she resolves to hire her to look after my brother and me. A successful author herself, Iris is staying with her stepfather, the writer Percy Lubbock, who has a property on the cliffs nearby. Something I say prompts him to prophesy — unforgettably for my mother — that I will be a writer.

Well, according to Wikipedia's entry (about which I don't give a rat's arse), I'm 'a writer and Holocaust denier'. I'm nothing else worthy of note. Earlier entries allowed me a somewhat wider experience. I'm not a writer, of course, just someone of my generation who learnt to write decently, in the same way that earlier generations learnt to play an instrument perhaps. I could never earn my living by writing. The modern custom of defining someone by their presumed occupation, in order to ascribe to them a particular worth or interest, is just another sign of the ongoing degradation of the race. Such postage-stamp nomenclature is only acceptable in the context of a cocktail party, where the alcohol-infused clamour renders all but a split-second's exchange incomprehensible.

My father's biographer, the Russian Robert Magidoff, however, is a writer and is staying nearby, so that he can consult my father. When we children are not on the beach immediately below the house, we are being taken into Lerici on shopping expeditions by Ma. Forever after, I associate the sight, sound and smell of Vespa exhaust with a particular bend in the road near Lerici. One evening, as I am lying in bed at dusk, with the fireflies winging about the room, my half-sister enters and tries to persuade me that one of them is Tinker Bell. Unlike Lorraine, my half-sister is basically unsympathetic, so she doesn't stand a chance of convincing me. What is it with these girls, or has a film version of Peter Pan just appeared?

Autumn 1956

As I am wheeling my bicycle on my way back from the village, a couple of local yokel's sons pop out of a garden and begin to make fun of me, because of my foreignness, and threaten to steal my bicycle. Because there are two of them and because I am, in any case, very easily intimidated, I just put my head down and continue on my way, under the hail of their jeers. When I get back to the chalet, I go straight to my father's study (he is exceptionally at home) and tell him how I feel and why. He shows not the slightest understanding, sympathy or support. I'm disappointed. The humiliation and subsequent lack of explanation, comfort, or resolution of this experience takes root within me.

I sense a burgeoning, overwhelming hatred. So far, it's unformed, unexplained. I am fundamentally unhappy. I resent my younger brother because he can stay at home and learn the piano. He and I, perhaps because he is three years younger and because his life is pleasanter than mine, have little in common. He has an easy, captivating charm and few sorrows, as well as a chosen path: music.

I feel certain there's nothing I can look forward to. Perhaps if I didn't know what life could be like, if I hadn't experienced the freedom and brilliance of California, I wouldn't feel so abandoned. Whenever I recall that earthly paradise longingly, I have almost to push it physically out of my mind. My parents made it happen; they marooned me at this excuse for a school, this outhouse of education, so I hate them. This is a pivotal betrayal, by those in whom the ultimate trust of their children resides. When they respond impatiently and uncomprehendingly to my frequent sulks, I go up to my room and take a photograph of the two of them which my mother has given me, and hurl it into the waste-paper basket.

In the depths of the winter of 1956, the skies lightened for six weeks, when my parents, who were in South Africa, sent for my brother and me. My father had undergone an operation to correct a slipped disc and was convalescing in a hospital in Cape Town. We flew over with Ma. What a glorious country was and for all I know still is, South Africa! (Apart from the 52 daily murders, of course.) We visited acquaintances of my parents in beautiful properties (as an eight-year-old normally deprived of such treats, the vanilla ice cream with hot chocolate sauce we were served at lunch at the Holt sisters is unforgettable) run by armies of black servants (note to subconsciously envious, too-young-to-know-anything critic: I know this is politically incorrect, but so are all my recollections), and settled for the remainder of the stay in a beachfront hotel in Hermanus, on the coast between Cape Town and Durban. There, my brother and I acquired the deepest, healthiest tans of our lives. The beach was long, wide and empty; the sand, clean and white. On the dunes, among the stunted brush, twisted explorable paths, and in the tide pools and rock crannies were crabs and jellyfish. It was heaven. One of the most rewarding sports at the beach, apart from dabbling in the briny and building sandcastles, was throwing periwinkles at my brother, who hated this and screamed most gratifyingly. On Christmas day, Ma put her Swiss durability to the test against a plate glass door and came off worse with a broken nose. Thereafter she wore a plaster cast. I was given a wooden tug boat which was promptly stolen by another child or born out to sea. I was inconsolable for days. If anyone has found this sixty-year-old vessel in the meantime, I would still be grateful for its return. One afternoon, we joined some people my parents had met, who had a cottage on the beach. Their daughter proposed a game wherein she was to lie on the grass and we were to run by and spank her buttocks. Unfortunately, this intriguing pastime was cut short by the proximity of the adults at their tea table; presumably, they just resented our fun. I wonder what happened to that interesting girl.

On the return journey, all five of us travelled by the *Winchester Castle*, a Union Castle Line ship, and a fine temporary home for an eight-year-old. I made friends with the crew, observed the bizarre rituals which marked the crossing of the equator, swam in the indoor pool and chickened out of seeing Laurence Olivier's *Richard III*. My brother, aged six, loved the beheadings and sat through the whole thing. (I saw it three years later, when my tutor used the film as a way to instil in me the circumstances of the battle of Bosworth.)

That was still the time when real ships carried real people to real destinations. Ships were merely a slower, more comfortable and relaxing method of getting there. People who mattered never hurried; they had others to do their hurrying for them. To have the time and the ability to savour the things that make life worth living is a sign that one is satisfied with one's lot. Now, the man who isn't running isn't getting anywhere — in his own mind, at least. No silly tourist on a cruise, however expensive, has any right to assume they know what the atmosphere of a great ship is like.

The ambiance of the *Winchester Castle*, the SS *Rotterdam*, on the two '*Queens*', and others of the period, was unique. Those ships were little floating cities, with every necessary facility, in which passenger and crew alike went about their daily routines in quiet settled ways, amid the subdued, elegant decor. There were large libraries, stocked with classics, thrillers and children's books, smoking rooms and card rooms, indoor and outdoor swimming pools, and cinemas, and hundreds of yards of deck to explore. Artificial, communal entertainment (karaoke, musicals, or comedy acts) would have been as inconceivable as it would have been contemptible. Passengers were assumed to be individuals and therefore sufficiently intelligent and sophisticated to be able to entertain themselves. A child could have the lifeboat drill explained to it more than once, and one could, in my case at least, have a tour of the engine room and the galley and even steer the ship. One could play deck quoits laughably badly between the huge red and black funnels, and inhale the unmistakable combination of salt air and fuel oil. One did not have to be introduced to Randolph Churchill or Noël Coward unless one wanted to be. And one might see the New York skyline from the East River at dawn, not yet a cliché, and relax while Customs and Immigration did their jobs unobtrusively, without a single prying inquiry. Ah, those were the days!

1957

Vacations were often exciting, but they scarcely balanced the bleak monotony of school. However, my penitentiaries were about to change for the better. Twelve years after the end of the war, intellectual and distinguished Germans were concerned about the negative effects of the rapid growth of their economy and the commensurate swelling of a plutocracy. At Salem, the school founded in 1919 by Kurt Hahn, an attempt was made to give all children, irrespective of background, an alternative to this materialism, with an education which emphasized sports and the outdoors in general. The upper school was lodged in a beautiful baroque monastery, not far from the Lake of Constance, the property of Prince Max of Baden. The headmaster in those days was an impoverished aristocrat, Prince Georg of

Hannover, a relation of the British royal family, one of whose youngest sons, Welf, was about to enter the system at my level. This boy, tall, ash blond and a year older than I, earned my envy immediately for his ability to drive the family's VW Beetle along the fire breaks in the nearby woods. He was an amiable fellow and universally liked, and he acted as my guide during the weeks it took me to acclimatize myself to my new surroundings.

In retrospect, it is not quite clear to me why, except for the undoubted advantages of the school's health-oriented principles, my parents sent me there. They must have met the founder or the headmaster at some social function and have been impressed by him. But the idea of raising an English- and French-speaking boy at a German boarding school was a peculiar one. It was certainly confusing for me.

The countryside was unspoiled and underpopulated. It consisted mainly of forests and hills, interspersed by small farmsteads, next to one of which was my new school, Hermannsberg.

This was one of the three prep schools, from which children graduated to the Upper School at Salem itself. Hermannsberg consisted of two buildings only. One, a five-storey block, contained classrooms and separate dormitories for boys and girls, and on the top floor, the apartments of the headmaster and his family. The other, rooms for the masters. Kurt Hahn himself then lived on the top floor too. Between the buildings was a gravelled courtyard where we played badminton. We wore a simple uniform. In summer, grey flannel shorts, white shirts and dark blue pullovers; in winter, plus fours with long thick socks protected bare legs. The plentiful food was supplemented by each child's personal stock of fruit, kept in his own locker in the hall. The daily routine began early with a run around the playing fields and a cold shower for the boys, before breakfast. A prefect ensured that each boy counted slowly to ten under the shower. Lessons followed. Musical instruction consisted of sing-alongs from a songbook. They were traditional, upbeat, tuneful songs. I remember one in praise of the potato. In our free time, we dug hideouts in the woods nearby, and searched the caves in a sandstone cliff for the bones of medieval monks or nuns whose adjacent convent and monastery were supposed to have encouraged secretive sexual liaisons. We never found any. In the autumn, we helped to pick apples on the local farm. The huge old barn, crammed to the rafters with fragrant hay, made a wonderful playground to tunnel through. At harvest time, a Thanksgiving service was held in a picturesque chapel, the altar of which was covered with a colourful array of produce. In winter, a steep slope below the tool shed was assiduously developed to provide the slickest possible surface for tobogganing. Once a term, we had fire practice. We were all awoken in the middle of the night and mustered at a window on the fourth floor. The mouth of an enclosed canvas chute was attached here, through which we had to slide down to a net held up by the staff. Climbing over the sill scared me, but once inside the chute it was like a fairground ride.

I made a fool of myself almost immediately, but it was in a good cause. Among the girls was a strikingly pretty twelve-year-old, with long dark hair. I confided my interest in her to one of the older boys, a playful type, who suggested that he take a message to her on my behalf. He told me this was an '*Angebot*', literally 'offer', and was the done thing. An assignation was arranged in an empty classroom. She came in, shut the door, and addressed me very seriously. My German was weak, but I understood enough of what she said to realise that she was telling me that, at nine, I was too young to interest her. Naturally, I was crestfallen. This event took a while to live down.

During the vacations, I joined my parents and brother in Settignano, near Florence, where they were now living. (That's Florence, Italy, for American readers, not Florence, South Carolina.) The house was a Villino, or small villa, rented from the art expert Bernard Berenson, whose grand villa was across the valley. Rarely, my brother and I were invited to accompany our parents for a meal amid its splendid but rather gloomy interior, intentionally kept sombre to protect the art from the bright Florentine sunlight, but I retain no memory of the owner himself who died later that year, aged 94.

The Villino was built around a small courtyard with a pergola, whose columns were girdled with wisteria. The kitchen was untouched by modern conveniences and the stove, wood-fired. On it, Settimia produced traditional pasta. Occasionally, Ma, my brother and I would catch the local bus at Ponte a Mensola and ride down to Florence itself, to do some shopping. Needless to say, back then, we were the only foreigners on the bus and probably almost the only foreign voices to be heard in the centre of Florence. I stress 'to be heard' because what tourists there were in those days were neither noticeable nor audible. I have a vague memory of staring up at the hole in the ceiling of the enormous Duomo. Beneath it, at our feet, a rectangular pool collected leaked rainwater from cracks in the plasterwork. The Duomo underwent extensive restoration in the Seventies.

During the summer holidays, I sat in the sun, at a table on the garage roof, while an Old Etonian, hired by my parents, tried to inculcate in me the basics of Latin verbs, so that I might, one day, be an OE too. I wouldn't say that this was a less than ideal way of passing the summer, but I still retain the scar on my wrist, incurred when I tried to kill a buzzing fly by putting my fist through my bedroom window.

I have never understood why my parents moved to Italy, while keeping the chalet in Gstaad, but it was only a short interval before they decided to settle permanently in London.

About twenty years ago, I returned to Florence one May, intent on recapturing some of the flavours and impressions of the rurality that had been Settignano in 1957. Of my memories of that peaceful pastoral backwater, with its rows of cypresses, its stands of bamboo and hilly fields, and its narrow, empty country roads, little remained. Berenson's villa had been sold to Harvard and was now a 'Center for Renaissance Studies'. As for Florence itself, its identity had become submerged beneath a foreign invasion. So obstructed were its streets by a dense swarm of American and Oriental tourists that it was impossible to stand still long enough to take in the sights. Beyond their role as service providers, the Florentines were conspicuous by their absence. In all the restaurants, the menus had been translated into English. The natives had surrendered themselves entirely to catering to the whims of foreigners. Never again.

Chapter III

A LIFE OF DUTY
or
YOU CAN HAVE YOUR CAKE AND EAT IT TOO

1959

No. 2 The Grove, Highgate, London.

Highgate Village lies along the crest of a rise in North London, across the Heath from Hampstead. Because of its distance from the centre and its height and greenery, the air is much cleaner here than in the West End. The Grove is a graceful row of protected Charles II houses. During my parents' possession of it, No. 2 was an agreeable home; wood panelled throughout and with its own composed character. The garden overlooked Witanhurst's grounds, which, in turn, ran down to Hampstead Heath. From my window on the top floor, the impression was of being in the country. The drawing room ran almost the length of the house and gave onto a good-sized lawn, with a crab-apple tree. It was a wonderfully peaceful room, silent except for the chimes of an 18th century ebonized clock. My parents' bedroom occupied the same space on the first floor. I used to sit on one of the four cushioned window seats and stare out, while my mother talked. My father was hardly ever to be seen in this room, although he slept in the right-hand bed. If I were early enough, I might catch him eating his breakfast (herb tea, yoghurt and very tough grains) at a table at the foot of the beds.

Reading in a window seat at Highgate.

A LIFE OF DUTY

I had my breakfast in the kitchen and paid my compulsory respects to my mother on my way back up to my room. My mother always had breakfast brought to her in bed. The bulge at the foot of my mother's eiderdown and a very loud purr denoted that Foxy, the large Siamese cat and most cherished member of the household, had installed himself in his regular place. The cat belonged to Millie, the housekeeper, and had been inherited along with her.

My mother lay on her bed, scratching her legs with her dark red nails. She had some kind of infection from catching phlebitis as a result of losing her third baby. "Don't you love to scratch an itch?" she said with relish. I was revolted. I don't remember ever climbing into my mother's or my father's bed in the mornings or ever wanting to. I don't remember receiving one spontaneous hug from either of my parents or ever wanting one. My mother repelled me and my father was cold and remote and important.

Actually, this is unfair. Before the Bernese Oberland was infested by day trippers, so that no secluded spot survived, and his schedule stuffed to bursting, my father sometimes found the time to join us for picnics. Memorable was the one when he tried to fuel the fire on which we were to cook sausages and melt cheese, with cow dung, a sample of which he had found nearby, in order to show us how this was done in India. As I recall, it didn't burn, maybe the result of the difference between Indian and Swiss cows' excretions. My father was also (once) to be seen on skis, an experiment curtailed after my mother reminded him of the risk of injuries to his hands. In the early Sixties, my father consented to being filmed on 16 mm in a silent surrealistic sketch in which he admonished my mother's collection of china animals, in the garden at Highgate.

My father's sense of humour was entirely in keeping with his gentle nature. The composer Haydn was hard to find because he was always 'hid'n'. Which opera took place in a garage? Carmen. The riskiest joke he ever told was one involving a Jew who asked another to guess what he had just eaten by breathing in his face. The answer was not as first and second guessed, garlic or onions, but strawberries.

Another sphere my mother did not enjoy was motherhood. According to my mother, I was born at 10 p.m. in a hospital in Edinburgh. Although it was wise to take all my mother's statements with a hefty pinch of salt and to halve all quantities, up to this moment, I have not uncovered any evidence which would seem to contradict this assertion. I know very little else about this event. As a matter of general information for the reader interested in such things, three further events of note in 1948 were the publication of the Universal Declaration of Human Rights, the UN Genocide Convention, and the establishment of the State of Israel — a curious juxtaposition.

My mother, never particularly reticent when she thought she could elicit pity from recounting her sufferings, told me just a few times that it was a difficult birth, long-drawn-out and painful. I apologised. The tone she usually used to impart this information belonged to her 'it's-all-part-of-a-woman's-role' variety of remarks, and was not a mood to be encouraged. However, apart from this initial pain which I caused her and with few intervals continued to cause her ever after, the ordeal itself must have brought her some satisfaction, if only because by going through it she wrote off some of the debt she may have considered she owed my father as part of the marital bargain. She was 'doing her duty', and my mother was always very keen on duty. I understand that when I was very young, for instance, my mother, presumably partly out of duty and perhaps partly because she liked the sound of her own voice, read to me. Although these must have been memorable occasions, as she was hardly ever at home, I don't remember her doing this, but maybe she did.

When she was away, she sent my brother and me weekly Beatrix Potter postcards, and later ones from the Railway Series featuring Thomas the Tank Engine and his friends, and later still, when she thought we were old enough to appreciate them, letters informing us how hard she was working at the packing and unpacking and the writing of letters, and what a strain all the travelling was. When I was at school, I wrote back during the Sunday letter-writing sessions, assuring her that I was all right and that life was fun with my pals. I must have felt that she would like to receive an account that did not contradict the style of *The Boy's Own Paper*, which I read. We were both dissembling, in our respective ways.

So why did my mother travel so much, accompanying my father and suffering countless *crises de nerfs*, if she hated it so much? This is a real puzzler, but I believe the answer is twofold: she didn't trust him not to have affairs, and she enjoyed the perquisites of her marriage, although the notion of enjoyment scarcely fitted her narrow view of life as a kind of affliction.

One could hardly blame my mother for having preferred to travel in luxury to far off lands that she never had the opportunity to see, in the company of a world-famous figure (my father in those days enjoyed the celebrity of a film star — indeed, he had turned down and had had turned down for him by his father, a variety of film roles), rather than to sit at home and supervise the upbringing of her sons by the humourless Swiss governess. It was true that my father's California property or 'ranch' as the newspapers called it, was a sort of nirvana, with every conceivable comfort a war-starved British ex-dancer could have dreamed of, but being a Londoner, she was accustomed to a more sophisticated environment than Northern California could offer. At least that was her justification for not enjoying herself. The servants, the unrationed healthy food, the enormous swimming pool, the perfect climate, last and (of course) least her two sons, just could not compete with the worldliness she had known, when as a second lead she had toured the Middle East with such luminaries as Cyril Ritchard in *The Merry Widow*, as part of a troop entertainment organisation, or had almost become engaged by Diaghilev in the Russian Ballet.

It is clear, too, that she was not about to abandon her husband, who, as his biography and her autobiography notes, relied on her to tell him who Greta Garbo was, an item of knowledge without which an accomplished concert artist is immeasurably impoverished — AND, and she was needed to darn his socks and underwear (as she would assert to anyone who would stop and listen), for my unfortunate father was earning such small fees that he could not afford both to pay for double accommodation at first-class hotels and to buy new socks.

If one examines under a not particularly strong magnifying glass this compulsion of my mother's to stay at my father's side, a more disturbing element than the mere excitement of being a celebrity's wife emerges. My mother was afraid of losing her catch. If one refers to a photograph of my father at the time, it is clear that he was a handsome man, and moreover one imbued with an irresistible charm and — silly word — charisma. These qualities made him very attractive to women. However, the man was so caught up in his music and his many other projects, and so attentive to his wife and influenced through book-learning with quaintly chivalrous notions, that even if he had been allowed the breathing space of the odd night off the stage and away from my mother, he would not have been able to discern the interest of women, so naive and innocent was he. No, no, this is true.

My mother was forever introducing into a perfectly innocuous conversation dark mentions of my father's current 'girlfriend' (I'm sure she did not say 'mistress'), who, in one case, poor maligned woman, was a talented painter, in her sixties, married with several children, was physically handicapped into the bargain, and lived in Canada — inconveniently distant one would have thought for my father to have had much of a fling. And yet, my mother, in her self-sacrificing way, insisted that she went into another room 'whenever' this woman called. Knowing my mother's capacity for exaggeration, not to say downright fabrication, I would guess that this woman had perhaps called once, probably to enquire about tickets to a forthcoming concert of my father's in her home town.

My mother never forgot that my father once nearly succumbed — according to her — to the charms of an Austrian

A LIFE OF DUTY

opera singer of great repute and substantial physical allure, by comparison with whom my mother would have seemed like a broomstick. Jealousy, even in a woman of seventy, can have its charming side, I suppose, but constant insinuations that what was merely mutual admiration between two gifted people was in fact sexual congress, was both degrading and insulting to a husband as faithful and devoted as was my father. So much for sexuality about and between my parents, which I must confess if I dwell on it, will make me ill.

No, there is more, come to think of it. I have totally and greatly to her detriment omitted to discuss my mother's own sexual recollections. Woven into the increasingly fantastical legend that my mother concocted around her premarital years in London, were a number of hoary strands, which, judging from their repetition, must have contained a thread of truth. Some of these dealt with her ballet experiences and disappointments, and were rife with suffering, for which a certain 'Black Fairy' bore considerable responsibility. Others, with the murkier atmosphere surrounding her social life as a young woman of good family living with her sister in a small flat in Belgravia. The former recollections were infinitely preferable (although equally dull), as much less embarrassing for the listener.

Among the latter memories was one about my mother's 'seducer', a young man of doubtful reputation but who possessed a Bentley. He took my mother on a wild drive into the country, cracking up the Bentley in the process (so smitten was he), in an accident with an American army truck, and as far as I can make out, had my mother in an attic amid some chickens, or it might have been cats. No matter the menagerie, the incident left a lasting impression on my mother, who used it — the whole tale — to prove a variety of points about herself. For these occasions could be turned to infinite advantage, as they all possessed some derivative quality which could be used to demonstrate my mother's allure, calmness, prescience, etc., etc. Thus, at the time of the accident which totalled the Bentley, she got out unharmed and hitched a ride with the soldier driving the truck. What happened to the luckless beau is anyone's guess, but his fate did not serve to display anything useful about Diana.

Sometimes, under the influence of alcohol and of her fascination with her own physical condition, my mother would complain that continual travel had affected her health. One of her most important grievances was that "your father dragged me around the world when I was pregnant with your brother". Allegedly, constant travel eventually led her to contract phlebitis and to miscarry her third child. When my mother was feeling particularly hard done by, she tended to augment the number of her miscarriages. I have heard her claim three, and once, after a lengthy rant, she mentioned four, in which number I believe she included my brother and myself, who it is true as far as having any ornamental value might as well have been stillborn. The ornamental, the decorative, in dress, food, furnishings, cars and all, figured high on my mother's list of essentials. Presumably, she was once a reasoning woman, capable of normal deductions and responses; now, only very occasional glimmers of a rational intelligence shone through a miasma of protective mantras, a list as long as your arm, all concerned with her own ineffable suffering. Condemned to spend a lifetime washing underwear and darning socks in luxury hotels across the globe, and checking matching towels and hangers at home, she had become the enchanted princess of the picayune.

When I still lived at home, we had our routines. "What's this?" says my mother, coming through the hall and picking up a shirt or a letter or some easily identifiable object that seems to her not to be in its proper place. "Oh, sorry," say I, rushing to remove the offending article, or, alternatively, "It's a shirt," remaining where I am, if I'm not feeling quite so compliant. "Well, who does it belong to, whose shirt is it?" she insists. I feel obliged to take it from her and to put it out of her sight, although I had probably put it there intentionally. My mother sits down with a sigh at the lunch table "Good morning," she says then with heavy emphasis. "Oh, good morning," says I, "I thought we had got past that."

A LIFE OF DUTY

When I was a child, I never seemed to have enough time to eat. It was bad enough at school, where meals were set to a schedule like everything else; but at home, my parents were always dashing off somewhere, often during the meal. I had to be ready to run down to the table within seconds of being called. The food was generally all right, but there was less time to eat it than there was at school. My mother kept up a monologue, pausing only to put food into her mouth. My father, brother and I had to eat and follow this performance at the same time. It started when she joined us at table and stopped about thirty minutes later, when she had finished eating. Unfortunately for us, she ate very little — lack of nutrition may have contributed to her nervousness — and her only concession to the presence of the food itself was her constant exhortation to finish it. The idea of eating for pleasure was unknown to her; eating was just another duty that had to be done. We had to clear our plates and the serving dishes too, if possible. Remnants of food conflicted with her pathological obsession with neatness. The God Neatness came close to ruling her life. Halfway through a sentence, her voice would take on a plaintive note and she would push a plate at me and coax "Will no one finish this bit of ham?" And I, striving not to disappoint her or the piece of ham, left so lonely on its dish, would take it although I felt full. Throughout her life, my mother was driven by unseen demons to accomplish innumerable tasks at great speed and to derive absolutely no pleasure from them. So you can see where I get my habits from.

Among the minutiae and the conventionalities with which my poor mother was possessed, greetings at first sight in the morning and before retiring in the evening were conspicuous. The omission of 'a proper good night' meant starting off the next day on a sour note. When I entered my mother's bedroom of a morning, bearing a load of guilt for having neglected this vital salutation on the previous evening, I was addressed by her in a curious whining tone, high and monotonous — my brother and I came to call it her 'still small voice' — with an injured 'good morning'. My father, if he had been similarly remiss, received the same treatment. The princess, or the star of whatever show she was currently in, had been neglected; it was as though Garbo's date had brought her carnations maybe, instead of roses, and she was darn well going to sulk until he rectified his mistake.

The problem was that my brother at seven and I at ten carried equal weight with our father (and possibly all our mother's previous boyfriends) as 'all my men'. My mother liked us all to pay continual tribute to her. My father tried his best, generally attaching the word 'wonderful' to his praise, as in "Isn't Mummy wonderful?" However, on these occasions, we failed her ideal of courtly love; we were not parfit gentle knights, or something. I found it difficult to accept that whatever I had done on the previous day continued to offend her now and required an apology. However, the slate could be wiped clean with the magic words 'I'm sorry', which also activated her voice-change button. Failing this expression, my mother was prepared to persist for hours, or until my father was roped in to exact penance from me for being 'horrible to Mummy'.

This was a familiar accusation and one of which I was often guilty, depending on one's definition of 'horrible', of course. According to my mother and contrary to my own hypothesis, it was simply my brother's arrival that had provoked my irritability. Not usually aware of modish trends, she had conveniently discovered the novel expression 'sibling rivalry'.

Once things were all right again, my mother might ask "What are you going to do today?" to which question I usually had no answer. By asking it, she was challenging me to submit whatever plans I might have for her approval, or testing me to come up with an occupation worthy of her son. I would twist my hands and hop about and say I didn't know. "What? You don't know? With all the things you could do?" my mother would say disapprovingly. And so one more spoonful of guilt was added to my already brimming cup. I would writhe and frown some more, and tear my eyes away from her feet, on which in my distress they had alighted. As a result of the tortures of dancing, my mother's feet were contorted and ugly.

Even if there had been something I wanted to do, I would not have imparted it to my mother. Her invariable condescension and simulated maternal manner were an insuperable barrier to any confidences, beyond the restraints normal between parent and child. She may not have meant to patronize me, but she simply couldn't help imposing her obsolete notions of children's behaviour, epitomized by the thirty-six-year gulf between us.

While I was slowly, desperately trying to inch my way out of my mother's bedroom, and my small stock of enthusiasm and energy dissipated, she continued to talk. I had come in fairly cheerfully, but now I was hunched over, longing only to get away from her. The effect of going through my mother's conversational wringer: from sprightly to ragged in half an hour. I would go up to my room and close the door and perhaps play with my toy soldiers, or lie on my bed and read the latest James Bond which my tutor had been kind enough to smuggle in to me and I kept under other books in my bedside table, but first, I must just get away.

Whatever I might do, I considered it to be no business of hers. Of course, what I would have liked to do, now that I was on holiday, would have been to play with other children or another child, any child. But I did not consciously sense that this was missing from my life. At no time did my mother declare that the presence of other children and the commotion they might cause were unwanted, but it was understood that the people who mattered would be inconvenienced by them. The implicit reason was that my father was not to be disturbed. In fact, it was my mother who would have been most disturbed. Apparently, she did not remember playing with other children as a child, although she grew up with a brother and sister. My mother's mental state resembled that of a patient in a sanatorium; nothing must ruffle her composure because she would then complain even more than she already did, and hamper my father's activities.

I was an imaginative child and loved to read, but apart from that or other solitary occupation, there was nothing to do in our house; nothing that did not intrude into my parents' living space, threaten the antiques, or make a noise while my father was practising. In time, this system came to seem normal, as my brother and I never had the opportunity to make any friends anyway. During the twenty-five years that my parents occupied the house in Highgate, a total of perhaps ten people of various ages penetrated into this shrine at my brother's or my invitation. Any change in this behaviour might have resulted in our being out of bounds at home.

If the subject of this deprivation ever arose, my mother would be sure to blame it on my father's habits and to waste no time in switching the conversation to one of her favourite topics: how his life had limited her own. "This house is just an upholstered office!" she would cry, and "I don't have one corner I can call my own, your father even invades the bedroom!" In those days, there were no MP3 players or smartphones, with which to listen privately to popular music. Until the late Sixties, we possessed no television and when my parents finally acquired one, the guilt associated with being caught watching it was so great that we hardly ever did. It was insinuated that watching television was somehow immoral. The sounds of the house were few and fairly predictable: my father practising, my mother talking at anyone who would listen; the vacuum cleaner, and the telephone. My brother and I, when we were under the same roof at the same time, were unobtrusively quiet. Sometimes, we played board games together or built houses in our rooms. We were very good little boys. Partly, this was because we were by nature not rowdy and had learnt to amuse ourselves; partly it was because we were ignorant of any alternative. However, the twins next door, two boys a year younger than I, played cricket regularly on their lawn and the balls they lost over the intervening wall reminded us of the existence of another world.

A LIFE OF DUTY

My mother spoke disparagingly of these neighbours because their habits were casual almost to the point of bohemianism. She resented the comparative nonconformity which reigned in their house, and could only come to terms with it by implying that the twins' mother was insane. My mother craved a permanent audience, but the only setting in which she was assured of one and in which she felt secure was one which she had designed herself. It followed that she never visited the neighbours. One of the reproaches she continually to made my father was that during the quarter century they lived in this house, she was only 'allowed' to have seven dinner parties. Sometimes, the culprit was the housekeeper, who was too infirm to undertake the catering; sometimes, my father, who had installed her in this house 'miles from anywhere, like a bird in a gilded cage'. My mother was fond of recalling nostalgically her youth in Belgravia, where, as a 'gel', she was wont to 'hop on a bus'. Now she had to be driven to the West End in the back of the car 'like a dowager duchess'. As my mother normally did not disdain duchesses, I could not understand her dread of the resemblance. The dowager duchess could simply have stayed at home or could have used her cartage to do charity work, but in the event, she merely went to the sales.

The real reason my parents did not have more dinner parties, apart from the fact that my father cared not a whit for them, was that they were both socially inept. The parties they did have were total failures. Their lack of discrimination led to the most improbable combinations of people. Their circle of acquaintance was huge and would have suited any number of casual gatherings, such as cocktail parties; but a formal evening, at which people with like interests and social backgrounds could converse in a relaxed atmosphere, was quite beyond either of them to arrange. Obviously, my father's own peculiar experience had given him no knowledge of how to go about this, but, if pressed, he could have been expected to give my mother some direction, to advise her of those he might have been interested to meet. My mother's own concerns, poor woman, hardly bear examination. Given the upbringing with which she endowed herself, this kind of entertainment should have been second nature to her, but the truth was that in company, she was like a fish out of water.

Whatever the impulse behind one of these dinners, it was doomed before it began. Millie, the cook-housekeeper, knew or claimed to know, only a handful of dishes. Of these, she could produce three or four competently. It would have been unwise to insist that she learn anything new. Having decided then on filet with Béarnaise perhaps, my mother would approach the second class vintner in the village for his suggestions. After scanning the shelves, laden with giant cans of Lager and jeroboams of cut-rate gin, he would discover behind the Liebfraumilch a couple of bottles of *soi-disant* Gevrey-Chambertin, interfered with by Cruse. If they were not actually corked, they had suffered such rough treatment during transfer from one branch of the chain to another as to render them undrinkable. It did not occur to my parents to keep a cellar until much later.

The crowning disaster among these dinners, to which I — then working in Paris — was grateful not to be invited, must have been the one given for the Prince of Wales. Although they had practically the whole artistic, financial and political world to choose from, my parents invited an obscure French musicologist and his wife, and my half-sister and her second husband, whose idea of convivial behaviour consists of a blank stare, broken by a sporadic monosyllable or irrelevant question, delivered with a sly smile. My unfortunate half-sister, a relic of my father's first marriage, is a colourless social aspirant whose only ability is to conform, which she does by reproducing the shrill, distorted vowels of her elected caste, to no clear purpose. To have chosen brilliant intellectuals with uncomfortably radical views or speech defects, or titled persons with whom the guest of honour was perhaps over-familiar, would have been far preferable to this collection of non-starters. There are those who would have spared no effort in their endeavour to produce a perfect evening; those whose lifelong (never to be fulfilled) ambition was to be able to invite the Prince of Wales to dinner. I would have liked to be present during the discussions which resulted in this choice of guests; I am sure it would have been a revelation.

If I had to say who among the hundreds of people my parents knew were their friends, without including the innumerable physicians they were constantly consulting in every land they visited, and who were in any case paid for their advice, I would have trouble deciding. After due reflection, I cannot name any. My parents seemed to know many of the most influential and internationally recognised people, but there was not a single person whom either of them could treat as a confidant. My mother, who felt most comfortable in the company of those who could not escape her because they were financially dependent on her, kept in touch with all her elderly and infirm former employees, even if they had been notoriously slothful, rude or even dishonest. For them, she collected little pieces of bric-a-brac and souvenirs on her travels; to them she sent postcards constantly.

My mother loved to think that she was accepted as a 'pal' by these people, though why this should have been is a mystery to me. She also claimed to be one of the few people to be able to understand and get along with a type she called 'the real gruff Cockney'. In order to please her, my father once engaged one of these rough diamonds as a chauffeur and general factotum. He turned out to be a well-known petty thief with an established criminal record. After giving him a credit card and a key to the safe, both my parents were surprised to lose £15,000, and to learn that the Jaguar they had bought through him had been stolen. Even then, it was touch and go whether my mother would forgo her companion, her audience, whether she would not make an attempt to reform him by further 'understanding'. Finally, the police took a hand and he was prosecuted and sent to jail for a year.

By way of contrast, my parents hardly knew their neighbours. My father led a very busy life and travelled for most of the year. He was rarely at home for longer than a fortnight at a time, but nothing prevented my mother, if she were not inclined to accompany him, from paying a casual visit to either of her neighbours, in particular to their wives who were both of an informal disposition. But, by doing so, apart from her fear of uncontrollable circumstances, of the need to behave herself like an independent, mature adult away from my father's side, my mother would have been giving the lie to her myth of herself as a constantly overworked person. The truth was that she had no notion of casual social intercourse, of how to share a conversation with or be interested in, another person, let alone another woman. She craved an opportunity to indulge without interruption in one of her plaintive yet curiously boastful monologues, and she could only be assured of this on her home ground, before a captive audience. A dinner party was thus the ideal venue. She was no more capable of dropping in at her neighbours' for a chat over a cup of tea than she would be of suggesting that I invite the twins to play at our house. To be fair, I believe my brother did once play cricket with them in our garden and unfortunately broke the plate glass window of the garden-room door, which must have prejudiced my mother further against them.

Chapter IV

PREP SCHOOL AND CRAMMING

August, 1959

Playing the bread violin, Edinburgh.

The Caledonian Hotel, Edinburgh. We came up by overnight train pulled by a steam locomotive, of course. At seven, the conductor knocks to ask if I want tea. Then there's a proper breakfast with white table cloths, in the dining car. My father is playing at the Edinburgh Festival. One day, the local citizenry bring him a violin and bow made entirely out of bread. I am photographed pretending to play it. I was born here, but, apart from my mother's ancestry, I have no right to call myself Scottish. Nevertheless, this country stirs me. Every morning, a different regimental band marches past, playing the pipes. The hotel belongs to British Railways and is suitably austere, but it's comfortable. There are television sets in the rooms and, naturally, I turn mine on. One evening, I watch an American gangster series. A couple enter an apartment building and ring a doorbell. A man behind them says, "I'm going there too." The door opens and they go in. So does he. Then he pulls a gun and asks for money. They refuse to tell him where it is, so he hits the man on the head with his gun. It turns out the money is hidden behind an air-conditioning vent. By my father's wish, at this time, there is still no television at home and so I have never watched it before, and certainly have never seen this kind of cold-blooded violence either. That night, I have nightmares and, in desperation, I seek refuge in my half-sister's room across the corridor.

The island of Eigg, one of a trio which also includes Rhum and Muck, belongs to Sir Steven Runciman, an expert on Byzantine history. His house is fronted by a classical colonnade. My parents and I are his guests. Of the doubtless fascinating discussions they enjoyed with Sir Steven, I retain only a waspish anecdote of his, concerning a couple of parvenus — apparently known to my parents as well — who recounted to Sir Steven how affronted they were when a fashionable hotel had disappointed them. "When they knew who we were, they admitted their mistake, of course." "And who were you?" responded Sir Steven. I climb the magnificent cedar next to the house and take many pictures of sheep with my Brownie box camera.

Inspired enough to disturb my parents before breakfast, which I would not normally do, I dash into their bedroom and announce that I have decided that I must learn the guitar. My father buys me a three-quarters Spanish guitar, made by a renowned luthier. He arranges lessons for me. The teacher, while likeable, insists on teaching me notation and theory exclusively, without at least adding a couple of simple tunes to make the instrument more accessible and fun for a child, so, after a month or so, I give up. To be fair, one of my chief talents has always been giving up, so my failure to continue with the instrument is as much due to my lack of confidence in myself as to the teacher's lack of flair. In addition, the kind of music I want to learn to play is hardly the kind my parents would want to hear.

An indication of how wrong-headed my musical tastes are can be deduced from my father's reaction to a Rolling Stones concert, to which he is invited a few years later, when the band is considering making a donation to the Yehudi Menuhin School in Surrey. He leaves after ten minutes, reportedly saying "I can't take it anymore. I have to leave." He describes the show in an unattributed newspaper interview, the gist of which is: "Meaningless cacophony. Overgrown children pandering to the worst emotions one can have, playing what they thought was music. All I could think of was some barbaric ritual. Awful!" In a way, he was right. Such events, attended by screaming fans, do have something of a devotional ceremony about them.

1959

Broadstairs on the English Channel is a favourite location for prep schools, although Stone House is one of the least distinguished. The school building is pebbledash faced. It is of course a boys-only school. England is still very insular and there are only two boys of foreign extraction: Theodorou, a plump Greek, and Wallis, a French string bean. Although English is my mother tongue, I am apparently so exotic that, within a short time, I find myself relegated and relating only to them. This is no problem, as I don't seem to have anything in common with any of the others, except possibly Plevin, of whom more anon.

Reinforced by our outsiders' bond, we get along fairly well. I join Theodorou on school walks and we invent long, involved stories of a sexual nature, in which letters substitute for the body parts. Casting a glance over his shoulder, Theodorou murmurs, "Then she took his X and rubbed it against her G."

"But I thought he had tied her hands."

"Yes, but she could move them so that she could just touch his Ws as well as his X."

Fire practice. We are gathered in a fourth-floor dorm. The paved drive looks miles down. We are supposed to slide down an open chute. I resolutely refuse and nothing will make me change my mind. Evidently, I must have undergone a change since my last fire drill in Germany.

It may have been at around this time that I was repeatedly plagued by two dreams. The first was definitely a nightmare. I was being pursued along a railway track by a steam train. Thankfully, I succeeded in wrenching myself off the track, but the black locomotive detached itself and pursued me down a bank. In the other dream, I had a view of the entire planet from space, giving me a sense of extreme detachment, of withdrawal and estrangement.

Usually, I awake to the sound of pigeons cooing. This morning, as, half astir, I crack my lids to the new day, looming a few inches above me are the hazy but unmistakable features of Mlle Crop, the deputy head mistress at Chalet Flora. (What can this mean, Doctor? Subconscious impulses from my id?)

The school has some interesting books. I read and reread *The Iron Pirate*, an imaginative, late 19th century work, about a marauding, gas-driven ironclad. I'm generally attracted to nautical themes, such as the Arthur Ransome series, although my experiences of the sea have been confined to voyages on ocean liners and channel crossings, the latter of which invariably induce seasickness.

Shooting practice. The red flag is up and the targets are placed against the mound which covers the WWII bomb shelter known as 'Mount Ararat'. Four of us lie parallel on straw paillasses in the shooting shack. The .303 is almost too heavy for me to hold steady, but, surprisingly, I'm not a bad shot. It's a collective but solitary activity.

Scouts. Four stone huts stinking of sooty fried eggs are headquarters to the school troupe. We dress up in khaki shirts and shorts and learn forest and tracking lore. I'm not much good at this. It's more fun to slink through the stinkweed with Plevin, pretending to be characters out of a Saint story.

In chapel this morning, for the first time for some reason, I'm struck by the roster of dead alumni from two world wars. They're just names engraved on panels, but the recognition of their senseless deaths contributes to the general gloom of my life.

At Stone House, what remains of my musical education peters out, without regret. The only subjects in which I do well are French and English. Mr. Biggs teaches English, he is encouraging. Mr. Childs, the maths master, terrifies me. After trying to learn mathematics in French and then in German, I am too timid to ask questions in this new environment and I soon fall behind. In fact, I do so badly at this school that there is a risk that I might disgrace my mother by failing to follow her plan. I don't know if I would ever have become a good student, but after trying to adapt successively to learning to read, to write and to count in American English, then in French, then in German, and finally in British English, and to these countries' respective teaching methods, during the first ten years of my life, I sit as quietly as I can, at the back of the class, and hope I will not be called on.

Spring 1960

Rubbish and I sit at the sturdy table in my brother's room, which is larger than mine. I run my hand repeatedly through my hair and watch the dandruff fall onto the pale green Formica surface. My mother put me down for Eton at birth, which she says you have to do. Her father and brother went to Eton, and, despite my poor scholarship, she is still determined that I shall go there too, so I have been removed from Stone House and a tutor has been hired to force-feed me with facts at home. Trevor-Roberts is a good-looking, dark-haired Welshman of about thirty, and not a bad sort. I call him 'Rubbish' anyway, but not to his face, because of the nuisance with which he is associated. He has a tough job. I am sulky, obstructive and resentful. "Hair is a nuisance," he says. Mortified, I stop immediately. He pulls the rubber bands off two packs of oblong white cards and spreads them out. He has a system for matching dates to events, which manages to drive even into me the basics of English history. He also takes me to see Laurence Olivier's films of *Richard III* and *Henry V*. The same efficiency enables me to pass the Eleven-plus and then the Common Entrance exams, which I scrape through sufficiently well to be accepted at Eton, oh joy.

I play hot and cold in my mother's bedroom to find the latest Tintin. It's a game I enjoy. I'm captivated by Tintin, especially *L'Affaire Tournesol*, which takes place partly in Switzerland, and *Les Sept Boules de cristal*, which has an extraordinary atmosphere. I type out all Captain Haddock's swear words on my mother's Olivetti portable. In so far as these interests may be regressive, I plead guilty, having only in my defence to say that they were familiar refuges from the latest turns my life had taken.

Summer 1960

Mrs. MacDougal fetches my mother's brother, Uncle Gerard, for lunch. Mrs. McDougal is our six-foot, two-hundred-pound chauffeur (why, oh why can't we have a normal person, instead of yet another cause for embarrassment?). I understand that Mrs. McDougal's father founded the British Camel Corps in Egypt. She wears a dark uniform and cap, and drives our pale blue Wolseley. Uncle Gerard is one of my mother's 'crosses'. Having him to lunch now and then is a duty she, but not her sister Griselda, does. My father has arranged to be, or has to be, absent. Uncle Gerard has pale, unfocused eyes. As usual his fly is partly undone. He sits in one corner of the red sofa, my mother in the other. She tries to keep the conversation going, but it's uphill work. I'm in one of the children's chairs watching the ash on his fourth cigarette grow longer and fall onto his wrongly buttoned waistcoat. He must be the only person who would be allowed to smoke in this house. Drips from his sherry glass join an older stain on his grey suit, it could be dried egg yolk. At table, he says nothing, but occasionally responds distractedly to my mother's remarks. Afterwards, she takes him for a short walk. Then he is driven back to The Priory, the upmarket home for schizophrenics in Putney, where he has lived for decades, or, as far as I can make out, since he was eighteen. He's the one who went to Eton.

Autumn 1960

Sir Bernard Miles, a renowned actor and manager, comes to tea. He mentions to my mother that he is casting a children's play, *Emil and the Detectives*, after the book by Erich Kästner. He would like me to audition for the main role. I learn some of Emil's lines and report to the Mermaid Theatre in the City of London. The Mermaid, on the Thames at Puddle Dock, is a small modern theatre with an open stage and no proscenium. Barges pull up right outside the dressing rooms. Marjorie Sigley, who is assistant director and good with kids, runs the auditions for the German director. I don't get the role, but I am offered the second lead, a boy who heads the gang of child-detectives. There's a show every evening and twice on Saturdays. The play is a success and runs for 120 performances. I get some flattering notices, open a bank account and deposit my salary. I buy a reel-to-reel tape recorder, a huge, heavy affair, covered with blue cloth. This appliance comes with a recorded music tape which includes some fast numbers. When my parents are away, I play these, but not too loud, and dance to them in my room.

'Return to Sender' resounds in the backstage corridors. It's the first pop tune I hear and the only Elvis track I like. There is also 'The Quartermaster's Stores', a good whistling number. Just about the best thing about being in this play is the chance to meet all the other children in the cast, a bunch of mainly Cockney kids without acting experience, like me. When the boy playing Emil, who comes from an acting school, gets snooty, the others hang him by his legs out of the dressing-room window. He dangles over the water until he swears to reform. I smoke my first cigarette, sitting by myself on the dock and watching the boats go by. I also learn my first smutty verses from 'The Good Ship Venus':

'Twas on the good ship Venus
By God you should have seen us
The figurehead was an old woman's head
Sucking a dead man's penis

The captain's name was Carter
By God he was a farter
When the wind wouldn't blow
The ship wouldn't go
So Carter the Farter would start her.

The First Mate's name was Copper
By God he had a whopper
Twice round the deck
Once round his neck
And once up his ass for a stopper.

The cabin's boy's name was Kipper
By God he was a nipper
He filled his ass with broken glass
To circumcise the skipper.
Etc.

There are a couple of girls in the cast. One of them gives me my first kiss behind the scenery and sends me affectionate notes.

(If you're still alive, Margaret Ann, please forgive me for not keeping in touch.) It seems that I could be leading a normal life at last. I make the mistake of inviting this girl home for dinner. The poor thing sits next to me on my bed; I am paralysed by the suffocating atmosphere of home.

It's an Albert Hall concert. As I have of course dressed in suit and tie, I try to slink past my mother's door, hugging the banister and pretending to be invisible, before she can spot me and say "You're very smart today!" or "How nice you look!" or worse: "What a masher!" (Victorian for a 'fop'). Apart from being the most inhibited person on earth, I am also very self-conscious about my looks and clothes, and hate having attention drawn to them. My mother's door is always open, except at night and when she's packing. It's always open because she needs to trap passers-by and engage them in endless conversations, driving them crazy with boredom in the process and preventing them from getting anything done. She sits at her desk, within view of the stairs, and waylays anyone going by. This she does, initially, by an enormous sigh, denoting how heavily the cares of the world weigh on her, and how hard she's working. Unless the addressed person responds to this, my mother will say something like "Well, that's out of the way, only two hundred and fifty more to go." Although I know she probably means Christmas cards, it would be churlish to disregard this remark and not to ask "Two hundred and fifty what?"

My mother intercepts Millie, as she goes past, in the same way, preventing her from getting on with her duties. Given time, my mother can undermine and corrupt the best trained and most industrious staff. Millie, who has known no other life except service since she was a girl (when, as I understand it, she worked for the Rothschilds at Tring), is dragged into a one-sided conversation whenever she ventures within sight or hearing of my mother. She tries to stay in her kitchen all day. Luckily, this is a large room, with, at one end, a breakfast corner. Here, at tea time, Millie relaxes, often with Foxy purring on her lap, and does the *Daily Mail* crossword. It's a quiet, private moment for her, so she resents it when my mother, who would otherwise have tea brought to her in her bedroom or in the living room, joins her in the kitchen, 'to spare Millie work'. My mother is firmly convinced that Millie enjoys sharing the crossword with her.

Teatime with my mother and Millie. My mother is exceptionally cheerful today, chattering away nineteen to the dozen, while Millie reads out the crossword clues. The phone rings, it's my father calling in from a rehearsal to check that my mother is all right. Immediately, my mother's voice takes on a doleful, harried note. As soon as she hangs up, she resumes her previous manner.

When it comes to the subject of servants, my mother sends a mixed message, according to how it suits her. As a child of the Twenties, when even moderately well-off people could employ a cook, maid and parlour maid, she was accustomed to a house with plenty of staff. As opposed to my father, she should therefore know how to run such a household. However, she continually blurs the distinction between employer and employee by confiding in her staff and spending much more time with them in general than is appropriate. Distracted from doing their jobs correctly, they soon grasp their mistress's compulsion for company, as well as the advantages of doing less. Fairly soon, even a professional like Millie, whose previous employer, a wealthy actress, had been a frequent and demanding entertainer, becomes simply an aging woman for whom a dinner party is an imposition and who, somehow, is capable of only four menus. "Take my tray, slave," my mother says jokingly to Millie, not understanding that this is a remark one may only make to a real slave, or to a friend of whom one is perhaps embarrassed to ask a favour. My mother, having demoralized her cook-housekeeper and turned her into a quasi-pal, can no longer require of her the comportment of a servant. When I point out that Millie is not pulling her weight, my mother asserts her superior knowledge and says of her own mother that she was 'always terrified of the staff', as though this were a given. (A favourite comment of my mother's when confronted with an irrefutable point is to say "I wish I knew as much as you do when I was your age." The temptation is to reply "You bet you do.") Having created this predicament herself, my mother can complain that she can never give a dinner party, or that in the last ten years she has only given seven dinner parties. In the final analysis, my mother gains another reason for complaint about her cheerless life, so that's all right.

I imagine that my mother is reproducing the relationship she enjoyed with her mother's servants, as a little girl who was humoured and allowed to get away with all kinds of mischief, or was, as the boss's daughter, even considered cute when she wiped her nose with the back of her hand or helped herself with her fingers from the serving dish — less winsome traits in a woman of forty-eight. As actual children, my brother and I would of course be strictly rebuked for doing such things.

During the concert, I sit quietly next to my mother as usual. No one has told me not to fidget; I'm just a well-behaved child. My father appears to the usual avid applause. As he plays, I think how lonely he looks on the huge stage, and how I would run up and protect him if anyone attacked him. (Can you make sense of this thought, Doctor?)

January 1961

We're at the chalet in Gstaad. I sit on the garden wall in my skiing gear, frowning at Rubbish. The poor man is not responsible for whatever ails me, but he must bear the brunt of my depressions, for there is no one else I can revile. I join Frau Caillat, the ski teacher, on top of the mountain called Eggli, for my lesson, but soon, I am overcome by the most painful stomach cramps. This is not unusual for me. The gripes clutch at my stomach and render me incapable of skiing. I lie on a bench at the back of the fortunately empty restaurant. Rubbish, who has been correcting my work or reading the paper, massages my stomach. The regular physical therapy represented by yoga lessons with B.K.S. Iyengar (my father's teacher) in no way mitigated this psychological ailment.

The Chalet at Gstaad.

PREP SCHOOL AND CRAMMING

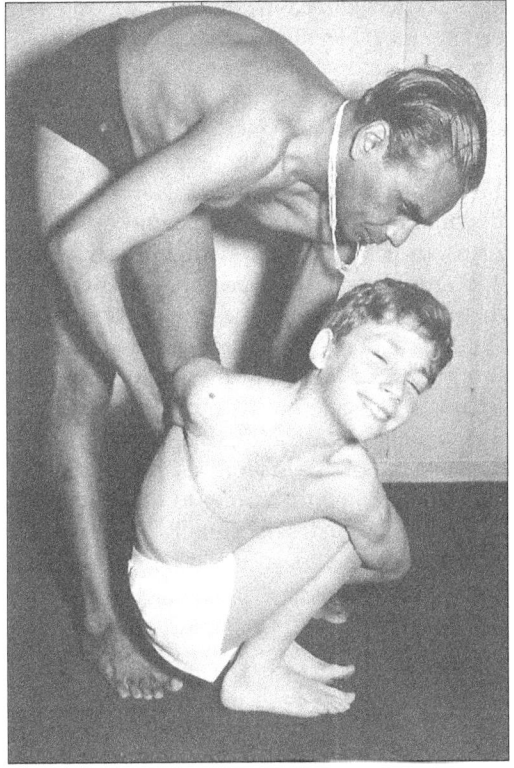

Yoga instruction with B.K.S. Iyengar.

August 1961

It's the fifth year of the Gstaad Music Festival, established by my father. It would be inconceivable for me to refuse to go to the concerts, which take place in the church at Saanen, ten minutes' drive away. We always occupy the same seats, in the fourth row. My mother sits in a chair at the end of the row, acknowledging all those who stop to pay court to her. In suit and tie, I walk down the aisle from the door at the back of the church, hunched over, trying my best to go unnoticed, knowing that people have recognized me and are pointing me out. Special guests who have been honoured by being invited to tea or drinks before the concert, sit next to me in the row, and I am obliged to be pleasant to them and answer idiotic questions like Am I musical and, if not, why not. When the music starts, I sit immobile on the hard pew, counting the movements, whose number I have checked against the programme, along the lines of 'Two down, three to go'. Every time the conductor or one of the musicians turns a page, I am thankful; every time the score requires the musicians to turn back a page and repeat something, I groan inwardly. Sometimes I try to delude myself that I have lost count, that they've played one less movement than is the case, so that I can feign a pleased surprise when the piece ends. I like some classical music, but I resent the formality of concerts, of having to listen, and I find most of the people associated with this kind of music lame, especially the public. During the interval, I escape thankfully to the graveyard. Beyond the spotlight that illuminates the church, the graves are in darkness, and I can walk the gravel paths and breathe the night air and think my gloomy thoughts undisturbed.

Chapter V

ETON

September 1961

As said, entirely due to Rubbish's cramming, I have scraped into Eton. I am in the Rev. Wilde's house, or RDFW. His nickname is 'Rubberneck', the rumour being that his neck was stretched under torture by the Japanese. In fact, he was a P.O.W. in Germany and the giraffe neck is a natural growth. He is a tall man with a fine head of iron grey hair, through which he often runs a hand. Tortured or not, he is said to have a partiality for South African sherry. Perhaps it's his shyness around the boys. His house is probably the most boring, lifeless one among the twenty-five houses. It never distinguishes itself at anything, nor are any of its boys in the slightest glamorous or even disreputable.

The building itself, by name 'Waynflete', is one of an adjacent, identical red brick pair, built in the 1920s, on a road which runs into the country in the direction of Dorney, a hamlet of council houses beyond the railway viaduct. The gravelled drive which leads into the 'Private Side', where parents may call on the housemaster, is graciously broad, but the boys' entrance is a narrow alley next to the 'arrears' or toilets, and always smells accordingly. Perhaps that accounts for the nickname 'Drainflete'.

The first thing new boys have to do is learn the catechism of inane nicknames and colours that make this asylum special. Each of the houses has its own colours, as do the school teams. The colours denote an awards system for achievements in sport.

All this mumbo-jumbo has to be memorized, and tested by one of the prefects, or, as they are known, the 'Library'. Everything at Eton has to have its own name. For a boy who has gone through the British educational mill, this nonsense may inspire awe or even seem like the initiation into some privileged sect, but for someone who has lived and gone to school in three other countries, it's just ridiculous and toe-curlingly embarrassing.

New boys live on the top or fourth floor, along the corridor from Mrs. 'Mac', the 'Boys' Maid', who brings each of us a jug of hot water to wash with every morning. I have been given a choice of three rooms and I pick the corner one, with the beam running diagonally right across the middle of the room, from floor to ceiling, because it has the most character. My mother has provided me with a series of prints of 18th century balloons, of the 'Montgolfier' type, to pin up. My recycled furniture consists of a clap-together bed, concealed during the day under a drape (tacked to a brown vinyl-covered board) whose pattern matches my curtains (yellow, with a brown design); a desk with a bookcase and drawers; a chair and an armchair; an ottoman, or chest, with brown vinyl-covered lid, for my sports and casual clothes; and a washbox, with lid and door, in which are basin and spongebag. The desk and washbox are a bit battered from previous service and are repainted the ubiquitous dark brown. A water carafe, capped with a glass, sits on a little shelf.

There is central heating in the corridors, but the rooms are heated only by coal fires, and tend to get cold during the winter, when the coal runs out. We are allowed one bucket a week, hauled up from the coalhouse, in the yard next to the kitchen. It's enough for about two real fires a week, so it's best to have friends one can visit.

I have a tiny Hitachi radio with an earplug, purchased with my acting salary, so I can listen to pirate radio under the bedclothes. Kenny Everett and Dave Cash, the DJs whose jingle is 'Kenny and Cash on London', are familiar and engaging voices. Although based on a ship just outside UK waters, they have revolutionized radio in the UK. Radio Caroline starts up later, but I'm loyal to Radio London.

Luckily, I am by far not the only boy who has not attained the magical height of five feet and two inches by the age of thirteen, and am, therefore, not the only boy obliged to wear a 'bumfreezer'. This uniform consists of a three-inch starched white collar, whose stud is covered with a narrow white tie, a black jacket which stops short of the behind, the regulation black and grey striped trousers, black socks and shoes. Taller boys wear the waiter's tails and a narrower starched collar. I have been issued with two of these uniforms, six collarless white shirts, six normal white shirts, grey flannel trousers and a tweed jacket for 'change', six handkerchiefs, underwear and socks, all with my laundry mark 'W60' sewn into them. We change uniforms every week.

At Eton, wearing 'bumfreezer'.

Fagging is a feature of the first year at Eton. Members of the Library have the right to call fags and send them on errands to other houses or to shops, or pretty much anywhere they wish within the school, or to set them to do chores, like cleaning their Corps equipment. Delivering fag notes — folded into a sub-origami shape — is also common. Fags also serve tea to the house captain and his cronies in the Library, toasting bread over the fire on a long fork. Fags are summoned with the long-drawn out call 'Boy up!' Until one gets used to its rising-falling-rising cadence, it is a startling sound and of course an interruption of whatever one is doing. All eligible boys in the house scamper towards the source of this howl, jostling each other so as not to be last, as it is the last one who must perform the chore. It's supposed to teach boys the importance of hierarchy or something. When the fags attain senior rank themselves, they will also have the opportunity of harassing their juniors.

Because I sang my best without knowing the purpose of the audition, I have landed myself in the Lower Chapel choir. This is a major indignity. Talking about music, 'Road Runner', an instrumental by the Gants, is my favourite 45rpm single.

The railway viaduct is a good place to explore and the arches are good to hide under. We put some copper pennies on the line and the train flattens them, distorting Britannia pleasingly. Coin box phones are another place pennies can be used, they take four of them. Of course they won't take them if they're flattened, but a good thump often liberates a few coins.

Lunchtime at No. 2 The Grove

Quoth my mother "Have some more Joo", as she passed the fruit salad or the gravy. This usage, which originated between her and my father (who never objected) and tended usually to be addressed to him, was already common during my childhood. There were plenty of opportunities for her to gratify this habit and she seldom missed one. What did it mean? To a woman not normally given to cute expressions for their own sake, although still possessed of a lamentably clear memory for juvenilities shared with her brother and sister, the utterance must have had a precise meaning. I believe it is no exaggeration to say that the pronouncement of the word 'Jew', or the phonetic equivalent thereof, represented for her a kind of deliverance, a talismanic relief from her own self-imposed political correctness.

Jews and Jewishness were often on her mind, both in an amorphous way and in the singular omnipresence of my father. As a child, she would grieve to us, she had been taunted by her blond siblings with the epithets 'elderly Jewess' and 'battling half-caste'. So she may have grown up with a natural contempt for Jews, even beyond the innate disdain normal among her compatriots. (The English are or were courteous and discreet, but they never made a secret amongst themselves of their distrust of Jews, unlike the overtly anti-Semitic French Catholics, a high percentage of whom recently responded to a survey by designating French Jews as foreigners.) My mother was wont to describe the wave of Jewish immigrants into Britain in the early Thirties as 'Refujews' and to designate those of particularly Semitic appearance as 'Hitler's posters'. I only became aware of the categories of 'Jew' and 'Gentile' in the 1970s, by coincidence perhaps around the time the word 'holocaust' was being distorted and promoted in the media. (Doctor, was I as a child the victim of subliminal 'antisemitism'?)

Yet, with her wavy black hair and slightly beaked nose, my mother could have passed for a Jewess herself. This must have instilled in her an irresolvable conflict, and raises interesting questions about the attitude with which she married my father ("just think what he can do for me," relayed her sister spitefully, but not necessarily truthfully, from her slough of envy). The possible duality implied by her marital commitment cannot have added to her peace of mind. Her mental state, rarely stable, was always tainted with potential schizophrenia: on the one hand an erstwhile danseuse and Semitic type, in danger of being mistaken for an actual Jew, and therefore with a stronger than average need to identify with her traditional if latent anti-

Semitic background; on the other, her marriage to an actual Jew. So her voicing of the sound 'joo', for 'juice' may have been sort of charm, a vocal juju, providing immunity from this infection. (Would you say, Doctor, that I'm attributing too much importance to this? Was it just the deliberate mispronunciation of the French '*jus*'?)

But it could also have been a provocation. Having lost through marriage to my father the medium of the stage, much of my mother's speech and manner was a substitute, a performance, intended to attract attention. My father, in his gentle, absent way, completely devoid of the experience or information which would have explained her behaviour (or of the realization that explanation was warranted), never corrected her. He did not understand what drove her. Her sons, divining the truth, sat by, grimacing and twisting their napkins. In fact, my mother came close to insulting my father at his own table every time fruit salad was served.

1962

It's my second year and I've moved down to a room on the third floor. It's larger but undistinguished and gives onto the road. Playboy centrefolds would stand out better against the flowered wallpaper and the dark brown wood than my balloons, but, apart from the fact that they would be forbidden, I'm a bit confused about the sexual attractions of women. Most or at least many of the boys I know and meet in class — outside those in this moribund house of course — chatter animatedly about other boys' attractions. The exceptions to this temptation are presumably those whose sexual vitality is low or undeveloped, like Plevin, who has followed me from Stone House. Unfortunately, perhaps because of this tentative connection, he and I are thrown together as messmates, which limits gossip of this kind. Messing means taking tea together and sharing whatever goodies individual pocket money will afford. I have bought a toaster, but it tends to short all the lights in the house — so inadequate is the good old English wiring — and we have to rush to conceal it to avoid confiscation.

Very few boys of my year are neither under-sexed nor obsessed with other boys. But John P., for instance, whose father owns a mill in Bradford, gives the impression of being without the need of this kind of stimulation, while being generally on top of things. John wears a handmade uniform. The pattern of his perfectly pressed striped trousers is slightly different from that of the baggy, stained norm. His hair is always beautifully cut and combed and he has a state-of-the-art Quad stereo system.

I have had a falling out with Plevin. He has placed my jars of Tiptree jam outside my door with a note which reads 'I believe these belong to you'. Plevin is nice but dull, he must have been offended when I made fun of him. But he does have a sense of humour. For example, he agreed that my scheme for selling 'Zacharia Cakes', seasoned human waste, would be a real money-spinner. (Isn't this an early indication of what your kind calls 'social alienation', Doctor?)

Chapter VI

MYKONOS, MOTHERS

April 1962

Mykonos house.

As usual, in April and September, we are spending two weeks on the Greek island of Mykonos. My parents have restored a shepherd's cottage, to which they continue to add.

The house has a great view over a bay towards an islet with the quintessentially Greek white chapel, and the property has three wells, so it's about the greenest spot on the island.

On Mykonos, our two main companions are Jim Price and Jinx Walker. Jim, a tall, lanky, gay American, who wears a dark blue fisherman's cap over his brown curls, has supervised the remodelling of the house. He and his dog, Sifty, often accompany us on picnics. Jinx, a slender American painter, also gay, an acquaintance of former friends of my parents, becomes a regular accomplice. To her, the island is 'Mickey Mouse'.

When we land at the port, we load the luggage into one of the half dozen taxis which are the only cars on Mykonos, and walk up through the maze of whitewashed streets. My father carries his violin case on his head, this being, as he tells us, the best way to maintain an equal balance. This may well be, but his appearance, in shorts and sandals, coupled with this porterage, which I have hitherto only associated with Arab women carrying water jugs in Hergé's *Les Cigares du Pharaon*, adds to my discomfort at being alive.

We quickly fall into our habitual routines. My hair stiff with salt, I laze with a book in a canvas chair on the patio, under the vines, and watch a large spider weave a web. The insect is an expert weaver, which is more than can be said for the island's weaving industry, one of whose amateur products, an almost injuriously rough pastel orange pullover with typically unreliable dye, I am wearing.

The daily chores are quickly completed. We all troupe down to the town in the morning, stopping at one of the local characters, English-speaking Vienoula K., a large, black-clad materfamilias, who runs the weaving store whence comes my orange creation. Having whiled away a few minutes conversing about her family and other matters, such as repairs to the house, we move on to the two or three shops where provisions can be bought. We don't need much and what we buy must be carried back to the house. On Mykonos there are two bakers: the 'German' baker (with a German oven) and the other one, which we frequent. He bakes his bread in a traditional wood-fired kiln. Down some steps between two of the alleys which criss-cross the town, into a large space, white-painted, dominated by the oven, a towering affair built into one corner. Two mouths in its smooth surface admit fuel and loaves respectively. A pile of the island's dwindling brush lies to one side. A dusting of flour coats most surfaces. The smell is heavenly. Only two kinds of bread are baked and, already on the second day, they're better toasted, but they form a staple of our diet, the remaining ingredients being yoghurt, Hymettus honey, coffee, sardines, feta cheese, tomatoes, oranges and figs from the trees on our land. We also have a plentiful supply of prickly pears, which my father once tries to cook in a pressure cooker, for some reason, maybe because he can't find another pot. They explode all over the kitchen.

The string shopping bags now filled, we move on to the port, where we usually lunch at one of several adjacent restaurants. Unless there is a cruise ship moored just outside the port itself, there are very few tourists and we have the place almost to ourselves. We children think the lukewarm moussaka or meatballs, chosen from the cauldrons in the kitchen, is a treat, although the baklava, or shredded wheat resembling, syrup-covered desert, is too cloying for me. Depending on the catch of the day, a more adventurous lunch might start with octopus tentacles, speared with a toothpick and dipped in vinegar, followed by a grilled fish. Washed down with Retsina, a wine cut with pine resin, the atmosphere is complete, Retsina not being an acquired taste but simply part of a Greek holiday's suspended reality. Allegedly, young Greeks these days mix it with Coca-Cola, probably because they can't afford more expensive alcohol, but the combination of this infamous soft drink with varnish must surely be exquisitely horrible.

Alternatively, we hire one of the blue and white caiques and putter around the headland to the islet opposite the house. Here, we snorkel and collect seashells, and partake of the invariable sardines and bread.

LIVED IT WRONG

This morning, when my parents asked me what time I got back the night before, I said midnight. In fact, it wasn't until nearly two and they probably heard me anyway, through the communicating wall. I was at the 'Seven Muses', as usual. It's quite a thrill, at thirteen, to sit in a nightclub among adults. Vasilis runs the place and always gives me free drinks. I have a crush on Danielle, who's French and twenty-five and probably Vasilis's girlfriend. Her boyish figure and short blond hair make her my ideal. I'm not sure what I want from her. It's not sex, as I don't know what sex with women consists of, apart from what I've deduced from Ian Fleming's fantasies. Neither should she be a substitute mother. Perhaps just affectionate proximity. She introduces me to the poems of Kahlil Gibran, whose name she writes for me on a packet of Greek gaspers. At two, she and I pick our way up the pitch dark and potholed road on the hill behind the town. When we get to the goat track which leads over the foreland and down to my parents' house, I pass her my flashlight, so she can get back to the oversized dovecot she shares with Vasilis. Years later, I learn that Danielle was Jinx's girlfriend. Ah well, not another missed opportunity, then.

A word about my parents on holiday. My father goes down to the kitchen every morning, makes breakfast for my mother, and carries the tray up to her. A casual observer might deduce that this is a husband giving his hard-worked wife a holiday by performing the household chores himself. In fact, of course, my mother is waited on hand and foot all the time. Why shouldn't she get up and make everyone breakfast? It's just as well she doesn't, as she wouldn't know how. My mother doesn't drive, never goes anywhere alone and can barely dial a phone number. On holiday, she spends hours lying in the sun in a bathing suit and sunhat.

She's a woman who doesn't lift a finger around the house, but affects to be sorely oppressed by her duties and responsibilities. She does have two daily, self-appointed tasks: writing her diary and reading a Christian Science-prescribed passage from the Bible.

But her most critical obligation is packing for her next trip. We don't interrupt her while she's doing this, as it takes her full concentration. Exceptionally, she closes her bedroom door. Suitcases are strewn all over the floor and wardrobes, packed with clothes, gape open. Don't you dare envy her clothes or her easy life, or you'll get an earful. Yet she's not like most Englishwomen of her class who don't expect to do anything, or to be anything, except decorative. She grits her teeth and does her duty. She may not be much of a mother, but she's an efficacious companion to my father. I must not forget that, to him, she's always 'wonderful'.

My mother is well-read and quick-witted. She quotes from the Bible, from literature, writes well and inventively, if ornately, and she even draws a bit, with charcoal. Something must have bust inside her brain though, if she really thinks life consists of such incredibly dull things as seem to belabour her in her relations with her children. At least Joan Crawford didn't only care about metal hangers. Another point which distinguishes my mother from Joan Crawford is her lack of performing talent. Yet she wants to perform all the time, by reading aloud from the newspaper, for instance, thereby spoiling the article for everyone else who could have read it, if he were interested, at his own leisure; or by suddenly throwing up one leg in front of the guests and in the middle of a conversation. Why does she do this? Because she wants to demonstrate how she can still do this ballet stuff? Because my father is getting too much, and she's getting insufficient, attention?

All I know is, it's highly embarrassing. Then there's the endless repetition of anecdotes. I can predict not only how she will react to something, but exactly what she will say. If you mention American humour, for example, you will hear about the New Yorker in the bar who said "Something has died inside of my bun." If you mention Shakespeare's speeches, you'll get her brother, before he went mad, exclaiming "If me no ifs and but me no buts." These snippets could have been marginally amusing the first time; at the fiftieth repetition, they tend to pall a bit.

I wonder, does she not notice how tediously verbose she is? Her speech mannerisms and her affectations are a throwback to the Twenties, when she was growing up, or even a direct inheritance from or impersonation of her own mother. She makes me jump when, halfway through a word, she suddenly shrieks one syllable. Her French is exquisitely discomfiting. She is fluent and her accent is fine, but her vocabulary is outmoded and she uses such ancient and cumbersome expressions as '*Je m'en fiche comme de l'an quarante*'. But she loves to go to Paris, where she can air her French.

I once proposed to my brother, to relieve the boredom of my mother's predictable anecdotes, that we play a game at meal times. I called it 'old chestnuts'. We were to agree beforehand on a few key words, calculated to provoke our mother's time-worn utterances, to see which of us could succeed in eliciting the most of these. Unfortunately, my brother never consented to play.

I must not omit to mention that I am grateful to my mother for taking me to the theatre, no matter how much this may have been due to her own need for this kind of amusement and my father's incapability of deriving much pleasure from it. On the few occasions when my parents shared some kind of non-musical public entertainment, like a film, my father was wont to inquire in a loud voice for information about what was happening. Beyond the classics, fiction in any guise was a mystery to him.

In the early Sixties, my mother would reserve two seats through an acquaintance at Claridges, say at the Old Vic, and we would duly be driven over the river to enjoy one of Shakespeare's tragedies, most of which I saw, aged about twelve. Sometimes, we would go backstage after the performance to intrude on the actors in their dressing rooms. I remember Barbara Jefford and John Neville, and today's eternal and omnipresent Judi Dench, as Ophelia. Later, we saw together Noël Coward in *Private Lives*, during a Coward revival in the West End, in 1963, and a memorable performance of Pinter's

No Man's Land, with John Gielgud and Ralph Richardson, in 1975.

To watch such great actors perform was unforgettable; to meet them, an enormous privilege. Particularly Gielgud and Richardson, both known for their modesty, were interesting to talk to as well. Gielgud explained to my mother and me how he had pondered over what shoes to wear in his part and decided on the sandals he still wore when we visited him backstage. Richardson spoke about his motorcycling when I had the good fortune to sit next to him at lunch at the Savile Club. These grand old pillars of the London theatre contrast sharply with today's media-friendly, all-purpose equivalents, like the ubiquitous Stephen Fry.

Noël Coward was kind enough to give me advice about acting, when I visited him in his dressing room one afternoon. He was adamant about the dedication required, which, in retrospect, I probably didn't have, although to be fair, I was not given the choice.

I next spotted Coward in a brown dinner jacket, sitting on a sofa at Buckingham Palace. The occasion was Prince Charles' twenty-first birthday party, in 1969 (a few months later than my own). I accompanied my parents to this celebration, having custody of the two green and three yellow cards with which we gained admittance to an inner sanctum. I knocked at the closed door, which was opened by H.M. the Queen herself. Much taken aback, I said "Full house", flourishing the cards at her, and we entered. It was also here that I heard from Welf's mother that he had been killed in India recently, allegedly by a karate blow at the Ashram he had been attending, of all unlikely occurrences. There must presumably be Ashrams of all types, from genuine retreats to those contrived to suit foreign demand, presided over by Gurus such as the infamous Rajneesh (recipient of 96 Rolls-Royces), or the more recent 'Guru of Bling'.

Winter 1962

Of course they don't play football at Eton, they play their own game called the Field Game, a sort of combination of football and rugby. It's played in the winter, when there's plenty of mud and it's freezing. I'm so good at this that I'm always relegated to goal, where I can doze off, waking with alarm when I realize that the ball may be coming too close for comfort. During a really dull match, like today's, it's possible to have a conversation, although it tends to be interrupted from time to time. The subject today is sex, for a change.

"What's it like — doing it with a woman?" I ask Selwyn, during a lull at our end of the pitch.

"The first time is special, they say, like a voyage of discovery," says Stubbs Minor.

"Yeah, it's sort of like a Voyage to the Interior with Captain Cock, you know?" says Selwyn.

"Very funny. You ever been?" I ask.

"No, but my mother promised to pay for me if I get through school."

"How, pay?"

"You know, with a prostitute," says Selwyn airily.

"Oh," I'm impressed.

"Your mother?" says Stubbs.

"Yeah. She says there's not a whole lot to it. Men just have to get their mechanics going. She says it's all a matter of mechanics, like running a car in."

"Doesn't sound like she has much fun with your dad," says Stubbs.

"Shut up, Stubbs. What do you know about it anyway?"

"As much as you. It's supposed to be fun, isn't it?"

"My mother says sex is disgusting because men do it with the part they use to pee with," I say.

"So do women," says Stubbs.

"No, they don't, it's next to it. I'll show you. See this?" Selwyn begins to draw with his boot in the mud.

"Get back into goal, Menuhin!"

"OK, I'll show you later."

I look up at the sky as another plane to or from Heathrow goes by. I don't care where it's going; I just wish I were on board. While I'm up in the sky, I can imagine other things planes could be used for. Bombers, for instance could bombard the school buildings, fighters could strafe the staff. I myself expand to a friend on a plan to man a Spandau machine gun from the Lower Chapel altar. (Shades of Lindsay Anderson's *if...*, 1968.) We are all familiar with the Second World War and its armaments, from 'trash', cheap comics that portray the invincible British against the Germans and Japanese. These are immensely popular. Occasionally, we play war games in which the Germans are usually impersonated by a luckless officer called Nerdlinger von Klein, who is always shouting '*Achtung Minen!*' When I'm not skimming trash, I'm reading the novels of P.G. Wodehouse, of which I have a number. One book no one can read is *The Fourth of June* by an Old Etonian, banned because it maligns the school.

25 December, 1962

Family Christmas at No. 2 The Grave is a marvel of controlled merriment. For days, my mother has set the stage on which we will express our wonder and gratitude. Behind the locked door of the living room, she has wrapped most of the presents herself and arranged them artistically under the tree, in order of size. Around the middle of Christmas morning, the door is thrown open and my father, brother and I are summoned to attend the ceremonious opening of the presents. We, the *dramatis personæ*, advance gingerly into the room, taking care all the while to deliver ourselves of appropriate cries of joy and praise. However vociferous Jeremy and I are, our father always outlasts us with expressions in which admiration and condolence are mixed. "Oh, my darling, how marvellous!" he exclaims, and then, moaning slightly, "You shouldn't have done all this. Isn't Mummy wonderful?" he asks us rhetorically. Then he is sent upstairs again to get his camera, which he has 'hopelessly' forgotten. Usually, he can't find it, or else it is so new a toy — he is always buying the latest model on his trips to the Orient — that he doesn't know how to use it, or if he finds it and it has film in it and he succeeds in deciphering the manual, he has no flashbulbs, or those he has don't work. We affect patience and await the order of procedure. There is very little of the festive anticipation in the air; too much is planned and formal. Once my mother has castigated my father sufficiently for his failings and he has recorded this miracle of artistry, my brother and I prepare for the signal that we may approach the tree and choose our first present.

"Aren't you going to open your presents?" asks my mother, somewhat plaintively. My brother and I advance tentatively, not quite on our knees but suitable humbly, on the tree. Carefully, so as not to disturb the symmetry of the arrangement, we extricate something with our names on it. Having spotted my pile, I pick the most accessible present and read the card. "Oh, it's from Mummy!" I say. I usually aim for the smallest object I can see. I unwrap it extremely slowly and painstakingly so as to preserve untorn the paper for future use (as I have been trained to do), murmuring the while such phrases as "I wonder what it could be" which, considering that most of my presents are books, would give an observer the impression that I am an imbecile. "Oh, it's a book!" I say, surprised, "Thank you so much, Mummy!" I also try to remember to say "Oh, what lovely paper!", for, if I forget to remark about it, my mother is sure to say "Don't you like the paper, I chose it specially?"

Then it's my brother's turn to complete the ritual. With becoming modesty, we then occupy ourselves by examining these presents. I leaf through the book, as if there are no other presents and I mean to read it there and then, at one sitting. After a suitable interval, my mother invites us to open another. If a single word defines my home life, it's 'unnatural'.

My father is put through the same paces and reproached with "Your father never notices anything", should he overlook some aspect of his gifts. He habitually receives a framed caricature of a famous composer or musician, for which rarity my mother has probably been gypped by the dealer. I cannot tell whether these objects please my father particularly, but he is always certain to greet them with the proper ecstasy. This is an integral part of the spontaneous living pageant that is our Christmas. So is the cry of surprise and joy when I discover a book. Actually, my mother knows my reading tastes, and the pleasure I derive from receiving a new Arthur Ransome, say, is genuine. A kiss is then exchanged and I read the blurb of the book, until, with further encouragement, I again approach the pile and unwrap another present decorously, first handing my mother one that is intended for her. It is harder for Jeremy and me to enthuse over the odd articles of male jewellery, such as tie pins and cuff links which our mother invariably brings back from various corners of the earth. These trinkets, often large misshapen blobs of lava or unprecious stones, glued into crude settings and packed by our mother into cotton wool in one of her collection of 'useful' small boxes, are absolutely unwearable. My mother holds up the proceedings to instruct us in the provenance and supposed exoticism of these objects, for instance: "Do you know what it is? It's malachite, the natives dig it out of pigs' trotters and use it to shine their noses. Isn't it extraordinary?"

My mother has told me with the sigh of the morally obligated about how she buys these and other gewgaws (doilies, scarves, soap) throughout the year wherever she finds herself, for what she calls her nest. I am not sure why she uses this word to describe erstwhile retainers and others for whom she plays Lady Bountiful, but I should like to see their expressions when they receive these gifts or read the cards on which my mother scrawls four or five lines of complaints about her dreary life. I shouldn't imagine that it would go down terribly well with a retired nurse afflicted with cancer, for instance, to get a postcard of a Greek beach, on which is written 'a scrawl from our fifth stop in ten days, just time to unpack and pack again before our next departure. Ah well, no rest for the wicked.' But my mother is much attached to these ex-employees because they listened by the hour to her monologues — they had no alternative — and shared with her the *Daily Mail* crossword or the soap operas on television. I don't know how many times I've heard my mother speak condescendingly of Millie, who, because of her swollen legs, cannot manage the climb to her room during the day and is therefore trapped by my mother in the kitchen at tea time: "Poor Millie, she does so enjoy our tea together with the crossword, it's all she has." I have it on good authority that Millie, after she retired, was heard to remark that now at last she didn't have to share her crossword with that bloody woman. Millie's spoken was perhaps richer than her cooking repertoire. It included such advice as "Steady past your grandmas" (when stumbling), or "Nothing's wasted where there's pigs" (finishing leftovers), or the unforgettable "Me no like Darkees" (pidgin-English, around the time of Enoch Powell's warning about the influx of African migrants; retributive justice for colonisation).

Whereas Millie's Lancashire roots are probably faithfully reflected in her conversation, my mother's claim to her Londoner's credentials is less well-grounded. Inquiries concerning this subject trigger the story about the pompous dinner guest of Nehru's who asked her where she came from. She told him she was 'a true Cockney, born within the sound of Bow Bells'. Surely this kind of verbal slumming was already outdated before the war. My mother gets along with anyone who is sufficiently attentive or pretends to think she is amusing. She prefers men, treating women with few exceptions as rivals for the attentions of whatever man is present, including their own husbands. If she likes a man, she usually describes him by saying "He has a great sense of humour, we got on like houses on fire and he rolled all over the floor." The number of men whom my mother has consigned to spontaneous combustion or to the bonfire of her sexual imaginings is legion. Depending on her mood or motivation, the anecdote will either serve to reflect her irresistible sexual allure or her incisive insight.

Arguably, there is not a great man whom my mother has met, sat next to at dinner or on an aircraft perhaps, who has not awarded her one of these accolades. Whereas most people in similar situations might attempt to elicit from their celebrated neighbour some information which he is peculiarly able to impart, my mother invariably reverses the positions. Thus, according to her, she told Henry Kissinger how to run foreign policy and he said, "You are quite right, Diana."

The image is always one of her interlocutor in paroxysms of pleasure, on his back with his arms and feet in the air, like a dog having its stomach scratched. The saddest aspect of the approval she claims she evokes in men is their sexual interest. According to my mother, there is probably not a man over twenty-five who does not experience an immediate desire to copulate with her as soon as he sets eyes on her. To the image of the sprawling dog should be added that of a rutting ram. "Pricks up, Diana's here!" was my ex-wife's verdict. Through this heated atmosphere of barely restrained desire my mother moves, ruefully aware of the frustration she causes. "And of course he liked me but your father disapproved", or "His wife doesn't like me because he and I get on so well." A certain member of the German aristocracy, famous for having had several younger and voluptuous wives, is supposed to have 'tried everything but' with my mother. "Everything but what?" I ask, provoked for once beyond restraint. "Everything but," repeats my mother mysteriously and with even greater emphasis.

Prompted once again by my sullenness towards her, while I was still at school, my mother refers to her recent response in matters of hairbrushes; at my request, she has remembered to buy me a new one: "Am I not, she says, the perfect mother?" I am speechless. This marked the height of my mother's self-deceptions — at least where I was concerned.

Eulogy. When a mother enters a room, all bow and scamper. A mother carries with her a measure of dread and holiness that commands respect. When a mother raises her leg (right or left) vertically to demonstrate her flexibility, all murmur their admiration at this feat. When a mother divulges her suffering, including miscarriages without number, endured stoically, and continual disappointment at the hands of her ungrateful and undeserving wretches of children, all nod along in mute compassion. When a mother sighs, all nature takes heed, for a mother's sigh contains all the world's regret, all of history's faults, all of man's failings; a mother's sigh is as the humid draft that spreads the seeds of fertility far and wide, and as the scorched breath of the desert that shrivels them up again. All women are potential mothers. A man may ponder and pronounce, but a woman propagates. All hail then, to the noble everlasting soul of women, of mothers, and, as they pass, on their eternal round of self-fulfilment and duty, pass me the sick bag.

Chapter VII

MORE ETON

Summer 1962

I'm rowing my fixed-seat rigger on the river. I'm a 'wet-bob', which means that I row for exercise. 'Dry-bobs' play cricket. Apart from cricket being a pretty lame game, overwhelmed by imbecilic expressions like 'short leg' or 'silly mid-on' or 'silly mid-off' or 'googly', I'm not a team person, so I'm pleased with the alternative. Except that I get terrible blisters until my hands have acclimatized themselves to the oars. Wet-bobs have to do a certain number of miles according to a chart on the house notice board, every week. It's possible to cheat, but it's not really worth being caught, and besides, it's not that hard work. If you don't do your miles, you must go on a forced run, usually on the river bank, with a member of the Library coaxing you along with a whippy bamboo cane.

I'm not making much progress with my guitar. I can just about play 'Wipe Out', the Surfaris' hit. There are a couple of quite capable boys' groups. I've just heard one of them doing a decent version of the Dave Clark Five's 'Glad All Over' on the stage in the School Hall. If I had followed through with my original desire to play, five years ago, I would by now be better than them. A couple of catchy lyrics from other memorable tunes from the era are 'Let me tell you about the birds and the bees, and the flowers and the trees, and a girl like you, on a night like this', and, of course, the unforgettable 'In the summertime, when the trees leaves are green, I'll be blue, 'cause you don't want my love.' These are less profound than they appear, but I like them.

As a member of the Film Society, I saw Franju's *Les Yeux sans visage* in the School Library tonight. A black and white masterpiece of unnerving, muted horror, and definitely an improvement over last time's film, *Babette s'en va-t-en guerre*, a so-so comedy with Brigitte Bardot.

Lady Crosfield has died and left her property to her adopted son Paul, who lives in the grand style, spending where his stepmother saved, on a Rolls Royce and peacocks. One of them dies in our garden.

Spring 1964

I'm not sure, but I think my father has just been trying to tell me the facts of life. He summoned me into the bathroom he shares with my mother, where, on the green carpet, he was sitting cross-legged in a bathing suit, doing his daily yoga exercises, and began to talk to me in a very roundabout way about relations between men and women. In any case, I was far too fascinated by watching him roll the muscles from one side of his stomach to the other to pay much attention. In fact, it was only after I left him that I thought I realized what he had been on about. It was even vaguer than the celebrated lecture which begins 'I don't know if you've noticed something at the base of your stomach.' He must have been put up to this by my mother. Why else would he accept to be distracted from his yoga? It was probably the only moment he could manage to spare.

Speaking with my father for longer than it takes to say something while passing him in the hall, or on the stairs, entails making an appointment for an audience. This of course implies having an important subject to discuss, so as not to waste his time. My mother acts as a sort of go-between with my father. She can mediate with him about the common things of life for which he has little understanding and less curiosity. To say he is a busy man would be an understatement. He can fill every minute of the day. If there seems to be an empty space in his official two-year schedule, he fills it without telling anyone, to my mother's irritation. If he's not practising, writing an article, involved in some project, giving an interview, or playing a concert, he's recovering from one of these exertions. So there's never any guarantee that he will be approachable. And that's when he's at home. While he's travelling, he has the happy ability to fall asleep for a few minutes in car or plane, so that he can't be disturbed. That's why my mother is a necessary intermediary.

Despite not being conversant with the tedious details of ordinary people's lives, my father is an authority on all sorts of subjects with which I know he has no or only minimal experience. Jogging, for instance, or women, of whom he has known two, maybe three. All women are to be exalted. I suppose that much of his knowledge comes from second-hand sources, like his goddess-mother, herself a proficient theorist, or from classical literature.

August 1964

Our neighbours, the Turners, have invited me to join their sons, the twins Richard and Roger, in Scotland with them. I take the train to Lairg, the northernmost station on the line. There, Sir Mark, the twins' father, picks me up in his black and silver Bentley. The car's soft suspension and strong-smelling leather seats make me queasy. We arrive at Ledmore Lodge, a simple single-storey building with a tin roof. Inside, it's spacious and comfortable, with a separate wing for us children. There's a hut for hanging game. Next door lives the gillie, or gamekeeper. The property, which the Turners have been renting every summer for many years, belongs to a shipping magnate and includes several lochs and fells.

Richard and Roger and I climb into our rubber boots and, behind the gamekeeper, trudge off over the heather to fish. The gillie rows us across the loch while two of us trawl lines over the rear of the boat. Sometimes we get instruction in casting, but this is the laziest fishing imaginable. As usual, we catch enough trout for lunch. The fish is cooked on a fire on one of the islets.

We are well protected from the persisting drizzle and, in any case, rain on a Scottish moor is part of the atmosphere and almost enjoyable, compared to sooty, acid city rain. The clouds of midges are a nuisance, though.

Today, it's shooting. We climb to the top of a hill and wait. Twelve-bore shotguns, broken, are under our arms. The gillie makes us lie flat and get ready to shoot. Suddenly, there's like a commuter rush of rabbits. It's my turn. I raise the gun, aim and fire, traverse and fire again. To the approval of the gillie, I have got a 'left and right', two rabbits with successive shots from each barrel. They're thrown, lifeless and limp, into the game bag. I feel sorry for what I've done; fishing seems less cruel. Later, some neighbours come over to dinner and we play charades afterwards, but I'm too shy to be much good at it.

We dam up the stream in front of the house. It's a big project. In the evenings, we play Whiskey Poker and Mah-jong with the twins' parents, in front of the fire. On another evening, in the absence of the adults, who have gone out to dinner, Margaret, the twins' sister, who's older and usually fairly distant, joins us in a raid on the liquor cabinet. We invent a cocktail and, feeling quite happy, run about in the dusk and swing wildly on the gate. It's harmless stuff.

November 1964

I'm in the house shooting team and am allowed to practise with the others in the shooting gallery above the gym. This means being able to leave the house after dark, having entered my name and time of departure in the roster. It takes about ten minutes to get to the gym. I enjoy the strange sense of power I feel, as I prowl through the usually empty alleys, sometimes in thick fog, pretending to be evil incarnate, like Jack the Ripper.

January 1965

I feel a frisson at the sign 'Kaltenbrunn'. Did Ernst Kaltenbrunner come from here? At sixteen, one has read something about the war. But not really enough to make any deductions. About what? About the sensational but unspoken nastiness of wholesale gassing and the general ghastliness of the Second World War. That's what. The Bavarian winter landscape goes by the car's windows. I'm certain Nazi gold must still lie at the bottom of the notoriously deep Starnberger See, as described in *Gold Is Where You Hide It* (Stanley Moss, 1956). We're on the way to Schloss Elmau again.

My mother snorts water from her nose into the basin in the mornings. She says "It's the only way I can clear it." I don't know if it's as a result of this once-too-often-performed observance, or because my father forgot to say 'Good Morning' right to her, but they have some kind of a disagreement, and my mother disappears from their suite during the morning. My father, panicked, alerts the hotel owners, who call in the police. All day, patrols search the surrounding countryside. My father fears my mother could be frozen somewhere in the snowy forest or even eaten by wild animals. Eventually, she is found enjoying a drink in a local tavern. Certainly, she hopes my father has been taught a lesson. Probably, he has.

The owner of the hotel invites my parents for dinner to an alpine hut, on the mountain across from the hotel. It's a kind of refined rusticity, meant to offer an alternative to the elegance of the hotel. There's no supervision, so I drink as much wine as I like, red and white both. Whether it's mixing the wine or its quality, as I stumble down the slope on the way back, despite the brisk winter cold, I begin to feel bad. Unfortunately, I don't throw up until I reach the bedroom I share with my brother. My mother is indignant and revolted, as she has never had to clear up this kind of mess.

Spring 1965

The headmaster, Chevenix-Trench (also known as 'shovel-shit-stench'), wants to see me. He understands that I am friends with a certain McP. What do I know about him? McP. is an amusing boy, with whom I occasionally gossip, I say. The headmaster tells me that McP. has been discovered in the act of whipping a boy he has bound to a tree, with a bicycle chain, and will be sacked. I am told that my year is the worst the school has ever had. While it undeniably contains its share of riffraff, including myself, I feel he must be exaggerating. There is a certain troublesome element, to use the euphemism common to schoolmasters, more concerned with music, fashion and sex than with studies, but this is not untypical for the Sixties, and the England of Carnaby Street and the Beatles and Rolling Stones.

I'm an old lag now and prone to an old lag's ways. For poetry, we have a substitute 'beak' or master, who is legendarily short-sighted. When it comes time for me to recite my poem, I go up to the front of class and, holding the book beneath the level of his desk, I simply read it out. Then I return to my place artlessly, amid sniggers from the rest of the class. "I know your type," the master tells me, sensing the truth despite his bottle-end spectacles.

A less successful attempt at cribbing, in Latin, before a humourless beak, results in my being reported to my housemaster and beaten by a member of the Library. In fact, cribbing is considered a serious offence and I could have been beaten by the Lower Master, a much more painful experience.

The spindly, timid history beak made a fool of himself today. He was advising us on probable exam questions, and said "I would avoid those like bargepoles." Naturally, we yelled and banged our desks and stamped our feet in derision.

Summer 1965

I can row in a sliding seat rigger now, a slim, very light boat with an almost transparent skin, which if rowed hard, goes quite fast. When stationary, you have to keep both oars flat on the water though, else it rolls over. I row up to King's Eyot and have a beer and row back again. Every time I slide under the road bridge before the island, I think of 'Ode to Billie Joe' which is a big hit and has to do with someone throwing themselves off a bridge. Being short and light, I also cox the house eight, as useless an enterprise as any of this house's sporting endeavours.

As I enter Addington Schools, where I have French with the famously eccentric and entertaining John Wells, I hear my favourite Shadows tune 'The Rise and Fall of Flingel Bunt' on a radio somewhere. My preoccupation with this number and the urgency of acquiring it from Andrea, the svelte but acned blonde with the beehive hairdo at the local record store, distracts me somewhat from a friend's whispered gossip about the latest rumour: a trusting boy has been waylaid by a vicious paedophile, tied to a desk in an empty classroom, and assaulted. As no one seems to know the victim's name, one wonders if this isn't just another product of our sex-obsessed society, or even someone's wishful thinking.

August 1965

Gstaad. An old friend of my father's is staying locally. She has recently been widowed and says she is thinking of moving to the Côte d'Azur. She is fun and probably in her mid-forties. She seems to like me and invites me to drive down to Cannes with her, in her rented Peugeot 504. At some point during this long drive I have to wrench the steering wheel over, when my host's attention seems to wander and we are in danger of hitting oncoming traffic, but we reach the hotel without further incident. The Carlton is undoubtedly the best hotel on the Riviera. Nice's Negresco has lost its allure and none of the other hotels, grand though they may be, can match the Carlton's glamour. Its pink doors with their golden letter boxes, discreetly silent corridors and irreproachable staff make it a model of its kind.

We settle down to a rather dull routine, whereby I spend much of the day walking around Cannes or lying on the beach, and my father's friend visits houses. One morning, as I pay my respects to her in her room, I find her still in bed. Whether it is on account of my neglect of this signal, if that is what it is, or because she is bored with house-hunting, she announces that she is leaving for New York.

A few days earlier, we had met in the lobby a small group, consisting of a mother, daughter and English nanny. Mariam and her mother are staying at the hotel too, as part of a round I later gather this good widow makes every summer between Gstaad, Cannes and Venice, in a desultory attempt, I suppose, to find a second husband. It is proposed that I stay on as harmless male company for Mariam, who is about my age. Princess Mariam is beautiful. Her father was the Sultan of Johore and her mother is Austrian. This inheritance has given her a tall, slender figure, opulent black hair, and elegant hands and feet to go with it. Flawless though she is, any intimacy in our relations is doomed from the start by the eternal presence of her nanny (amiable but authoritative) and my own hopeless naiveté. There is a romantic Twenties song called 'And Her Mother Came Too'. In this case 'nanny' would do as well.

Assisted by my inarticulate admiration, Mariam and I hit it off quite well. We while away the morning on the Carlton beach, where Mariam's mother has secured deck chairs in the front row, eat lunch at the hotel's splendid buffet, which must extend over six yards (I have always regretted the inborn restraint which prevented me from sampling all the dishes presented), and spend the afternoons shopping in Cannes' narrow streets or at a pelota match. (For those familiar with Sixties 'gear', the dark green herringbone-patterned hip-huggers with flared bottoms which I bought myself, may ring a bell. They were too revealing for a shrinking violet like me and I never wore them.) One day, we are treated to a ride along one of the corniches in the new Mercedes 230 SL (I sit across the back on the occasional seat), which has appeared recently. Our conversation, such as it is, is limited to the kinds of superficialities with which Mariam, as a gossip-conscious teenager, is conversant, and my own tongue-tied and ignorant responses. In the evenings, Mariam and I eat in the hotel's bar, chaperoned by the nanny, while Mariam's mother dines later in the dining room.

Most memorable is still this restaurant's *pot au chocolat*, the best of its kind I have ever tasted.

Mariam and I at the Carlton, Cannes, 1965.

A few years ago, when moored at Cannes, I dropped into the Carlton out of curiosity to see if it had retained any of its earlier aura. As a member of the Four Seasons chain, however, it had shed all individuality. The dining room was a sea of empty chairs, probably waiting to be filled by some dreary conference or other; the bar, drab and vacant, and the outdoor area, crowded with as sad a crew of everyday vulgarians as populates any self-conscious watering place. I left in a hurry. Never again.

September 1965

We are met at Athens airport by Jinx and her dog, Jason ('he has golden fleas'). Jinx is a riot. Besides being a talented painter, she's great fun. She asks me if I want to ride back to Athens with her on her tandem. Picturing the two of us panting all the way into Athens on a bicycle built for two, the self-conscious English schoolboy in me declines, and my brother accepts instead. I join my parents in the British embassy's stately black Rolls. When we arrive at the embassy, I see with surprise and mortification a white two-seater Alfa Romeo convertible pull up behind us. "This is my tandem," laughs Jinx.

We board the *Despina*, the old patched steamer that does the Piraeus to Cyclades overnight run. Jinx is along too. She and my parents get on very well, which is surprising, considering how repressed and unnatural my poor mother is. Jinx makes them laugh, something they don't seem to do too much together. In this area, they are incompatible: my mother's humour is arrested in the Fifties and earlier; my father's is ponderous and unsubtle, and rare.

We are all at lunch, at a restaurant by the beach. I drink far too much Retsina and swim fully clothed in the sea with Jinx and Jason. My parents don't seem to notice, but, on our return, I throw up copiously and discreetly, as I think, into the oleander bushes outside the house.

10 September, 1965

It's time to return to England. My father asks me if I would like to stay on for a few more days, with Jinx. I accept gladly. When we have seen my parents and brother off at the airport, Jinx and I drive back, stopping at an outdoors stadium to admire the view of the sea. We sit alone on the bleachers. "Do you have a girlfriend?" Jinx asks me. "No," I say, "there's no one on the island, except Danielle, she's beautiful, but she doesn't take me seriously." "Well, there's always me," says Jinx. I laugh nervously. I am too encumbered by my public school development to recognize this offer for what it is. The crippling combination of English inhibition and adolescent homosexual romance, and the fact that Jinx, slim and fun as she is, is also rather plain, make this offer unthinkable. Instead of seizing the opportunity, I am scared and repelled.

Jinx has a tiny, three-roomed house. She places a mattress for me in the corridor which connects the kitchen and her studio. She decides we should go on a camping trip to Delphi. Once we have picked up a friend, a butch Greek woman, the car becomes very cramped. It's almost dark by the time we arrive at Delphi. We set up the tent under the olive trees, between the ancient Olympic racing oval and the oracle's temple. The moon is full and casts long dark shadows. We are quite alone and there is no surveillance. The women share the tent and I use a sleeping bag.

The tourist season is over and we ramble around the site undisturbed. On the way back to Athens, we take a ferry through the Corinth Canal. Sheer cliffs tower over the boat on either side. It's late when we get back to Jinx's house, so I change and lie down on the narrow mattress. After a while, Jinx, still in her t-shirt and cut-off jeans, gets in beside me. I go rigid with embarrassment, and after a minute or so, without making further advances, she gets out again. As I lie still awake much later, puzzling over this unexpected and awkward episode, it occurs to me that, as a confirmed lesbian, she might only have been doing my father a favour.

20 September 1965

Back at school, the familiar smell of the freshly painted grey corridors embraces me. I have what may be the best room in the house. It's on the top floor, a few yards from the room I had as a new boy, but it's about three times larger. From the central beam hangs my hammock. There's a door which gives onto the top of the fire escape, ideal for slipping out at night and bicycling to Slough, to drink and bowl. In the wash-box is the miniature Sony television I share with John P. (transported to and from his house in a canvas holdall) and next to it, usually, a bottle of Teacher's Scotch. The radio and gramophone are now permitted, and I can play the first record I ever bought: the Beach Boys' 'Surfin' Safari' (1962), as well as such 45rpm pop as 'Woolly Bully' (Sam the Sham and the Pharaohs).

Three of us have been caught out of bounds and smoking, by a nosy junior Library member. He comes officiously into my room to question me. Evidently my replies are unsatisfactory, for he utters the fearsome phrase "You'll hear more about this." We are all beaten.

26 May, 1966

John P. and I take a taxi to London to get haircuts and shop for clothes. John buys a pink-and-white candy-striped jacket in a boutique off the Kings Road.

The Lansdown Hotel, Bath. My brother and half-brother, Krov, and I meet during the Bath Festival, of which my father is musical director. Krov has just completed his stint with the U.S. Army Green Berets. We are joined, apparently fortuitously, by a pretty young woman who seems somehow to be related to my mother. As my mother came from English/Irish/Scottish stock, she must have had relatives in the UK and might have been expected to introduce her own children to our cousins. But they have remained invisible throughout my life. Apart from her sister and schizophrenic brother, and her own mother, whom I met when I was too young to take her in, my mother's family apparently didn't exist. As I recall — I'm of necessity vague — the only comment my mother made about this girl, when we told her about our meeting, was to dismiss her as 'mad Sonia's daughter'. We never saw her again. Why wouldn't my mother have wanted to maintain contact with her relations — or they with her? The result is that my own extended family is limited to the descendants of my father's side of the family, none of whom interest me. The younger generation doesn't attract me in general, but I would have liked to meet others of my own or my mother's age.

Summer 1966

I have been elected to the Library. The only privileges I enjoy are the Library room itself and its gramophone, and various minor advantages to do with dress and the increased extent of my liberty. The music this summer, if anything, surpasses the previous four years'. Apart from preparing for A Levels, I do very little work. I don't have to row anymore; I'm a slack bob, which means that I may, if I can be bothered, play the occasional game of tennis. I'm also allowed to drink beer legitimately.

On the Fourth of June, my mother comes down to take me out in the family Mercedes, Mrs. McD. at the wheel. A gold Rolls Royce Silver Shadow glides by, with 'L' plates tied to its bumpers; it's John P., learning to drive.

21 July 1966

A celebratory lunch at Pruniers with John P. and Dominic S. We are free of Eton (as I recall, we got food poisoning). I believe I managed to get three A Levels. So the world is open to us. In those days, there were only a few English universities, all of them beyond the intellectual reach of academically average boys like us. (It would take Mr. Blair's populist egalitarianism to transform polytechnics — useful training institutions — into 'universities', at the wave of a wand.) I doubt if it crossed any of our minds to prolong our scholastic lives, even if we had had the requisite qualifications. In any case, further education was unnecessary in mid-Sixties Britain. Those who had achieved a few A Levels at a good public school could expect to find employment without any trouble.

As far as John was concerned, this new freedom was a welcome challenge. He moved to Japan, where he taught English at the University of Nagoya. A couple of years later, he used his Japanese connections to establish a bubble-wrap business in Milton Keynes. On the proceeds of this and a course in architecture, he set himself up as a minimalist decorator, a new departure in London and one which he justifiably and with some success claimed as his own. Later in this seemingly seamless advancement, he acquired a bright and attractive Dutch girlfriend, the director of a prominent art gallery, produced a son, and could be seen driving a Renault 4L about town. John eventually married another woman who bore him another son.

While I was living in Paris, in the Seventies, John gave me the name of a French girl he knew there, asking me to 'look after her', if I remember rightly. I interpreted this to mean that I was supposed to represent John's interests until he chose to take up with her again. The girl was very pretty and I would have liked to try my own chances with her. John may well have meant me to do so, as I doubt he ever saw her again, but my loyalty to him prevented me from being more than friendly. Such a relationship would have lightened the slog of my life in Paris considerably, might even have prevented me from returning to the States, had things gone well between us. (Would you say this was a form of self-handicapping, Doctor?)

For Dominic, burdened as he was by a more complicated family history of divorce and by numerous step-siblings, the future looked less clear. Tall, bearded and blond, and with a good sense of humour, we shared my flat in Bina Gardens for a while. I remember his enviable girlfriend, the shapely and vivacious Alex. Later, doubtless drawn back to his Scottish roots, he retired to Findhorn, where he joined the local New Age community, an esoteric order that claimed to produce larger vegetables (reportedly, a 40-pound cabbage) by 'co-creation with nature'. Here, he met and married a homely Canadian woman of dour and heavy temperament, in striking contrast to Alex, by whom he had no children.

July 1966

The war in Vietnam is going strong. As an American citizen, I'm liable for the draft. At age eighteen, all U.S. citizens abroad must make themselves known to their local embassy and enrol in the Selective Service System. I duly report to the London embassy. My father accompanies me, because he has something he wants to say to the ambassador. When I've completed the formalities, I join my father. As we're leaving, the ambassador calls my father back and says that there's someone who wants to meet him. It's ex-Vice President Richard Nixon. We shake hands. My father and he exchange a few words. His nose is really very striking.

August 1966

To Venice with Mariam, her mother, and nanny, plus grandmother, this year. The Excelsior lobby is dominated by a huge poster for one of the films running in the Venice Film Festival, *La battaglia di Algeri* by Gillo Pontecorvo. Mariam looks as fetching as ever. In the intervening time, she and her mother have driven down to Eton to see me (chauffeur-driven dark blue Bentley S3). Then they come to visit my parents in Gstaad, in the aftermath to which Mariam is unkindly christened 'Princess Nitwit' by my mother. Now we're at this Lido hotel, down the road from the Festival buildings. There are some fascinating Festival hangers-on staying here, among them a voluptuous woman straight out of a Fellini film, far from young, with shoulder-length wavy black hair, a revealing white dress and very long red nails.

My duty is to accompany Mariam's grandmother, a crusty, bejewelled dame in her seventies, to the casino. I must leave her at the entrance, as I'm not old enough to be allowed onto the premises themselves. One day, we're invited to a screening of the Peter Fonda motorcycle film *The Wild Angels*. We also see *Fahrenheit 451*, whose political message I am far too innocent to grasp. I film Mariam on the beach with my 16 mm Beaulieu camera. A motorboat trip to Piazza San Marco and a trawl through some boutiques in the narrow streets nearby yields a pair of white Gucci shoes, my first.

This summer, Mariam apparently has matured to the point where she is ready for the next step. My chance to see her alone comes at last, when she invites me to her room to receive a birthday present: a Georgie Fame record. To my everlasting shame, I am too backward to recognize and take advantage of this unique opportunity. The combination of my insuperable inhibition and fear of being rejected, as well as the hitherto constant presence of the nanny, prevent me from taking the necessary initiative to break the barrier between us.

Back in London, where the family live at Grosvenor House, I visit a few times, but the friendship peters out after a while. It turns out later that Mariam has thrown herself at the Italian singer who sang in the Excelsior bar, a young fellow called Mimo or Pipo. This warning may have encouraged her mother to take a hand. She had introduced me one day to an Englishwoman with whom she was having a drink at a table in the bar, a Mrs. Ryan. This woman's son was already then a minor English pop luminary of the same name, born Sapherson; a Jewish crooner obviously better attuned to Mariam's interests. They married, but their relationship ended after a couple of years, fortunately without issue.

November 1966

My father and I are in California, visiting his parents. Los Gatos still retains the unblemished charm of a small, sleepy town. It's hard to imagine that, in the Eighties, it will become a favoured dwelling place for Silicon Valley commuters and retirees, with soaring property values and its own 'Ferrari of Los Gatos'. Speaking of which, at a lunch given for my father at the Fairmont, where we are staying, I befriend our host, Norman Stone, who has just added a Ferrari 275GTB to his collection. Karen Stone's wild brother agrees to teach me to drive on his VW Beetle, a car whose gear shift is famously accommodating to learners. I pass the test for my California Driver's License, my first. A Ford Galaxy is rented for me. It's a huge two-door car, in robin's egg blue. I feel quite safe surrounded by all this tin, which is just as well, as I lose myself on the freeways and tend, in desperation, to swerve across four lanes, when I think I've spotted the right exit or changeover. After dinner at Norman and Karen's, in Atherton, Norman invites me to drive the Ferrari.

Chapter VIII

PARIS AND ROLAND

November, 1966

Paris. I'm staying with Nadia Boulanger in her flat in rue Ballu. I'm going through a period of uncertainty and doubt. Terminal doubt and intermittent uncertainty are twin viruses of my existence. I'm certain about all kinds of things which could never affect me, but which I know for a fact are true and right and indisputable. Things that concern millions in money and people, the solutions to global problems, are for me the work of minutes, elucidated between mouthfuls of croissant and coffee. Breakfast is the ideal time for solving the hoary questions of starvation, disarmament, inflation and unemployment. The position can be pondered over the newspapers and disposed of before the last cup of coffee is drunk. Then the terrifying and insoluble riddle looms, huge and sinister and overpowering: what should I do today — and every other day of my life?

On this particular day, everything seems to have an equal value or non-value. For instance, should I shave? Is the occasion worthy? Should I change my shirt? The one I've been wearing is not quite dirty enough to require changing, I think. Is it worthwhile taking the Metro across town to see this film, which I've already seen anyway; but if it isn't, wouldn't it call into question the point of having lunch at the *brasserie* near the cinema? Well, what's so great about that *brasserie* anyway? But if I don't go to the film and don't have lunch at the *brasserie*, what am I going to do? I look again at the poems of Mallarmé, recommended to me by Nadia, a volume of which I'm absently exploring. Maybe

I should run through my address book in case there's someone in it I might feel like calling. I get up and trip over the carpet. Why is it always so dark in here?

In my room or cell, with view over the dismal inner courtyard, the death mask of Nadia's sister (a cosy custom of earlier times), suspended from a nail by a piece of string, imparts a sepulchral gloom. I fumble for the light switch. Apart from the mask, Nadia's spare room contains a filing cabinet and a narrow camp bed, in which I sleep and under which I keep my suitcase. I drag it out and extract my address book. How depressing! The only valid entries relate to hotels, doctors, taxi firms and suchlike practical information; the other items concern people who are for the most part boring beyond bearing, or dead, or in disfavour. Those in disfavour wear little pencilled brackets around their names, to distinguish them from the damned, who are struck through again and again with a ballpoint. I use a pencil on the disfavoured against the day when they might be reinstated. The dead, the damned and the disfavoured easily outnumber the few who could according to my strict definition be called friends or acquaintances and who might consequently be eligible for a telephone call or a visit, were they not invariably located in other parts of the world.

I close the book, replace it in my suitcase and shove the case back under the bed. In the living room, the lamp I have been reading by has been switched off during my short absence, despite the presence of open Mallarmé on the crimson velvet couch. Even at midday, Nadia's apartment is too dark to cross without the aid of electric light or a seeing-eye dog, but Nadia is a certified miser and her servant has been instructed to turn off all lights. I'm persuaded that the man lurks behind the arras, waiting to go for the switch the moment I cross the threshold of the room.

Nadia is an elderly spinster and a friend of my parents. A music teacher of international renown, in her youth she suffered an unrequited passion for Stravinsky. Nadia has loose teeth but a rigid discipline. She has acquired a useful reputation in the

United States and most of those who can afford her fees are Americans. A major reason for her chiefly American draw is that people accustomed to judge on the basis of received information instead of by observation and experience are naturally given to indiscriminate adulation. Americans are on an eternal quest after those they like to call 'mentors', ultimate authorities at whose feet they can cast their empty minds. Nadia's autocratic manner fulfils this need admirably and her pupils revere her.

I'm not sure what I'm doing at Nadia's (hardly every eighteen-year-old's idea of a fun place to be), but I imagine it has something to do with my parents' character-building goals for me. Nadia knows what's best for everyone, even the unmusical. I know that she doesn't know what's best for me, but I suppose a sort of purpose might reveal itself in Paris, somehow; might whisper to me over the rooftops from the Place Pigalle perhaps, where the hookers traditionally hang out, or from the Seine, where the suicides traditionally drop in. Not that I'm suicidal, I can't think of a more positive act. Suicide is taking a hand, making a decision, with a vengeance. I'm not even attracted by the choice between sudden death by drowning and lingering poisoning by a venereal disease, which I would be sure of contracting from a prostitute, even if she were the only one I would ever visit. I contemplate the curious misnomer whereby venereal diseases are called 'social', when they're basically antisocial. The only social disease I can unhesitatingly identify is Man himself, that irresponsible spreader of the disease of bad ideas, generator of the rot that sets in wherever he passes. Karl Marx had a social disease. The society of Man is unhealthy, as is the society of flies or mosquitoes.

Paris is not very much like the city most Americans have been given to understand was practically invented by Hemingway and Scott Fitzgerald and that tendentious ugly fraud whose art consisted in repeating herself. When I first arrived in Paris, I tried to track down some of the rare old atmosphere that had animated those seminal authors. I searched high and low for it. In the *haut monde*, where the Parisians dressed like the English, they told me all about myself and about great Frenchmen like Napoleon (a Corsican) and Madame Curie (a Pole) and Yves Montand (an Italian) and about great French inventions like television and the telephone; in the *bas monde*, where they dressed like American college kids, all they wanted to do was to hang out at Le Drugstore and talk about Le Western as an art form.

I soon discovered that the worst thing about Paris is not that it has definitively been put on the American summer migratory routes by these apparently unforgettable, prototypical expatriates and that it is now regularly overrun by other transatlantic explorers eager to chart their own experiences for *Travel + Leisure* or *Gourmet* magazines; the worst thing by far about Paris, as any discerning traveller knows, is the Parisian. What he greedily absorbs of American culture and coinage on one day, he rails about on the next, so that the more Americanized his sacred capital becomes — by his own choice — the more he resents it. It is this obvious duality that has sanctioned McDonald's on the Champs-Élysées, and foreshadowed the gigantic scam later perpetrated by the French government on French citizens that resulted in the multicoloured wart-like excrescences known as Euro Disney; while government-appointed guardians of French national patrimony raged impotently against American cultural imperialism. This would have been a genuine crime against humanity, if humanity had not already rendered itself insensible to injury by its renunciation of self-worth.

I'm replacing Mallarmé in the bookshelf as the doorbell rings again. I've watched Nadia's disciples succeed each other all morning and have almost made up my mind to take the leap, to trust in fate and chance the film, when an exceptional person is admitted. His three-piece plaid suit bespeaks volumes, as do his gold-rimmed glasses and loosely-bunched breast-pocket handkerchief. He looks me over and somewhat condescendingly introduces himself.

"Roland von B.," he pronounces, dropping onto the couch next to me, *"Est-ce que vous êtes un élève de Nadia ?"*

When he hears my father's name, his manner becomes more gracious. "Shall I show you Nadia?" he asks. Placing his glasses on the end of his nose, he takes a cup from a display cabinet, pretending to stir several spoonful's of sugar into it with a gold pen, then, leaving the 'spoon' in the cup, he slurps from it, clattering the rim against his teeth. It's a good imitation. He follows this heresy with an invitation to lunch. It appears that he has merely come to call on Nadia, whose courses he has taken some years previously. Roland is a cellist, he tells me.

As we drive in Roland's Mercedes coupe or actually his grandfather's as he presently admits, he begins a series of confidences which I am to hear regularly with few variations over the next years. I take them as confidences until I realise that they are just a recitative of anecdotes and ambitions, which Roland would impart to anyone he considers worth impressing. The purpose of his sojourn in Paris is to arrange among other matters a music festival.

"I am having concerts at the chateaux of friends. There will be symposiums, with famous people from all over the world." He mentions a few famous people. I am fairly impressionable, despite my ability to see through the French, and I'm not about to challenge Roland's claims, even though they sound very vague. His indeterminate age (he could as easily have been 35 as 25) and his dignified demeanour lend weight to his statements.

"They give me a special rate," he confides of the Ritz, up to which we soon glide. We leave the car in the charge of the doorman and stroll back up to the Champs-Élysées and over to the Avenue Montaigne, where Roland offers, "Shall I show you Charlie Chaplin?" and performs a duck-like walk all the way past the Plaza and up to the door of Chez Francis, a nondescript restaurant, favoured by colourless fogeys and conventional French snobs from Passy and Auteuil, accompanied by their beribboned rodents. Roland blocks the doorway for a moment, while he considers something that evidently requires him to be standing absolutely still (he's concentrating on a fart), and then proceeds into the dining area. The effect of Roland's aplomb, as I'm discovering, induces his friends to defer to him. I now hang around foolishly in his wake, like an ingénue at a cocktail party. Eventually, he chooses a table and sits down on the banquette. The waiter, who has been attempting to seat us elsewhere, has gone about other business, so that it is ten minutes before he responds to Roland's imperious calls for a menu. When it arrives, he doesn't look at it, but says airily to the waiter, "*Je prends quelque chose de léger.*"

"*Oui, monsieur?*" says the man, pencil poised.

"*Un paillard de veau. Non, une omelette. Avez-vous des raviolis?*"

"*Non, monsieur.*"

I dictate my order while Roland dithers a bit longer. Then, when it looks as if he's at last going to deliver himself of a conclusive choice, he says to me, "I am playing the sonata in La Majeur." The waiter turns to go. "*Alors un paillard de veau!*" Roland yells at his back, "*Et du pain!*"

As soon as the bread comes, he tears into it hungrily. It takes me a while to deduce that Roland has no taste for food, but likes the ambiance of fancy restaurants. He goes to these, orders something inexpensive and stuffs himself with bread. He drinks practically no alcohol, for reasons of health he claims. I reckon that he saves considerably on this miserable regimen.

I realise, when I come to know Roland better, that he must have trouble maintaining his image. His handmade clothes, petrol for the Mercedes, and the room at the Ritz, whatever the discount they give him, could not come cheap. But Roland never spends money on other, less ostentatious things. He never consults a doctor or a dentist unless in dire need or under the influence of hypochondria. So far as I can tell, he never buys a book, but only newspapers and magazines, and only the latter are well-thumbed, usually about the horoscope pages.

PARIS AND ROLAND

I see a lot of Roland while he is in Paris, and when my parents' French experiment fails and I return to London, Roland follows some months later, with the stated intention of giving some concerts (the singular never comes easily to him). To my certain knowledge, he has not once performed in public since we met, but he has several times expressed an interest in meeting my father.

Roland manages after his usual fashion to persuade some people that his presence in their city has a purpose. London, however, cannot hope to pander to his illusion quite as successfully as Paris. British snobbery being of a subtler kind and generally unconcerned with the arts, it requires of him at least some semblance of accomplishment in one of the fields he regularly claims as his own. It's still not clear to me what forms the basis of Roland's existence, beyond his pretensions of being a professional cellist. He keeps the average listener off balance with remarks about his musical or social engagements, which he flings about with equal importance, according to how the mood takes him. He benefits from the freemasonry of the old world and the ignorance and negligence of the new.

As his grandfather has reclaimed his car, Roland is constrained to use a lesser conveyance while he is in London. I can tell that this irks him by his regular assurance that his convertible Volkswagen Beetle had been made especially for him. He is living in a furnished flat in Knightsbridge and making desultory attempts to enter the musical mainstream of the city. Roland's problem seems to be that he takes himself and his slight ability too seriously. If he detached himself from his self-image of the soulful interpreter, he might make a career as a comedian of the cello, telling risqué stories interspersed with snatches of music. But he would have been insulted by such a suggestion.

Roland's method of publicizing himself is perforce genteel, as no agent could be bothered with his amateurishness for long. He distributes among his acquaintances — with the unspoken assumption that they will pass them on in turn — leaflets, on which a large, sentimental photograph of himself aged nineteen is accompanied by a necessarily brief resume of his concert career. As an easy life had spared him the wrinkles of care, this photograph is still a reasonable likeness.

While he's in London, Roland develops a fondness for my half-sister. Her dietetically restrained fleshiness and general appearance of availability, her endemic air of having just got up or being about to lie down, seems to fit his ideal of a woman's role. As far as I can gather, from glances into my half-sister's chatty diary, their trysts take the form of a kind of mutual rubbing up against each other, a sort of almost accidental reciprocal frottage perhaps, resembling animals relieving an itch against a convenient surface; tangential engagements in the vertical, fleeting mode, as with trains passing, rather than in the horizontal, considered one. I can't believe that my half-sister, an experienced object, derives much satisfaction from this, but Roland is clearly thrilled. My half-sister's appeal extends particularly to men of undeclared, undecided or ambivalent sexuality. Her demimondaine allure must have spared her suitors from having to feign virility.

In sexual expression, Roland is given neither to locker room crudeness nor to circumlocution. When he proclaims proudly that he has 'got at' a woman, or that she has 'coordinated with' him, he is clearly describing some function, but it remains moot whether the dread act of *immissio penis* has actually taken place. I haven't wanted to disconcert him by asking how he's doing with my half-sister. I've discovered that Roland is a habitual fabulist, in sexual as in other matters, but I consider that it's kinder to allow him his illusions. Roland customarily volunteers information about projects of his that are in the making or close to fruition, when they are in fact only pipe dreams. He's forever talking about organizing music festivals or symposia, which the distinguished of the world will attend. The venues are to be the castles of his friends. One of the main reasons for the failure of any of these projects to materialize is the basic incompatibility of the two worlds of serious music and international café society. Roland bestrides both like a restless gnat.

Chapter IX

FILM AND FRUSTRATION

January 1967

I join a jokey institution called The London School of Film Technique, which professes to train aspiring film makers. In fact, it's not a deception. There are lectures and viewings of classic films and even practical instruction. Most mornings, we sit in rows in the loft of the building under a skylight, about fifty of us, in our overcoats because it's so cold, and take notes. Among other optimists, there's an enormous black actor called Harcourt Curacao, from some island, maybe Curacao. It's only a bit jokey because of the terribly serious but misguided young people who have signed up to study here. Their problem is that the film industry is a closed shop, controlled by a classic Catch-22. You can't get a job unless you're a member of a union (the main one of which is the Association of Cinematograph and Television Technicians — ACTT), and you can't get into a union unless you have a job.

I'm genuinely interested in film, but I also hope that being a student will help me to avoid the draft. The director of the LSFT has sent a letter to the Draft Board to explain my status and hopes for a career. Unsurprisingly, this petition is ineffective. I am classified fit for service.

I don't know why I let it happen, but I got involved in another of those interminable, pointless arguments with my mother about my upbringing and about Eton, in particular. My mother, of course, extols Eton. Her father and brother went there, so why would she want me to go anywhere else? It's a school where boys can be themselves, she says, as if she knows what boys are about. She sent me there to make me independent. Incensed by the recollection of my unhappiness, I stomp out of her bedroom, flinging over my shoulder the taunt "How would you know? Your father died when you were three and your brother's mad." My mother pursues me down the stairs and flings her hairbrush at me from the landing. Naturally, I leave, knowing that I have sealed my fate as far as my father is concerned, and must live elsewhere. This is probably a good thing, except that I have forfeited my wardrobe as well as my books, among which a growing collection of film reference works. With her usual neatness, my mother has effaced my presence from her house.

I'm living in a furnished bed-sitter in Earls Court. It costs £6 a week. There's one telephone in the building, a pay phone on the landing below. Because I have to use it occasionally, I've met my downstairs neighbour, Valerie L., an aspiring actress with luxuriant dark hair and a fabulous figure. She also seems friendly. I fantasize about getting to know her, but I'm far too insecure to suppose that she could be interested in me, too timid to know how to start a conversation, and too poor to be able to afford to entertain her.

March 10, 1967

Through a chance meeting with Maggie A., an agent, I am given an introduction to Joe S., an American film producer, recently arrived in England. Joe has made a pile of money from *The Untouchables* series, and is developing a film at Twickenham Studios.

Twickenham, mainly famous for its rugby stadium, is also home to Britain's smallest studio. It's in a cul-de-sac, bordered by a modest residential area, the railway and a main road. There is no room for expansion. Because of its proximity to London and its professional staff, it's also very active. There are two sound stages, a sound department, a modern dubbing studio, a block of dressing rooms, a block of cutting rooms, a row of one-room offices for visiting productions, and the executive building. There is also a bar, of course, the essential hangout and meeting place. Joe occupies the best, if not the only suite of executive offices. He turns out to be a very short man in a beautifully tailored sports jacket of Italian cut. His first English production is *The Bliss of Mrs. Blossom*, with Shirley MacLaine and Richard Attenborough. He offers me the position of production runner. As no qualifications are required, neither is union membership. In fact, unless one has written the screenplay or has optioned the property oneself or has some other financial interest in a film, there is no other ground-level entry to the profession. There is no easy way into the union, period.

22 May, 1967

I start work at Twickenham. I sit on a hard chair next to the door in Fred Slark's office. Fred is the production manager. He's a Cockney with a chip on his shoulder. He resents my accent, he resents my car, and he resents the fact that I have been imposed on him by the producer, even though I am just a runner, the lowest of the low. Otherwise, I feel entirely welcome in his office. Fred and Daphne, the production secretary, are a team. Daphne chain smokes. The ashtray on her desk is always filled to overflowing with cigarette butts stained with her blood-red lipstick. She is accustomed to speaking around the cigarette which is permanently stuck in her mouth.

My training as a fag and my familiarity with hardship at Eton on the one hand, and my pride and pleasure at earning a salary on the other, make Fred bearable. He keeps me on my toes. When I'm not fetching cups of sickly sweet tea or sandwiches from the catering van, I'm copying scripts on a mimeograph, edge-numbering reels, or buying condoms for one of the actors.

It's five months into the film and I get to be third assistant director. This means yelling at the crew to be quiet when shooting starts. It's fun to watch the film being made, even though they tend to do an enormous number of takes. It's less fun to have to pretend to have authority over a group of men twice my age and more, and with considerable experience. However, they don't seem to object.

I'm summoned to the producer's office. His secretary, Hilary, whom I fancy — from afar as always — is in tears. It appears that the second assistant editor, a lively and good-looking young man, has killed himself by running his VW into a lamppost on the previous evening. Joe offers me his position. It's a great opportunity. Shooting is over and I have little to do. The chance to get out of Fred's office and to learn something new is a godsend.

My life has definitely changed for the better. Bill B., the editor, is a convivial boss. The ceilings of the cutting rooms are festooned with bouquets of champagne bottles he and his assistants have shared. I thank him for accepting me, although I imagine, that, like Fred, he had no choice. Mike C., the assistant editor is a really nice guy, who drives a red E-type. Sometimes he and I go to lunch together. Occupying the passenger seat, one has the impression of being directly behind the engine, extended at near street level in one of a pair of narrow channels, with the air scoop looming much larger through the windscreen than seems possible from the outside, and the end of the bonnet miles away.

I'm keen to take the next step and enrol in the union. It's been over a year since I started work on this interminable film, so I ask Fred if he will co-sign my application to join the ACTT. Geoffrey Unsworth, the lighting cameraman and a kind person, has already agreed to be the other signatory. Fred refuses, saying "We don't want to put you straight into the executive suite, do we?" He reminds me that he started as a uniformed page boy at Pinewood. "Last week, I couldn't spell Production Manager and now I are one," says Mike, consolingly.

I'm synching rushes. This means running separate sound and action reels over their respective heads on the cutting room bench, until the sound and picture of the clapboard match. Each take has to be synched and assembled with tape from the joiner into separate sound and action reels for viewing. Usually, there's plenty of time to do the previous day's rushes in the morning, as they're shown after lunch. The sound is no problem, as the studio's sound department transfers the sound recordist's reels to strips of magnetic tape as soon as they are delivered, after shooting terminates. However, if the labs deliver the picture late, or shooting has continued until late on the previous day so that development has been delayed, there's a fearful rush. In an emergency, I am delegated to drive to Technicolor to pick up the rushes.

During viewing of rushes, the director chooses which take he wants to use, or, conceivably, which scenes he may need to reshoot. Back in the cutting room, the reel is dismantled, and the individual takes numbered with a chinagraph pencil and rolled onto separate bobbins. Mike assembles the chosen takes into scenes in a general way, and Bill begins the creative job of making the scenes work, so that, when joined together, they tell the story. His skill depends in large part on his understanding of what the director wants, and the desired rhythm and mood of a particular scene. The editor runs the scene repeatedly through his Movieola, rolling his chair back and forth between the Movieola and the bench, drawing the sound and picture out in long loops with his white-gloved hands. Sometimes he shaves a few frames off a scene until a cut seems to run smoothly. Lengths of film, from several feet to only a dozen frames, hang from nails, stuck into a wooden frame over a canvas bin. The more advanced a cut gets, the shorter and more numerous the 'ends' of film become, as the editor compares various possibilities, often making alterations. At times, he will call us over to get our opinion on the progress of a scene. Shirley MacLaine doing take after take of the same scene, rather than boring me, now impresses me by her professionalism.

Frustration sometimes mounts as the director realizes that he hasn't shot what he needs. He and the editor may be at odds about a particular cut. Bill has been known to pretend to alter something and Joe, the director, to assert his satisfaction with a cut that has remained unaltered. Often, the editor will call out for a particular take or alternative take, and Mike and I drop whatever we are doing and try to find it as quickly as we can. Bill is very laid back, but time is always pressing, if for no other reason than the cost to the production company of renting the premises. It is not unusual for us to work weekends. I don't mind, as my social life is non-existent. Besides, Saturdays pay time-and-a-half and Sundays, double-time.

If an effect, such as a dissolve, is required, Mike orders this from the laboratory, filling in the form and sending in the take with the effect drawn in, in chinagraph. A dissolve may cover several feet of film, it looks like a *diminuendo* and *crescendo* in a musical score. Often, sound effects are needed. The sound of an explosion or a ship's horn, for instance, can be ordered from a sound library. They arrive on a sound reel, and Bill runs them through the Movieola too, choosing the one he likes best.

Towards the end of the marathon editing process that has defined this film, during which the cutting crew have moved from Twickenham to Shepperton and back to Twickenham, I am often sent to deliver cans of the umpteenth amended version to, or pick them up from, a London screening room. This allows me to spend my lunch hour watching an emaciated stripper disrobe to Chris Andrews' 'Yesterday Man', among the raincoat crowd in a Soho basement. These places are special. You can't just walk in. You have to apply to the Tropicana Theatre Club, say, and they issue you a numbered card which declares 'Members concessions only valid on production of this card'. Whatever that means, it's more likely to be soft-porn than popcorn.

I drive a tiny, hotted-up car, a Sunbeam Stiletto. Drink and dissatisfaction sometimes drive me. A couple of collisions, one in the snow and one with a double-decker bus, don't do much to calm my temper. I drive my mother to my father's music school in Surrey. All goes well until we are on the school drive, about thirty yards from the building itself. Then, for some reason, prudence deserts me. I accelerate around the last corner, blind due to the shrubbery, and run into another car coming the other way. No one is hurt, but my car receives a sizeable dent. Luckily, the engine is in the back and so it can still be driven. My mother is surprisingly unruffled by the incident. I, on the other hand, fling myself out of the car and run about, swearing.

9 September, 1967

Due to parents being in Teheran and Millie's holidays, I am billeted at the Royal Court Hotel, in Sloane Square. Clearly, I can't be trusted to live at my own home alone and fend for myself for a week.

22 April, 1968

Rome. Shopping and lunch with the lovely Tonina Dorati. I am astounded at the practised manner with which she bargains in the elegant shops along the Via Condotti. Evidently this is what Italians do, but it helps to be a beautiful woman. I acquire a suede jacket and a wool shirt for my father.

26 April, 1968

Grenchen. My father has been awarded Swiss citizenship; a dinner is given in his honour. This small town lies at the base of the Jura and is known chiefly for its watch-making enterprises (including Eterna-Matic, the first watch my father gave me when I was nine). My parents, brother and I are seated at a long table in the town hall, speeches are made. My father reveals that he has been desirous of becoming a Swiss citizen since boyhood, when he studied in 1929 in Basel with the violinist Adolph Busch. The movers behind this most welcome gesture have been local businessmen and politicians, including a family with which I remain friendly to this day. A few years later, we are made citizens of Grenchen itself. In return, my father establishes a small foundation to encourage the teaching of music in local schools. Gstaad, with which my father has been associated since 1954 and at whose request he founded in 1957 the festival that bears his name, has been too parochial (not to say, cretinous — cf. *Oxford Concise*: 'cretin, n. Deformed idiot of a kind found esp. in Alpine valleys') to initiate a like gesture but, presumably out of shame, eventually makes him a burgher too.

June 1968

The interminable *Bliss of Mrs. Blossom* is finished. Instead of hanging out at the studio bar in customary fashion, in the hopes of hearing about a new job, I leave for Germany with Roland, in his Fiat 850. This smart little car's 52hp engine is strained to the utmost under the weight of two adults, a cello and assorted luggage. It barely makes it, via Cologne and Munich, to Hannover. I rather like Roland's sister. She comes to stay a few days at Gstaad, but we are both on our best behaviour and the visit is frustrating. A more convincing explanation is that I just can't get over myself.

September 1968

Admitted to the ACTT. The little red booklet, in which annual dues are entered with a rubber stamp, is mine at last.

November, 1968

Helen and Alan Dowling are a curious pair. She is a well-known violin teacher, short and feisty and Jewish; he is tall and spare, invariably morose and Gentile, and publishes his own poetry. I meet them for lunch at the Westbury. Helen has on her leopard-skin coat. Alan wears his perennial Prince-of-Wales check suit. He barely says hello and remains silent over his scrambled eggs, which are all he can eat. I believe this is typical alcoholic's fare. They want me to meet a friend of theirs who is producing a film. I drive out to some godforsaken suburb their friend inhabits. He turns out to be a portly doctor in his fifties. He offers me a drink and tells me he is a partner in this film, which is to start shooting next week, and will take about ten days. Then he makes a pass at me. I leave hastily.

I report to a young woman with a good accent, whose name the brazen doctor has given me. The accent is a relevant point, as in Britain, it's unusual for women with upper-class accents to get involved in movies, let alone in the kind this turns out to be. She may be part of the production team or the cast or both. I drive her around St. John's Wood, where she wants to drop in on a friend who is also in the film. While I sit on her sofa and pretend that I'm used to this, or that I'm oblivious, they kneel on the floor in front of the three-bar radiator and compare breasts. "Don't you think my boobs are too small?" asks one of the other. They look just fine to me. Much, much later it occurs to me that these thirty-something women might have been trying to seduce a handy twenty-year-old.

7:45 a.m. Esher, a rented house at the end of a wooded street that serves as location as well as production offices of this minifilm. The cast and crew are assembled. Victor Spinetti, a fine actor, is the star. He has a voluptuous, full-length fox coat, which he allows me to try on. One of the rooms will serve as Victor's living room, where he will be discovered, lying in front of his gas fire, a towel wedged under the door, on the verge of suicide, when an available blonde just happens by. A couple of her friends then show up too, because you can't get too much of a good thing, especially in soft-core. All are revealed down to their waists, in Esher. In Soho, I saw it all. It's not as if I was up to anything but spectator sport yet anyhow. When will I be?

How odd that the Dowlings should have such friends! Maybe they don't realize what kind of film this is. As for Spinetti, either he's down on his luck or the film gives him a chance to screw and get paid for it.

As assistant director, one of my duties is to pick up the blonde, Vanessa Howard, from her apartment in Ealing. Vanessa turns out to be attractive and vivacious. We enjoy a pally relationship, along with the radio, during the half-hour drive. One day, when I drive Vanessa back to her place, a girlfriend of hers is there too. They offer me a drink and then seem to invite closer acquaintance. I plead an urgent engagement and escape, terrified. Terrified of what? That my inexperience will be detected, that I will be inadequate, probably.

25 December 1968

I drive up Highgate West Hill through several inches of snow, expecting the car at any moment to give up or to slide dangerously in the wrong direction. When I arrive at The Grove, anxious and tense after the drive, my father exhibits his usual sunshine in the breast and will put up with no grievance. When I try to explain how anxious I have been, he exalts the beauty of the snow. Our subsequent argument has less to do with the weather than with the subterranean baggage of past years. After a while I simply walk out and return to the flat I am sharing with my half-sister in Westmoreland Street. When my father drives down to knock at the door, presumably at my mother's urging, I pretend not to be at home. I call Nola, my father's first wife. Red-haired and in her fifties, Nola possesses a *joie de vivre* entirely foreign to my mother's understanding of life. She immediately invites me to dinner. At Jean Gutowski's flat in Eaton Place, which she rents, we decide to cook a fondue. When the fondue is unsuccessful, despite a call for advice to the Swiss embassy, Nola resorts to the steaks she has bought from Allens, opposite the Connaught, the only English butcher she deigns to frequent. After dinner, she calls her children from the bedroom extension. As she sits on her bed and dials, I am aware of her effervescent appeal.

January 1969

My half-sister's Italian ex-boyfriend, generously but unwisely, has offered to lend me his brand new Alfa Romeo Spider. I take the train to Busto Arsizio, near Milan, where his parents live. It's a typical Italian industrialist's house, all marble and gold fixtures. I'm ready to drive back right away, but they beg me to stay the night. In the morning, despite their misgivings, I drive off in the car. In fact, throughout the four-hour drive, I am all caution and responsibility, until I am a few yards short of the chalet, when, in a spirit of relief and carefree optimism at having managed so well, I accelerate into the garage door and knock off the emblem — unprotected, due to Italian

FILM AND FRUSTRATION

design priorities. A couple of weeks later, I am on my way to Zurich to drop off the car for its owner. The driving conditions aren't great: it has been snowing and only one lane of the freeway is clear. I stop at a filling station and ask the attendant how fast he thinks I should be driving. "Can you control the car?" he responds. "Yes," I say confidently.

A few kilometres further, I try to overtake a truck in the fast, uncleared lane. The car goes into a spectacular series of figure eight skids, hitting the central metal divider repeatedly. I am lucky in that I do not also hit the truck, which meanwhile goes by, blaring furiously. When the car calms down, a hundred yards further, I pull onto the shoulder to assess the damage. The hood and the left side are a mess, but the car is drivable. I take it to an Alfa Romeo garage in Zurich and ask them to do all they can to put it back in its original state. It costs me almost all I have.

Zamira meets the man of her dreams: he runs his ski-bob into her on a slope in Gstaad. He's a British snob with a minor honorific, tall, thin, and good-looking, and fun is his priority. Neil spends his time increasingly with us. On the face of it, he should despise Jews, but my sister's name and her obvious availability, possibly even an assumption that she may have money, keeps Neil in there. As for me, I enjoy the addition to our company.

February 1969

At the Hotel St. James & Albany, in the rue de Rivoli. It's a well-situated but shabby hotel. My parents have been staying here for years and always occupy the same suite, on the top floor with view over the Tuileries. The antique wardrobe is held to the wall by a piece of string. The bathroom fixtures are antique too, the bath itself has claw feet. I am to work on a film in Africa, directed by Georges Clouzot, famous for *Les Diaboliques* and *Le Salaire de la peur*.

Today I am summoned to meet Clouzot, at last. I have worn out two packs of cards, playing Solitaire. The days have gone by without word from the great man about when his film is due to start. I don't have enough money to amuse myself in Paris, so I am more or less confined to the hotel. Occasionally, I take in a movie (two films are always playing in Paris: Billy Wilder's *Some Like It Hot* and Polanski's *The Fearless Vampire Killers* — for some reason scorned in the U.S.), or buy a record. My meals are in the dining room, where the food is poor and the choice limited. Every day, the headwaiter with the long fingernails flourishes at me the same menu, bound in embossed black plastic, and every day, I pretend to be inspired by one of its three unchanging items.

Clouzot lives in a top-floor apartment in the Avenue Montaigne. He, his wife and I sit in their over-decorated living room and talk awkwardly. He asks me who my favourite French director is. What am I to say? To mention his name would be sycophantic. *Les Diaboliques* is certainly a masterpiece, but I haven't seen any others. Perhaps because it is one of the very first films I have seen and because I will never forget its doom-laden atmosphere, I think of *Les Yeux sans visage*. "Franju," I answer. The response is immediate: disdain. Whether this evidently unsatisfactory answer damns me, or whether Clouzot's poor health, or some typical film industry disruption is to blame, his planned film is never made, and I do not hear from him again. However, he has passed on my name to another production, and I am duly informed that I may expect to work as second assistant editor in Nice.

March 1969

My parents are in Paris, at the Plaza Athénée. President Nixon, with the obvious exception of JFK, in those days probably alone among American presidents to recognize the existence of Europe, travels to Paris soon after his inauguration. YM and his sister Hephzibah have been asked to dinner and to play for him. My brother and I are invited after dinner. When we present ourselves at the gate to the ambassador's residence, we are met by a very sceptical French policeman: "*J'en doute*," is his response to my information that we are expected. However, after a whispered confabulation with a colleague over the proffered printed invitation, he grudgingly relents. The concert is over and a band plays what I am told is one of Nixon's favourite tunes: 'Sentimental Journey' (familiar to me from Booker T.'s version). I meet Nixon again and am allowed a few minutes with Kissinger to ask him about *Time*'s report about Communists in Nicaragua. He treats the subject dismissively. Apart from the unserious nature of *Time Magazine* as a source of hard news, my question seems to demonstrate my early interest in political developments.

Orly to Nice. I am billeted in a pension on the rue de France, a block behind the Negresco. My room contains a bed, a cupboard, a table and chair, and the space to move between them. The shower is at the end of the corridor. Every morning, I am served *café au lait* and a second-rate croissant. Some way up the rue de France, I catch a bus for the Studios de la Victorine, on the hill behind the town. The film is *L'Arbre de Noël*, a French/Italian co-production. The director is Terence Young, of James Bond film fame, and the main cast is William Holden, Virna Lisi, and the French comic Bourvil. Young drives a convertible Chinese-eye Rolls and wears a red-lined cape. He is very full of himself. The cutting room staff is relegated to buildings some way across the lot and our contact with the rarefied milieu on the set is limited. I have lunch at the canteen every day, where the food is unreliable except for the *Bœuf Tartare*, presumably because the cook leaves it alone. The lot is totally unmemorable except for an enormous piece of scenery left over from Bryan Forbes' *The Madwoman of Chaillot* which for some reason no one has dismounted.

The screenplay is incredibly, revoltingly sentimental. It tells the story of a boy of twelve — whose wealthy and doting parents live in a castle — who has been diagnosed with terminal cancer. He is due to die on Christmas Day, under the Christmas tree, surrounded by wolves, with which he has a special relationship. It's pretty stocky for the European producers to have caught Holden, one of Hollywood's finest and most durable stars, but maybe his career is in decline. In any case, he is treated like an African potentate and fetched daily from the Negresco in a Mercedes 600. La Lisi is supposed to attract the Italian audience, and Bourvil accounts for the French quota. The boy is unknown but too enticing for his own good, as a shared taxi ride during which he is groped by a production assistant demonstrates to me. In an early flash of misguided enthusiasm, I approach the producer with some suggestions to make the screenplay more lifelike, but I am soon reduced to apathy and my paycheck. Between the cutting rooms and the main sound stage is a piece of waste ground on which the wolf tamer keeps his charges. They seem in no danger of getting out of control.

My boss, the editor, is a good-natured Frenchwoman (in France, most of the editing personnel seem to be female) with great experience. However, her colleague, the sound editor, is a traditional middle-aged Frog harridan who will brook no criticism of France. When I question the validity of the French coins with holes in them, which might just as well be phoney money from a kid's game, she turns near-apoplectic in an effort to defend *La Grande Nation*. Her assistant is a plump but not unattractive girl, a couple of years older than I. She seems friendly and invites me to dinner at her apartment not far from my pension. One weekend, we drive around together in a car I have rented. When I pick her up, she's still in bed in her night dress, but I overlook this resolutely. I pretend to myself that it's because she served me canned *ratatouille*, or because she's overweight, that I'm unwilling to take the hint, but the truth is that I would rather be considered obtuse, gay, physically disabled, anything, than inexperienced. I am equally determined to rebuff the aggressive and sometimes quite nice-looking prostitutes that frequent the rue de France in the evenings. To make my free time bearable, I have bought a portable gramophone from the local FNAC electrical outlet, on which I play my records: *Super Session* and *The Live Adventures of Mike Bloomfield and Al Kooper* (a classic). The latter is my introduction to the Blues.

FILM AND FRUSTRATION

May 1969

London. Blades the Tailor is in a bow-front-windowed building opposite one end of Savile Row. It's a business created by a couple of titled people for those for whom Savile Row is too stuffy. Blades materials are high quality but more showy. They also have a unique line of shirts. Blades clothes are my principal extravagance and comfort, in the absence of human company. I buy half a dozen wonderfully patterned silk shirts, and have several suits and a sports jacket made. The fact that I scarcely have occasion to wear them seems irrelevant. My grey flannel suit turns out to be a bad choice. Whether global warming or simply better heating is responsible for today's fashions, the mere fact of finding grey flannel about an eighth of an inch thick in a tailor's swatch indicates how much cooler conditions were then.

I've moved into a tiny service studio at the White House Hotel, just off Regents Park. It's on the eighth floor and has a dull and depressing view over some shacks. This is a so-called residential hotel. There's a world of difference between the ground floor, where are the expensive restaurant and swimming pool, and the dingy living amenities on the upper floors. When I can afford it, I dress up in my Blades blazer and treat myself to Lobster Thermidor in the restaurant, before slinking back to my dismal bedsit.

January 1970

Glancing out of the cutting room window today, I see the most monstrous airplane descending towards Heathrow; it's a new type, a Boeing 747. They'll never get me into one of those; imagine being cooped up with four hundred other people! I'm at Twickenham again, as second asst. editor. Besides me, the cutting room staff consists of Ernie H., and his overweight first asst. They both smoke. Ernie arrives every morning with a serious-looking black businessman's briefcase, for transporting a bottle of gin. He works in the afternoons. That winter he slips on the iron stairs up to the cutting room and twists his ankle, and needs help going up thereafter. The first assistant is memorable only for his jokes, one of which concerns the man who is arrested for squeezing women's breasts in a theatre and claims he's a 'titter running through the audience'.

Some tunes have been played so often at one stage of one's life that one simply can't hear them anymore, for example 'Layla', or 'A Whiter Shade of Pale'. Satie's *Gymnopédies* is another. It was used as a working score on *Ask Agamemnon* (later *Goodbye Gemini*), a typically late Sixties counterculture blunder. I propose something livelier for one of the scenes: Booker T's 'I Got a Woman', thus unintentionally consigning this fine track through repetition to the same outcast status.

Apart from the indubitable fact that most films are rubbish and infinitely forgettable, and are made for the wrong reasons, most of the films I worked on were also terrible. As a summary of the industry, that will do as well as any other to explain my gradual disenchantment with my chosen career. Work is work and all experience adds to one's professionalism. Surely I didn't expect to be apprenticed to some brilliant director? Well, subconsciously, I did, of course. Unfortunately, my main access to the business was through a producer who seemed to have no instinct for quality or even for good entertainment. He may have been under some financial pressure to churn out films, but it's hard to see why all twenty-two he produced had to be so bad. Still, I'm grateful to him for hiring me.

March 1970

My father has very generously bought me a flat. My peripatetic living conditions — from Highgate to Earl's Court, to a friend's, to Westmoreland Street and Cheney Walk via the Royal Court Hotel, all within a few months — may have persuaded my mother and him that I need a respectable and permanent base of my own. We settle for a top-floor conversion in Bina Gardens SW7, a duplex with a circular staircase, which at first seems picturesque rather than just awkward. I think of this apartment as a toy or unserious residence, because of the quality of its conversion. This betrays two overriding traits of the British construction industry: rapacity and incompetence. There is at once a desire to cut corners to make a profit and an inherent inability to understand that quality lasts and is appreciated, and may lead to a recommendation. For instance, the bathtubs are made of some composite that makes them bend ever so slightly when one gets into them.

May, 1970

I join a gym in Kensington High Street and buy a BMW 2002. Herbie Mann's *Memphis Underground* is a favourite companion in the car (still with me now, although a CD has replaced the cassette). I now have an apartment in a fashionable area of London (even though I find the name of the street faintly embarrassing), one of the most enviable cars, a handmade wardrobe and even some fledgling muscles. I am still absolutely clueless about how to go about attracting women. Things have obviously become my substitute for people. I simply cannot make the connection to real life. (Am I sociophobic, Doctor?)

June 1970

I discover Elmore James. As far from the Beach Boys as conceivable; hard to imagine Elmore singing 'She's real fine, my 409'. Dominic tells me later that I have the reputation of having introduced Elmore James to swinging London. For a while, I share the flat with Dominic and store the car in a garage which belongs to his father. Dominic is a good sort and I profit from his circle of relatives and acquaintances. His girlfriend, Alex M., is very desirable and reminds me of my own miserably solitary state. Keeping my hopelessness to myself is second nature, but it's feeding my inhibition, one of the chief national tendencies of the British. 'Hanging on in quiet desperation is the English way,' says Pink Floyd.

July 1970

Gstaad. It's time again to renew my U.S. passport. At the Bern embassy, the vice-consul informs me that I will lose my citizenship if I do not spend four years in the U.S. before my 28th birthday. This comes as a thunderbolt.

August, 1970

To the Bürgenstock, stay with Nola at the chalet she has rented. Krov and his wife, Anne, guests too. Tennis lessons. Not quite sure what I'm doing here, but it makes as much sense as anywhere else. Krov and Anne are a good-looking couple, but neither is interesting. They may have travelled extensively while making their marine films, but none of what they have experienced has rubbed off on them, except in terms of the often pompously related and for the most part terminally tedious technical details of these expeditions. Lawrence Durrell, a neighbour in Provence, reportedly called Krov 'The most boring man in the world'. His wife, perhaps in response to years of dissatisfaction, has become a shrew, as she later demonstrates when she cuffs my six-year-old son for hitting her arm unintentionally with a pebble he has thrown.

August, 1970

Peggy and her mother are staying at the Park Hotel. Being a late starter and then some, crippled by innate repression as well as an English upbringing which separates the sexes, I have had no natural opportunity of spending time with girls, apart from my very brief experience at the Mermaid and around the seemingly untouchable Mariam. I have known Peggy, on and off, since my public school days. Her mother, a pianist, is a pupil of my uncle's. My aunt, in her usual charitable way, calls the daughter a retard. So, according to my relatives, my girlfriends until now have included a nitwit and a half-wit. It's true that Peggy isn't bright, but she's a pretty girl and approachable too, which is something. However, the curtain that inhibits actual physical contact still hangs invisibly between us. If anyone is retarded, it is I.

August, 1970

My brother and I report to the local schoolhouse for Swiss Army physical induction exams. We intentionally arrive late and incur the animosity of the village's military man-in-charge, otherwise the manager of a shoe store. For reasons never revealed to us, neither my brother nor I hear any more about this corollary to Swiss citizenship.

November 1970

I've been invited to a coming out party at the Savoy. (A coming out party, in the traditional sense, is a debutante's introduction to society, not the disclosure of latent homosexuality.) I've heard about these things from my mother, but didn't suppose they still took place. The young woman in question is practically unknown to me. I feel a mixture of dread and excitement. Will something actually happen to me, influence my life? I have on my ridiculously expensive three-piece Blades blue suit. There is a huge crowd of Hooray Henrys and correspondingly jolly women. Purebred English girls and women, especially of the middle and upper classes, invariably remind me of furniture, because there is no definition to their ankles or wrists. Their hands and arms, calves and feet, fuse into each other inelegantly, without the slightest, or with very little, concession to, or variation in, bone structure. If you add to this appearance of physical clumsiness a loud laugh, affected mannerisms, an inability to cook or to make general conversation, let alone to discuss current affairs intelligently, you have a most undesirable product and an explanation as to why sex between English men and women is often neither gleeful nor impulsive. To give them their due, I also am undesirable because I cannot join their conversation or dance. I have a few drinks, but not enough to encourage me to make a fool of myself, or perhaps so many that I withdraw entirely.

Chapter X
PROGRESS

Anthony Lewis, a distinguished journalist and an acquaintance of my father, learns of the problem with my U.S. citizenship and recommends taking it to court. He puts my father in touch with Leonard Boudin, renowned defender of left-wing causes. Boudin believes the law is unjust and chooses to fight my case as a precedent.

July 1971

Cambridge, Mass. to cooperate with Leonard Boudin. After undergoing the rigours of an unexpected interrogation in a windowless compartment, presumably by some FBI types (so different from my experiences at SFO), I am picked up at the airport by Barbara, a bombastic woman in her sixties, an old acquaintance of my parents and patron of the Boston Symphony. She drives an Austin Princess Vanden Plas, which she tells me has a Rolls-Royce engine. Her sister Frannie and brother-in-law Burke have been friends of my parents since I was born. In his retirement from SHAPE (Supreme Headquarters Allied Powers Europe), in Paris, Burke writes thrillers. The two families own adjacent properties on the cliffs at Swampscott, outside Boston. They are typical East Coast WASPs of the old school.

Barbara suggests that I stay with her or with Burke and Frannie, but I don't want to offend Boudin, who has kindly asked me to stay. I occupy their daughter's room upstairs. It has a single bed, whose off-white sheets smell as if they haven't been changed. Gradually, I sense a peculiar, depressive atmosphere in the house, emanating mainly from Mrs. B. It's more than just laid back hippyism and dislike of household chores. One day, Boudin volunteers that life is difficult for him and particularly for his wife, as their daughter Kathy is a member of the Weather Underground, the closest thing in the U.S. to a terrorist organization, and she is wanted by the FBI. (Does this connection account for my airport interview?) They haven't heard from her in a while. Her mother has left her room as it was when she last occupied it, including apparently the sheets.

LB is a brilliant lawyer and a nice man, but being around them is a major drag. It only takes a call to get myself invited to stay in Swampscott. At a family dinner, I'm introduced to my host's daughter-in-law. Ann is 31 and very attractive. After dinner, I'm sitting next to her on the sofa. Our eyes meet; there is a strikingly warm expression in hers. I have never encountered such a candid look from a woman. We move outside onto the deck to talk. Later still, we drift over the lawn to the cliffs and sit talking and just looking at the ocean, until three in the morning. It's probably the most thrilling night of my life. I return to my room in the old house, and she to hers, in an annex of her in-laws' house. On the next day, she comes over to practice the piano and we snatch a few moments alone. We meet on a hillock, surrounded by brush, between the houses, she in her bathing suit and carrying a towel. I walk along the beach with her and her four sons, ranging from five to ten years. I'm fussy about cold water and in an unguarded moment she pushes me in.

Vitalized by love, I set off on the next day to jog along the cliff top. The family's golden retriever trails me. For him, it's better than a walk. It's strange that I, who have no time for dogs, am invariably adopted by them. I reach the midway point and turn back, but the dog refuses to follow. Because I am not absolutely sure that he will find the way back by himself, I feel compelled to carry him. I feel a right ninny staggering along under the weight of a full-size dog. He seems not to mind however.

PROGRESS

July 1971

Joe has offered me a job as second asst. editor on his next film *The Assassination of Trotsky*, at Cinecitta, in Rome. (Where does he get these screenplays from? Can't he find something the average moviegoer wants to see?) It is to star Richard Burton and Alain Delon.

I drive to Rome, to stay with Alberto Lysy at Monte Savello 30, also the home of the Origo family, all the while thinking furiously about my U.S. citizenship. It means a lot to me. I also think of Ann. The Lysys are away. I sit at the kitchen table with a green glass decanter of the Marchese's wine and call Joe: I decline the job as I must go to the States instead or lose my citizenship. Joe asks what a U.S. citizenship means, besides taxes. I insist and apologize.

My disregard of the sense behind Joe's observation leads to the second biggest mistake of my life — unless one counts my even more futile yet innate urge to turn back the clock in order to try to recapture the essence of the only carefree times I have known. Sometimes it's better to do nothing and simply to let events happen. In my case, it is not just my nostalgic and outdated vision of Northern California as it was in the Fifties, but my yearning for Ann that tips the balance. I wonder how my life might have turned out if I had had a normal sexual experience at, say, 18 in Europe; if, in that case, my retention of an American passport would have seemed less significant. At 23, I was simply pleased to own three passports and did not see why I should be forced by some arbitrary law to lose one of them. With the wisdom of hindsight, I can see myself enjoying the Italian experience, however mediocre the film, perhaps even breaking the sexual barrier with an Italian girl and avoiding the American trap entirely.

September 1971

The Marchese's chauffeur is to spend some time in the UK, so he and I drive back in the BMW. Once there, I return the car to the garage, and get a good price for it, as it's almost new and very desirable. I'm able to get a $99 'repatriation' flight to New York, from Pan American Airlines. Once established with acquaintances of my mother's sister, I send a cable to my parents which reads 'Am here, not there, Gerard'. The Bina Gardens flat is rented. This provides me with a small income.

A powerful society woman introduces me to the bearded chairman of Doubleday. My future is assured. The only condition for my employment at Doubleday is that I learn to type, a skill few Europeans outside the 'secretary class' have mastered. At Eton, we still submitted handwritten papers. I buy a Smith-Corona and join a typing school, the only male. There is a woman here who can type 145 words a minute, sounds like a machine-gun. With the assigned textbooks and multiple repetitions of 'The quick brown fox jumps over the lazy dog', I eventually manage 45. However, in some ways, it's a repetition of Paris, with days spent in my hotel room, meals in the dining room, and not much else, but with the added woe of heartache. With time and without contact, doubt about the sincerity of the Doubleday offer, whatever it turns out to be, sets in. Ann and I speak often. I decide that I really need to return to the West Coast, after all the region I know best and which means the most to me. It has an irresistible nostalgic allure. If I travel west, I would logically go via Denver, where Ann and her family have just moved. We meet at Stapleton airport and fly on to San Francisco. There, Ann has friends she can ostensibly visit. I rent a purple AMC Javelin and we drive to Alma. Finally. I'm only 23 years old. But it has been worth waiting for.

With $1,500 I buy a four-year-old Firebird 400 with a four-speed Muncie shift and no refinements, like air or electric windows. It's just a muscle car with a great sound. I add a cassette player. It's a typical American sports car: despite the gears, there's just a parking- but no handbrake. This makes driving in San Francisco difficult, so I get into the habit of parking and walking when I go to the city.

PROGRESS

Driving the twenty hours through Nevada and Wyoming, on the way to Denver, is an adventure. First I replace the alternator, then the battery. On the way back, the fan belt breaks, not too far from Wells. Ann shows me the call box on Arapahoe Road she uses. It's hard to think of her standing there, on this anonymous, dusty through-street, in her red corduroy jacket with the fleece collar, calling London for thirty minutes at a time.

Back in the Bay Area, I apply for work at Saga Food Services, at a chemical products company and at a bank. The response is always the same: go to college and reapply. I get the message. I apply to Stanford, Denver and UC Santa Cruz.

January, 1972

Ann arrives at SFO. As we turn off Highway 17 and onto Idlewilde Drive, Ann confides "I would like to have your baby." Wow! I mean, I'm touched, but what does an inexperienced twenty-three-year-old say to that? I don't want to have a baby yet and — does she mean she wants us to get married? Obviously she means it as a compliment, so I take it as one. I swallow and say something conventional like, "That would be nice." Then I pull myself together and get practical. "What would we live on?" I ask, "I'll be in school for four years." "I know," she says, like she's worked it all out, "I could give piano lessons, just like I do now, but more of them. I could sell my ring. It's an expensive one."

At an interview in a San Francisco hotel, I'm accepted at Denver. This means I can live at Ann's house. They have moved to a great location, a comfortable street in Littleton, with large lots and an uninterrupted view of the Rockies. I occupy the spacious guest room. However, D.U. is not a resounding success. For one thing, my choice of a useful major, accounting, is about as far from my nature as it would be possible to get. The text books are unfathomable and, despite my best efforts, balance sheets, with their accompanying concepts of assets and liabilities, plunge me into despair. Face it: I was not born to be an accountant.

In my determination to be industrious, I attend a promotional meeting for students at a company that makes a minor brand of motor oil. From the dais, a junior executive bombards us with a standardized pep talk about how much money we will make from selling this oil door to door or by phone. He cites a 19th century English statesman as his role model in life, a certain 'Desaray'. Largely English-educated though I am, I still cannot place this famous historical figure. A few days later, it occurs to me that the fellow was referring to Disraeli. Somehow, the guiding light that Disraeli represents, as he rouses the typical American house owner from his Barcalounger to hawk motor oil to him, is not persuasive. It looks as if I'm not going to fit the ideal of the self-made Yankee millionaire.

Against this, we go skiing often, at Winter Park or Vail, where we are once privileged to have in the neighbouring apartment no less a personage than ex-President Gerald Ford ("I'm not a Lincoln, I'm a Ford"). Ann and I enjoy many happy hours while the house is otherwise empty, or simply share the shopping chores. The ancient Chrysler Town and Country wagon is filled with double brown paper bags at Safeway, enough to feed four hungry boys, a husband and a lover. (A note about WASPs: while booze and food are always more than adequate, in terms of quantity and quality, Harvard-educated Dennis has inherited his parents' admirable trait of counter-ostentation. He drives an ancient Toyota Land Cruiser, ideal for a doctor's midnight distress calls in the snow; the once-elegant station wagon, loaded with four children, three adults, and provisions for the weekend, struggles to climb the highway into the Rockies. Dennis buys his black shoes from Navy surplus and dresses in every sense as if he belongs in the Fifties.) Evenings feature powerful drinks for the adults, endless pool games with the boys, barbecued flank steak and baked potatoes, and Dennis's renditions of Gilbert & Sullivan operas.

PROGRESS

Then, unexpectedly, comes news of acceptance at Stanford. My dilemma, of course, is that by opting for the better school — which anyone would — I will lose my proximity to Ann. Nevertheless, it's the only sensible decision and I take it, glad also to be returning to Northern California.

I move in temporarily with the Stones, in Woodside. Turn left off Manzanita Way, through a gate and up the hill, to come out onto a plateau on which is a circle around a majestic oak. The handsome Spanish house sits on one side of it and the tackle house and garages on the other. Mine is a small guest room. In the kitchen hang the keys to the cars: the Rolls Silver Wraith, the Ferrari, the Maserati, the Jeep Grand Wagoneer, the (new) Chrysler Town and Country, etc. My own modest Firebird, I park discreetly behind the kitchen. The Stones' property extends over several acres and contains a horse corral, a darkroom and of course an Olympic-size swimming pool. I spend many hours playing pool, alone of course.

Chapter XI

STANFORD

Stanford in the Seventies retains the aura of 'The Farm', as it is also known. The core of traditional Spanish architecture is pre-eminent. Green spaces and a leisurely ambiance imbue the campus. While the engineering, law and medical schools are acknowledged to be among the best in the land and some call the university 'Stanford Tech', little of the zeal associated with the study of these professions percolates through to the undergraduate hordes. For my part, I live off-campus and only occasionally frequent the library or the cafeteria. The small town atmosphere of Palo Alto shares the pleasantly low-key atmosphere of the university. The arty film programme of the 1920s Stanford Theatre, on University Avenue, is often compelling, as are the hamburgers and beer at The Oasis, a typical undergraduate joint on El Camino.

Karen Stone has pulled a few strings to get me a studio apartment at Oak Creek, a new development. It has a big deck and an uninterrupted view over fields towards the Stanford Shopping Center. Oak Creek thinks it's exclusive. It's certainly snobbish, but it's convenient to get to school from, just across Sand Hill Road.

It's not as if I was ever a natural 'joiner', but the five years that separate me from the rest of the undergraduates as well as my Britishness, add to my feeling of being an outsider. My major is Liberal Arts, or nothing in particular. I take courses in English Literature, History and Italian, and the required science units. Apart from two native English professors, whose learning and vocabulary grant them unquestionable authority, the faculty members who teach me are inferior to their European equivalents. Of course, if even one of the best American universities needs to teach 'remedial English' to the majority of its freshmen, their intellectual level cannot be compared to that of a British public school graduate. Consequently, the faculty's attributes are commensurately low. (My own contribution to the essay entry requirement, relating my recent breakdown in the Nevada desert, frees me from this.) In particular, a popular teacher of Shakespeare, whose ingratiating habit it is to make the bard seem almost a modern citizen, perhaps an inhabitant of neighbouring Menlo Park, and who speaks of him as one would of a pal, goes down well with his students, but not particularly well with me. I dare, in one of my essays, to quote the well-known commentator, Logan Pearsall Smith (born in the U.S. and educated in Germany and Britain), who wrote the much-appreciated *On Reading Shakespeare*, only to find my work returned with the remark 'Who is he?', admittedly from a teacher's assistant. This experience succinctly demonstrates the general subordinacy of an education which concerns any ambition not closely associated with making money. I understand that the teaching of 'Western Civilization' itself is being questioned at Stanford.

On most Sundays, I drive over to my grandparents for lunch. Their life together has been divided into 'departments'. My grandmother does the housekeeping and cooking and light correspondence, and my grandfather, the shopping and accounts, but also runs the washer and drier. Thus one may be referred by one to the other grandparent with 'that's Nonnetto's/Nonnina's department', if one inquiries into the wrong area. Their appearance is overall modest. My grandfather's wardrobe seems to contain only a few thick woollen shirts in lumberjack patterns and a couple of pairs of olde-worlde trousers, which he wears with braces. To these, a pair of brown elastic-sided shoes. My grandmother caps her wig with a bonnet, but is otherwise unremarkably dressed. Greeting my grandfather is always a minor ritual. "Be careful with the old man," accompanies the handshake, however gentle. Subsequent conversation sooner or later necessitates "Speak slowly and more loudly," as he is hard of hearing. My grandfather is a sufferer and worrier in general, his chief bane being 'arthur-itis'. Guests from the Middle East are often present at lunch, over which my grandmother presides, ladling out generous helpings from a collection of dishes. She is sure to reclaim her primacy with an interruption of "would you like some more?" whenever the conversation becomes too interesting. Before I leave, she will ask me if I would like one of her 'soufflés', an egg-and-vegetable mixture resting in the freezer.

Winter

To Tahoe with the Stones. Strange to think that my father spent time here when he was in his teens. It's a beautiful environment, even now. The deep blue lake sparkles in front of the house and the richness of the mixed foliage around it provides a fitting backdrop. Helpful as ever, Karen Stone introduces me to the head ski teacher at Alpine Meadows, with a view to my becoming an instructor. The idea is not unwelcome, but I doubt if my skiing ability would be adequate to the job, to say nothing of my inherent inability to socialize with strangers.

With my gradual acclimatisation to Stanford, comes the realisation that Oak Creek is rather confining. Despite the prospect of a forty-five-minute drive, I cannot resist the longing to move back to Alma. The earlier excitement of sharing a bed with Ann kept a confrontation with old ghosts at bay. Now, I return with full, solitary concentration, breathing in the surroundings of my earliest childhood. Unfrequented Alma Bridge Road follows the pipeline, which, in turn, skirts Lexington Dam, built on land scammed from my father. I unlock the brass padlock on the tall steel gates at 19750, drive through, relock the gates, wind my way up the potholed drive, one whole winding mile past the bay trees with their fragrant leaves, later to be used in spaghetti sauces, past 'Hell's Corner', so-called because little seems to want to grow there except the tall poplars, past the mimosa trees, over the culvert, to park next to the tiled pond. One of the figures in the twin niches flanking the front door seems to have been lost. The hall imparts its quiet aura, faint and yet so familiar. A strange and powerful mixture of nostalgia and loneliness envelopes me for the first time. Here is my parents' bedroom, with the wondrously thick Chinese carpet, here the spacious walk-in cedar wardrobe, here, the playroom, here, the sunroom, with the Capehart television and bunch of multicoloured Mexican corn on the wall. Here is my own bedroom, with the fabric wallcovering depicting fairy-tale scenes and, yes, the red drum containing my wooden train. Here, the little bookcase, with its row of green-and-white Penguin crime paperbacks; the grass cloth walls, the familiar smell of ginger in the basement dressing room; the kitchen with its twin Kelvinator refrigerators, bought sometime in the Forties and still going strong (did 'built-in obsolescence' start after WWII?). All the paintings and family photographs still adorn the walls. All is as it was left in 1956.

Of course, the mere introduction of one person, however devoted and attached, into this otherwise slumbering estate, doesn't bring it to life again, as it was when an entire household inspirited it — as it was before my dreams of a perfect world were shattered. Naturally, the upkeep now is at a minimum: the pool is empty and the flower beds are bare. Deer and foxes, emboldened by the air of dereliction, are often about. Bats sometimes fly into the bedroom.

My days start with a pre-breakfast patrol to the mouse trap in the kitchen. Once or twice a week, a poor creature is caught there. The house has been empty for so long that rodents have become habituated to it. I fetch the shovel from the fire irons in the living room and, opening the window, heave the dead mouse in a long arc, out over the canopy of brush and oak trees.

I go for long walks through the property, trying to find places that my pictorial memory retains; certain trees here or rocky outcroppings there. Once I go over the hill and down to Cathedral Oaks, now looking forlorn. Listening to the radio while I do schoolwork or read becomes a habit. I've been privileged to have been a listener to three excellent radio stations. As a teenager, to Radio London, the first offshore pirate radio in Europe, at the height of the great British groups, in the early Sixties. At Stanford, to KSAN ('Jive 95') in San Francisco, with as inspired and original a bunch of DJs as can have existed anywhere, and the greatest music I've ever heard. This station was like a friend to me during my college years, 1972 to 1976. Then, in the early Nineties, to KLCC/KLCO in Eugene, Oregon, with three hours of Blues every Saturday, hosted by the encyclopaedic Gavin 'Roosterman' Fox. My collection of music has been enriched by these broadcasts. In today's severely but quite unnecessarily troubled world, radio which combines such carefree and iconoclastic views and music could not overcome a wilfully ignorant and intimidated public, abetted by the all-intrusive agencies of government.

I leave for school at a time calculated to miss the rush hour around San Jose, park on campus, and attend whichever classes my timetable specifies. The most enjoyable and interesting of these, as implied, are the Eng. Lit. ones; the least, those concerned with science. One of these, enlivened by field trips, is about earthquakes, a fitting subject in the Bay Area, where the San Andreas Fault is a constant threat. Another, about astronomy, might have been informative, except for the impenetrable accent of the Mexican teacher. I even make a useful contribution to another, when I suggest that fresh water might be gained in southern lands, if icebergs were to be towed there. This idea, while not new, at least shows that I am trying.

Sharing one of my Eng. Lit. classes, is Bob M., the drummer with the school band. An unlikely friend for me, perhaps. However, his ever-present and engaging sense of humour is irresistible. With his curly hair grown to maximum extent in Afro-mode, he's definitely a wild card. We often meet at the Oasis or peruse the naughty magazines at a kiosk together. About a year after we first meet, Bob tells me that he's found a new girlfriend. Eva is very pretty, a tall blonde with blue eyes and the antithesis to Bob's obvious Jewishness. They eventually move in together. In the continued absence of any companionship of my own, we three often go out together, to dinner or to take in a film. It becomes a familiar friendship, in which I'm simply the third wheel.

I've been trying to persuade myself to get a date on campus. Also taking the Eng. Lit. course is a tall, thin, short-haired blonde, with a mean expression. One day, in true self-sabotaging mode, I steel myself to approach her. She gives me an immediate brush-off and later I learn from Bob that she's known to prefer football players. Not quite my type then. In my year is also Terri P., with black bobbed hair and very soignée, who drives a BMW. She accepts to have dinner with me, but I seem unable to capitalize on this in any way, even to the extent of making myself interesting.

Bob invites me to stay with him at his parents' home, in L.A. This is fun, as we hang out at various favourite places of his and I see L.A. from the inside. Bob's mother is a decorator, and a vivacious, amusing person.

September 1973, Gstaad

Ann fits in perfectly with my parents' environment. For one thing, her background makes her a known quantity and she genuinely likes classical music and so is happy to attend the concerts. The family still goes on picnics on the surrounding mountains and Ann and I go for long walks, during which physical exercise takes different forms. Of course, when she has to leave, I'm thrown back into the usual routine.

When the atmosphere in the chalet becomes untenable, I often beg Nesta to let me spend a few days with her. Nesta O., an English widow, has resettled from Hawaii to a villa above Lausanne. Tall and spare, white-haired and elegant, Nesta's exuberant company is a solace to all who know her. To cross the threshold of her house is to experience instant calm and peace of mind. It works every time. It's as though her aura repels all unseemliness. When one has been born in the late 19th century and has outlived the upheavals of two world wars, one tends to be relaxed around other events and other people's foibles in general. So, harmony reigns; the staff is discreet; no domestic difficulties vex the household. The furnishings are unobtrusively luxurious. A couple of hens provide fresh eggs daily and around the house prowls a large Persian cat, which sometimes springs into the guest room from the mansard roof where it has been sunning itself.

Nesta never speaks about her past, which I gather has been fraught with incident and accomplishment, but her present is intriguing enough. Whether meeting one of many British expatriates of her acquaintance, eminent writers or retired MI6 agents, or sitting for her to draw, or sharing an excursion into the Lake of Geneva in her amphibious car, a new experience is sure to ensue whenever I'm with her. Besides the amphibian, her other car is a Bristol 409 which she drives with verve, not letting her lack of a valid driving license impede her. Speed being one of her pleasures, she understands my desire for a sports car and finds me a bright yellow, second-hand Maserati Ghibli.

In keeping with her healing regard for all people, Nesta carries on a correspondence with my mother, whom, according to her generation's habit of nicknaming, she calls 'Rags'. Only all-embracing, all-forgiving Nesta can sense in me the grotesque, crouching, frantic and fearful gnome, still hoping to enjoy life; an embryo of vivacity, enjoyment and pleasure, morally certain that any pleasurable development will rightfully be curbed; any expectation disappointed; any joyful act justly paid for and punished, as it surely cannot grow in the soil in which it has been nurtured.

Nesta died in 1984, in her 92nd year, of quite unnecessary complications incurred at the private Clinique Cécile, in Lausanne, where I visited her. She had in my estimation lived the most rewarding span for an individual: the Victorian Era of Empire, the turn of the century, the coming of the motor car, the exhilarating Thirties, the descent into two violent conflicts and the ascent from both. She was spared the fall into the age of undiscriminating masses and the complete degradation of all a connoisseur of life holds dear.

Much later I learned that Nesta's marriage had been one of convenience, her nature being lesbian, and that she had lived both a daring and a distinguished life, long before I knew her. No one could have had a better friend, but I wish I had had the maturity to ask the right questions and to gain from her at least some of her adventurous spirit.

I drive the yellow tractor — I think of it as a streamlined tractor because of the sound of the engine, coupled with the lack of power steering and the heavy clutch — to my daily tennis lessons until my father discovers it and, declaring it an absurd extravagance, makes me sell it. I see his point. So I use it one last time to fetch Ann from Geneva airport and sell it to someone in Lausanne on the way back.

In a rented Fiat, Ann and I make a tour of some Michelin-starred restaurants in France. Starting with a tiny place where the mattresses are literally troughs, we move on to the Hotel de la Poste, in Beaune (one could still lunch outside then, undisturbed by today's constant traffic on the circular road). Then to the Hotel de la Cloche & Toison d'Or, in Dijon, which preserved its pre-war décor of brass bedsteads and claw foot baths, and Lameloise at Chagny (then with only one star), and the Hostellerie du Vieux Moulin, at Bouilland. Here, the accumulation of rich food upsets Ann's stomach. So we return a bit downcast to Gstaad.

Stanford

A tearful Ann visits me. She wears a red wool patterned dress which becomes her very well. We're both uncomfortable: the relationship is over. Distance from Ann not only inclines me to look elsewhere for comfort, it encourages her to take a cruise with her mother-in-law to France, where she seduces a Parisian, even younger than I, effectively releasing me from what increasingly seems to be a hopeless friendship.

1975
Dating

I've moved again, to a ground floor flat in Menlo Park. It has a small garden and a huge redwood tree. I plant some ground-cover and a few roses and feel quite at home among my material companions. There's a girl in one of my courses that I think I could handle. In bed, I change my mind when she announces she's a virgin. Then there's the one-night-stand I pick up in a bar in Mountain View. She looks all right, but when she rolls down her pantyhose, her legs seem to double in size. They're like sausages that have been packed into a membrane. My gay friend, Del C., introduces me to the daughter of a friend. She's muscular and as lean as a board, like Jinx, except that she's unsmiling. Del has told me that this woman is gay, so why she accepts to spend time with me, I can't imagine. In bed, I reach out for her tentatively. She's naked but she doesn't respond. I really regret this failure, as she's just my physical type. Let me rephrase an earlier remark: if there's one word that defines my *whole life* it's 'unnatural'.

My dilemma in no way explains the light-hearted mood in which this was written, which I can't now account for at all:

<u>The Party at the House of Lights</u>

There was Buggery in the Snuggery,
There was License in the Lounge;
There was Sodomy in the Orangery
And Corruption of the Hounds.

But there was Prudery 'mid the Rudery
(Veneration despite Depravation)
In the Loo no one disturbed the Silence
Nor not in the Chapel, the Reverence,
But on the Patio, Fellatio.

I'm following up an ad in the *Berkeley Barb*. Even at night, it doesn't look like a prosperous neighbourhood. I've crossed the Bay Bridge to Oakland and parked my yellow Alfa convertible a couple of blocks away. A pale light glows dimly on the porch. I ring. A squat and dowdy woman lets me in. It looks as if she and her husband are just finishing their dinner, which, at a glance, seems to consist of canned baked beans of Heinz or similar variety. The blinds are down and the atmosphere is drab and close. They appear to be saving electricity. I suspect that daylight, even through louvered blinds, would reveal the nadir of grottiness. I am asked to wait until they have consumed their victuals. Humbly — or neutrally, as I haven't decided which I should be — I lower myself onto a double sofa in Naugahyde black, barely visible in the gloom. The woman confides that their in-house slave has just had her nipples pierced and it's sort of a celebratory occasion, which I am lucky to witness. Hence the baked beans, presumably. I suppress the urge to ask if they are normally reduced to subsisting on their own bodily fluids. Presently, a delicate young woman with short curly hair enters and takes off her top, revealing the predicted accessories. She has nice small breasts. Each erect nipple has a golden ring through it. As a greenhorn in this domain, I'm fascinated. The couple applaud, as though at a show, so I do too. It seems to be some kind of inauguration rite, or maybe she's moved up a grade. A very skinny, sluttish girl in her late teens, with lank black hair, follows her.

The woman simpers, "I couldn't have done it without Althea," she tells us. The man raises his face from his plate, which he has been assiduously mopping with a piece of bread. "Would you like to see the games house?" he asks me, "Althea will take you round."

Althea's expression is sullen, closed, but she exudes a pleasingly depraved air. She leads me next door, where an entire clapboard house is given over to various practices, each allotted a room with its particular accoutrements. We seem to be alone, judging from the lack of screams and groans.

"Are you passive or dominant?" Althea asks.

"It depends on my mood," I say, resolved not to give an inch, and wilfully obstructing my own pleasure, one way or the other. "How about you?"

"I enjoy both."

"Do you play chess?" Althea asks unexpectedly. I confess that I do.

She produces the board and pieces from a rack which is crammed with periodicals. "We subscribe to all the trade magazines", she pulls out a few at random from shelves piled to overflowing. I see titles like *Rack and Pinion*, *Dungeon*, *Slave Master*, etc. I riffle through a couple with the air of an habitué. Why am I determined to appear blasé?

"Would you like to see the other rooms?"

"Later, perhaps." I would like to see the other rooms, but some perverse instinct prevents me from admitting the truth.

"I'm a very good chess player, I never lose. Do you want to play?"

"OK." Is the cerebral a prelude to the physical, mastery in chess the groundwork, or merely a way to pass the time? The atmosphere is tense and hostile. I wonder whether it's me she dislikes, all men, or just her standard manner. We sit on the L-shaped sofa which skirts the hall table, like two patients passing the time in a waiting room. We begin to play. She is indeed quite adept, or maybe I'm just rusty. It's unclear if she is a permanent fixture or employee, on hand to administer punishment when required. Her nature is dominant rather than submissive. Silently, we compete for supremacy over the chessboard, perhaps as a prelude to precedence elsewhere. Part of me likes the idea of submitting to her, but part of me is scared of the unknown and doesn't want to reveal itself. While the contest is still unresolved, I take my leave and sneak out and around the corner to where I'm parked. Another near-experience.

I have on my tan leather suit from Wilkes Bashford. It has a fur collar, entirely appropriate for San Francisco in the winter.

Despite or perhaps because of the suit and the attitude it requires, I'm a bit troubled. I have the yellow convertible Alfa, I have the clothes, but I still have no clue what to do with them. Maybe it's this subliminal question which is bothering me, as I carelessly accelerate through what I think is a yellow light. That's what I insist to the police afterwards, anyway. As luck would have it, the driver on the cross street sees it as green and we seal our differences with a crash in the centre of the intersection. The Alfa takes a bad hit and has to be towed, but at least this time, it's mine.

As it's very late, I'm not about to consider returning to Menlo Park. Instead, in a mood of self-pity, I take a cab to the Mark Hopkins and check in. I'll stay there a few days before escaping to Europe, putting the whole sorry incident, as well as my current life, behind me. It's an indication, see, that it's time to change venues. I must have been disregarding subtler signs about my inability to make my life work. A more persuasive hint was due. So this decision is logical and in no way an overreaction.

I don't sleep too well, but on the next day, the manager calls me. He's Australian and recognizes my name, on account of my aunt who married an Aussie the first time around, and has children there. He's a jovial sort and I don't bore him with my story. In fact, he invites me to stay as long as I want, as his guest — which I interpret as a day or two — and he hopes to see me in the bar at six. There's no way to get out of this invitation, so I show up obediently. In the bar is a collection of long-term lushes, including a man who accompanies himself at the piano in a version 'Moon River', which he calls 'Blue Liver'. He's drunk, see, and it's a huge joke. I wonder how he's different from the other regulars, but I laugh dutifully. It's not so funny on the next day, so, without saying goodbye to the manager, with my toothbrush and some clothes I've bought at Jaeger, I drive the chipmunk-powered Hertz Honda Civic back to Menlo Park.

STANFORD

As soon as the Alfa is repaired, I decide to get rid of it. It hasn't brought me luck and now it makes me feel vulnerable. A student from some expensive private school in Oakland answers my ad and pays my price, without noticing the filler around one of the brake lights. At one of the dealers on Stevens Creek ('crick', as some Californians have it) Blvd., there's a used white Buick LeSabre 455 convertible. Where the Alfa was small, cramped, European, noisy and underperforming, no one can overlook the Buick. It's Detroit at its confident best. The bench front seat easily accommodates three and the acceleration its huge V8 provides is quiet but real. There is the minor matter of a distinct lean to one side, but once the body shop has inserted something or other, it looks level, and sports wheels add the *dernier cri*. One day, as I'm disembarking on campus from what I soon call the White Whale, in patterned silk shirt, white jeans and white Guccis, I overhear what must be a passing visitor comment, "Typical Stanford student". Ah, if he only knew of the anguish behind this blithe exterior!

My favourite colour, yellow, is still part of my transport: I have a yellow Motobécane bicycle, which I try to remember to ride to school, if the traffic isn't too heavy. I believe I should be able to manage a ten-minute ride without mishap and I'll get exercise and feel closer to other students — and younger — than I would in a car. However, whereas some people can't walk and chew gum at the same time, I'm unable simultaneously to maintain my equilibrium on a bike and mail a letter. As a result of this daredevil stunt, performed late at night on campus, after a date, I fall against the mailbox and ride back with my nose streaming blood. Because of this incident, when the bike, although chained to a pillar in the closed garage, is stolen a few days later, I don't feel too bad. Of course it isn't insured.

Sometimes, when I'm collecting my mail, I'll glance through a Scientology publication, destined for my upstairs neighbour, Gloria. Gloria has got it bad and seems to be paying her way towards getting 'clear', the mysterious and no doubt expensive aspiration touted regularly in the journal. Her devotion doesn't stop her sex life, of which I'm all too aware as it occurs directly above my head. The sound of her bouncing bed acts as a further disincentive to me, as if I needed it. I'm a good watcher of life, just not a participant.

Le Voyeur is in the library today, not doing research with the help of a volume of Macmillan's Quotes, and watching girls. Just watching. For something to do, I get a film reference work and look up *Les Yeux sans visage*. The book says it's a classic and speaks of Franju as a unique director who developed his own style. So there, Clouzot!

January 1976

To Bahamas via Miami (one night), arrived 2 January. To North Eleuthera Island, Moved into Pink Sands Hotel cottage with my parents. I'm sitting at an outdoor restaurant, when two black men in army uniforms walked through, while seeming to check the guests. I experience mild paranoia: it occurs to me that the local government could arrest all foreigners at a whim.

Return to Stanford. First Class as coach full ($79 extra). Play cards with beautiful black stewardess. Contemplate asking her for date, but 'can't get bold' (Mike Bloomfield). Speaking of whom, Eva and I go to the West Dakota, Berkeley to hear Bloomfield, Gravenites, Naftalin. 'Dancing Fool very good,' says my diary. San Francisco, in the early Seventies, is still a haven of good live music. While I will always regret the laziness that prevented me from attending an Allman Brothers concert in 1972 at Winterland, at least I don't miss the one there which featured Paul Butterfield, Elvin Bishop and Mike Bloomfield. Where else but in the Bay Area could you hear one of the world's foremost guitarists for little more than the price of a cup of coffee? This is the second time we have heard them play. The first time, at the Old Waldorf, I introduced myself. My father was in San Francisco and I had some wild notion of getting him to hear Bloomfield. "Does your father improvise?" Bloomfield asked me. Forgetting my father's musical adventures with Ravi Shankar, I responded lamely that the great classical composers didn't lend themselves to improvisation. I wonder if Bloomfield might have suggested some kind of musical collaboration. He gave me his phone number, which I managed to lose. On reflection, I judged that my father's interdisciplinary musical interests would not have stretched to Blues. This was born out when I played a Bloomfield cassette to him in Greece much later and saw his eyes glaze over immediately.

The ad in the *Berkeley Barb* promises something different, but it's mainly her name that has attracted me: Alice. Why? Alice in Wonderland, perhaps. A name associated with childhood innocence and yet seductive. Her rabbit hole is on a sloping street in Oakland, in a semi-basement. It's dimly lit and very cramped, consisting of bare fibreboard walls surrounding a double mattress. It's a green and white striped mattress, with straps at each corner. Apart from the mattress-burrow there's a tiny entrance hall and a bathroom. Alice lives above the shop, as it were. She's in her mid-twenties, gratifyingly surly of expression, slender, and with long, dry, dark hair and very thin lips.

"I want to make one thing clear: I don't do role-playing," she informs me, straight off, when I have handed over $50.

"Right," I say, nonchalantly. This is a major disappointment; apparently, I have opted for the discount version. I figured that all this kind of stuff requires some pretence. Maybe she doesn't have acting skills.

"Do you want me with my clothes on or off?"

"Oh, off," I say casually.

She strips with the minimum of movements, revealing a rather nice body: tanned all over, with small breasts.

"Shall I spank you?"

"Yes, OK."

"Aren't you going to take off your clothes?"

"Oh, sure."

With my usual self-consciousness, I take off my jeans, t-shirt and underpants, but not my socks. I'm aware of having shrunk to the size of an acorn. It isn't just inhibition; I can't help thinking of all the other people whose naked bodies have preceded me. I flop onto the mattress and Alice secures my ankles and wrists with the straps. Then she sets to with a will. There's nothing fake here, anyway. I feel the pain fairly soon, but although my buttocks seem to be on fire, I'm not aroused. Her manner is neither depraved nor imperious, just indifferent. Perhaps that's the problem: she doesn't seem to enjoy her work. I'm prepared to suffer pain in exchange for arousal, but not otherwise.

"I guess it's no good," I tell her, "I'm not getting anything out of this."

"Maybe you need something stronger," she says, untying me, "My boyfriend just had his penis pierced. We're very excited about it."

"Really? No, I don't think that would do it for me either."

"Have a look in this box, maybe there's something here you'd like." A large cardboard box in a corner contains a collection of bizarre items. She picks up a couple of blocks of wood joined by a screw thread. "This here's a nut cracker," she explains.

"Ah yes, I see what you mean."

"Let's try this." She presses the ends of a couple of electrical wires, which seem to be connected to flashlight batteries, to my testicles. The sensation is pleasant, a not very powerful shock. I don't have the week to spare, is all. "Let's forget it," I say. But it doesn't seem to be $50 worth. I take in her long slim body and the tuft of dull brown hair at her crotch. "Can I go down on you?"

"Sure."

She lies on her back on the mattress and spreads her legs. I kneel and then lie flat and apply myself. I do my best, but as she remains silent, I can't be sure I'm making headway. Discouraged, I raise myself. "I'm sorry. I guess I'm not doing it right."

"You have to do it harder," she says, but she must be fairly excited, because she rubs herself and then gives a couple of subdued gasps.

Now she seems more agreeably disposed towards me. As she's pulling on her clothes, she says "I have a girlfriend. We do things together. You just have to call ahead."

"OK, I'll think about it."

"You should take care. Some of these adverts are just a blind. People have gotten killed."

"How do you mean?"

"You know, it's like mugging, only worse."

Slightly shaken by this information, I let myself out and walk down the hill to the corner where I've parked the Buick. I've learnt something valuable anyway. It makes sense when you think about it. That puts an end to further adventures of this kind.

Chapter XII

PARIS AGAIN, NEW YORK, LOS ANGELES

1976

The man plonks down $1,900 in hundreds on the kitchen counter. The White Whale is sold. Its last duty has been to transport my potted plants to Bob's flat. Bekins will store my furniture and my boxed possessions. I'm off to Paris to work for ICM. Rather than returning to the companies at which I tried four years ago to find employment, I take the line of least resistance and go back to what I know: the film business.

International Creative Management, at the time the most important agency of its kind, spans the globe from an office block on Beverly Drive, Beverly Hills, aided by various satellite stations overseas. Its little yellow client booklet mentions every sort of famous person who can be promoted and from whom a fee may be charged: directors, writers, actors, loosely known as 'entertainers', but also politicians, etc., etc. ICM is venturing into a new field, that of film sales through pre-financing, to be based in Paris. It sounds as if it's a rather tenuous method of funding an independent (non-studio) film and adds merely to the uncertainty surrounding all such enterprises, but apparently it's currently all the rage.

Accepting the genuineness of this commercial speculation, which of course I do unquestionably at the time, I am thrilled at my prospects. In view of what I have learned since about the general development of the world, I now wonder if the true purpose of this new department was, from the outset, not quite another. I have been engaged as the assistant to the new director, himself previously a senior executive at 20th Century Fox, which he has left under a cloud and which he seeks to sue for wrongful dismissal. Throughout my three-year tenure at the firm, he exchanges calls with his lawyer on the subject. My French language ability and of course my experience in the field, but also my perceived ethnic origins, must have been helpful in landing the job.

We are situated at 66 Champs-Élysées, a prestigious address, until you actually visit the offices. This world-renowned boulevard, broad, tree-lined and architecturally impeccable, has lately been gnawed at in its nether recesses, by the rats of contemporary city planning. Under many a superbly-designed, symmetrically perfect facade on the Champs-Élysées, runs, like a sewer, a so-called *arcade*, a corridor of brightly lit, tacky boutiques, dispensing anything from costume jewellery to hamburgers. These arcades, the expressways along the Seine, the clump of high-rises at La Défense, Beaubourg Museum, the dehumanised Halles, and the Perspex pyramid which so neatly obstructs the view of the Louvre — this is the sum of 20th century France's contribution to one of the greatest cities on earth.

Two floors above the hectic burrowing and the miasma of age-old frying fat in the arcades, an often no less hectic atmosphere reigns over the sale of films so minor and miserable that it is a constant mortification even to name them, let alone to be compelled to sell them. Initially, I am calmed in my distress at my enforced association with such contemptible guff, by the assurance that our product would get better. Indeed, eventually, one or two laudable films do come our way, but their presence is smothered by such fare as *Planet of Dinosaurs*, a full-length, semi-animated el-cheapo, in which you can almost see the shoestrings on which it has been made. In it, plastic Triassic monsters chase real, but third-rate actors in jerky movements, like puppets in a Punch and Judy show, in and out of clumps of rock, probably in the neighbourhood of Sonora. The producer calls from California every week to inquire about sales. He must spend whatever he earns from distribution on the phone. The poor sap would be easier to handle if he lost his temper once in a while, but he is always utterly reasonable, as if his goofy film really deserved an audience.

All the films this company represents are different in their individual lousy ways. What they have in common is that none of them have been made for the right reason: entertainment. People sometimes imagine that films are made because some director or producer has found a good story and some great actors are keen to play in it. This is the last reason films come to be. Films are made for one of the following reasons: someone stands to make a quick profit; someone owes something to someone else; money can be laundered through creative accounting; a star is available; the producer/director is downright deluded; the film has achieved its own momentum and it's too late to stop it.

My boss is a genial fellow, tall and well dressed in handmade suits, obviously an old hand at this kind of shenanigan. He's a salesman par excellence. I, on the other hand, am a very bad one. I figure that a good product can sell itself, whereas a bad one is simply something to be avoided. Here, I'm buried alive in bad ones. I know my theory is false. Most job advertisements are for peddlers of one kind or another, even if they don't use the word. Everything, good or bad, has to be pushed. A true salesman is someone who can sell an obviously useless object to someone who can't afford it; he's worth his weight in gold.

Through my boss's brother-in-law, Hubert Cornfield, I find a flat in the rented house of his uncle, Bernie Cornfeld, a notorious white-collar criminal. In those days, $2.5 billion was a lot of money. That's how much Bernie and his managers have managed to corner through the sale of mutual funds, via his pyramid scheme, Investors Overseas Services, often to U.S. servicemen overseas. Hubert is a film director, although not a very successful one. He is also quarrelsome, as my frank assessment of a screenplay, of which he has asked me my opinion, demonstrates. His main claim to fame is a film called *The Night of the*

Following Day, a freakish piece, starring Marlon Brando. Brando, reputedly, has done much of the directing himself.

My flat is a poorly converted upper corner of this '*maison particulière*', itself in the courtyard of an apartment building in the 16th arrondissement. There is a cheerlessly dark bedroom and a cheerfully light-filled, tiled bathroom, and the passage connecting the two, off which an alcove with a hotplate. Standing here, I consume my breakfast coffee and croissant. A large mirror leans against the wall, for decoration, presumably. Bernie occupies the main downstairs rooms, whenever he is in Paris, and lets the remaining space.

Bernie is short and tubby and habitually topped by a blue Greek fisherman's cap. He speaks so softly that only the most attentive listener can catch what he is saying. For his financial knavery, he has spent a year on remand in Switzerland. However, he seems not to be too much the worse off for that. He still owns a chateau, several villas, forty-two cars, and a couple of modelling agencies. Hence, he is often surrounded by attractive girls when he's in town. When he tires of catching up on business or playing backgammon with his closest cronies, he invites the whole crowd to lunch. At one of these occasions, I meet a beautiful model, Shaun C., strikingly white-haired for the season, and a really nice person. Being me, even an intimate conversation with her leads nowhere. She nicknames me 'Preppie', because of my three-piece suit, but affectionately. I also fail to take advantage of another girl, who lands in my bed as a consequence of all others being full, after Bernie has crammed two he has picked up into his 1965 Corvette on a trip from Geneva to Paris.

With the best intentions to keep fit, I start to jog in the Bois de Boulogne, before going to work. It's not the best time, as my body is still stiff. Bad weather and distracting glimpses of the occasional couple doing intimate things in the underbrush (at 7:00 a.m.!) undermine my resolve and I join a gym instead. Unfortunately, this is no better, despite being distinctly upmarket, in central Paris. The French don't seem to have got the hang of this kind of training. It's cramped and there are no lockers. During my second visit there, someone steals my tie, one of my favourites. That puts an end to my exercise routine.

Every day, I catch the Metro on Avenue Georges Mandel. When the train pulls in, I place myself level with the edge of the doorway of an uncrowded car and slip in on the tail of those exiting. Even so, the only available seat is often one of those marked '*Réservé aux mutilés de guerre*', which I take, having to the best of my knowledge never seen a war veteran, however mutilated, claim his rights. Given that the sign was affixed after the Second World War, surviving veterans might now be expected to lead retiring lives and not be keen to subject themselves to the crush of the Metro. As if to mitigate this evidence of a caring state, an unofficial notice next to the sign decrees '*Mort aux Juifs*'. Paris would always be Paris. I take out my Magic Marker and discreetly amend the first message to read '*Réservé aux mutilés de la paix*'.

As I emerge from the FDR station onto the Champs-Élysées, I am aware of the remarkable quality of the light striking the trees around the Rond-Point and the unusual freshness of the air on what happens to be a perfect spring morning. Resolutely, I ignore both. Head down, I cross the street to the office.

One positive thing I've been able to achieve is to option one of my favourite books, a thriller by Anthony Burgess called *Tremor of Intent*, through an excellent but expensive firm of lawyers in Paris. I should really have known better than to invest my own money, as I've met several would-be producers who have come through the office, trying with urgent insistence to persuade the company to back their properties. One even sold his wedding ring. A basic lesson in the film business is always to spend other people's money, but this is hard to do when it comes to controlling the rights to a book.

July 1978

My thirtieth birthday is a rather splendid affair. My parents happen to be in Monaco on the date and they have invited

Anthony Burgess and wife (a somewhat forceful Italian woman), and Princess Grace and Prince Rainier to lunch. Naturally, we have the restaurant to ourselves. Burgess has chosen to live in Monaco, probably for tax advantages, as this concrete paradise has nothing much else to offer. If it is possible for an actress to look more seductive off than on the screen, that actress must be Grace Kelly. I challenge any man not to fall in love with her at first sight. Burgess gives me a signed copy of his *Cyrano de Bergerac*. Princess Grace gives me two ties, which I still treasure. Rainier is probably very bored. The conversation isn't memorable. Burgess asks my father if he may send him a violin piece he has written, in the hope that he might consent to play it. On the next day, my parents and I are invited to drinks at the palace. Unusually for me, conversing with Princess Grace puts me at ease. She exudes the same casual warmth that I had felt with Ann. Her voice, low, soft, melodious makes me want to draw it over me like a blanket (sorry about that).

A few weeks after this, I receive an invitation to dinner at a house on Avenue Foch. My hopes to continue our conversation at this event are dashed however, as I am placed at the second table, between Grace's two notorious daughters, whose conversation consists uniquely of comparisons between winter resorts and the like. I remain mute and pining throughout the meal. In September 1982, Grace died after a mysterious car crash, under circumstances which have still not been satisfactorily explained. Stricken like so many others, I had sent the standard, futile bunch of flowers, but by then she was probably dead anyway.

1979

Inexplicably and certainly not because we have been doing so well that the office requires additional staff, we have been joined by a man called Zeev, who is inserted between my own position and the director's. This imposition is a short, grey-haired Israeli, who, as far as anyone can make out, has had nothing to do with films at all, except as a Jewish fan (he often alludes to some minor Hollywood star he has met, whose name it turns out was previously quite another). He doesn't even speak French, but communicates in guttural English. However, he is treated with deference, has the use of a car and driver, and a decorator for his rented flat, and seems to spend his day — when he is at the office at all — yelling down the phone in Hebrew, presumably at some crony in Israel. As we haven't sold any films to Israel, he could theoretically have been hired to do this, but Israel is too insignificant to warrant the expense of exclusive attention, particularly from such an apparently well-paid executive. So why is Zeev here?

Obviously he is not a waste of space to someone, whoever that might be, but to say that his presence is demoralising would be an understatement. Not having then the insights I have now, I couldn't hazard the guess that he might be engaged in some possibly clandestine endeavour on behalf of his homeland, and using the office as cover — this of course with the complete knowledge and support of the company's president and owner. In any case, I have had enough.

It's three years later and I'm coasting joylessly on the long downward slide out of my job. Joy is singularly absent from my existence. Some men dare to climb mountains or otherwise expose themselves to danger, but I don't dare to be joyful. There have been times when I've come perilously close to it, but at the current rate, I run no risk of snatching joy from the jaws of death. Never in the history of this legendary city has an intelligent, moderately good-looking, French-speaking, fully-employed and eligible young male so successfully squandered its opportunities. Occasionally, I try to do better. Although I know that the times of Henry Miller and his ilk are irretrievably over, and the 16th arrondissement no Clichy, I try once or twice to create my own quiet days there, on weekends when I don't feel obsessed by the need quite unnecessarily to complete some work at the office. But all I seem to be able to do is to add to the already record-breaking number of women with whom I have spent uneventful nights. A girl I had been seeing had recently imparted to me with some excitement that she had just been fitted with a contraceptive device. This, just when I was trying to figure out a way to end our relations, short of telling her that, at certain times and angles, her face resembled a pig's.

After the Cannes Film Festival, in which as usual we participate with minimal success in the market, I summon the courage to declare my intention of leaving. With an enormous sense of relief, I board a flight to Los Angeles. Here, Bob invites me to share the flat he and Eva rent, until I find a place of my own. This turns out to be a small Spanish bungalow in West Hollywood, a few blocks from the Design Centre or 'Blue Whale'. Bob, who has a true amateur-expert's eye for used cars, finds me an irreproachable 1976 Oldsmobile Cutlass. My life in L.A. is pleasant, if uneventful. West Hollywood is a friendly residential district, interspersed with small businesses. The architectural uniformity of tile-roofed bungalows, with the occasional apartment block, means that the few taller buildings, like the 'Blue Whale', tower like cliffs in a sea. Walking here is not an eccentricity and prone to police intervention, as it is in Beverly Hills. I invest in a stereo, buy music at Tower Records on Sunset, join a karate club on Santa Monica, and jog a mile regularly at the Beverly Hills High School track. I'm trying to make up for three years of physical slacking in Paris. I take in a lot of films, mostly in the afternoons, when the cinemas are empty and the prices, cheaper. To sit practically alone at Grauman's Chinese Theatre on Hollywood Boulevard and watch some recent release on the huge screen is always a marvellous experience. I also make desultory attempts to find work, of course.

The few contacts I still have prove useful in this regard. I apply for the position of assistant to the head of production at United Artists in New York and manage to get the job. United Artists, was founded in 1919, by talent as the name implies, not by exploitation, by Charlie Chaplin, Mary Pickford, Douglas Fairbanks Sr. and D.W. Griffith. In 1967, a group of lawyers took it over. Later it belonged for a while to Transamerica, an insurance company based in San Francisco. I have a large fourth-floor office and a secretary. To familiarize myself with the company's projects, I am given a cardboard box of screenplays to read. This I do, with growing dismay and disappointment: it appears that not a single film contemplated, or actually in production, is intended for the general public. Apart from the hugely over-expensive *Heaven's Gate* (a prime example of the 'too late to stop it' film-production category, and singly responsible for the company's failure about a year later), there are many lower-budget films, which can only be described as losers in the making, and apparently the choice of some sensitive intellect. Low-budget coming of age stories with no-name actors are bound to lose money, as films are simply too expensive, particularly with a major company's overheads, to recoup costs for such fare from the minute section of the public that might want to see them in the first place. The habit of senior executives only to see films at private viewings among their privileged equals, but never at cinemas among normal people, leads naturally to ignorance of the typical audience's taste, and the tendency to promote personal preferences. By contrast, I continue to pay my entry fee to see the latest releases, no matter how debased and plebeian.

Heaven's Gate itself is directed autocratically by a man who wilfully disregards the Anglo-Saxon film-going public by engaging a French actress in the main female role. It is said that he has made fifty takes of one scene. With the pride and fanfare expected and required of such organizations, UA publishes full-page announcements of its 'slate' of upcoming productions in the 'trades', a shameful revelation at best. My conclusion is that the company has a death wish. There are two Heads of Production, one at MGM, in Culver City, and one in New York, necessitating bimonthly flights across the country for production meetings. Management remains at the company's original building on Seventh Avenue in New York. The CEO is an accountant, whose directive to his main creative subordinates is simply "More T&A, boys", a vain hope from a group headed by aesthetes. One is tempted privately to rechristen the company 'United Autistics'.

For the first time, I become aware of the colossal sums spent extravagantly and most wastefully in this business. Huge figures are regularly flung about and used as measures of an actor's success. Executives are just as greedy about their perks, which may include company cars. No amount of first-class travel, limousines, fancy restaurants and hotels can alter the fact that all this money is squandered on failed entertainment. It's Paris all over again, except for the luxury.

Ostensibly an ideal job with considerable potential for advancement, it is in fact a dead end, as the company has sealed its own fate through years of mismanagement. Only the Foreign Department and the tiny office halfway up the building which deals with the James Bond franchise are profitable.

My chance comes when I recognize a screenplay I have read in Paris, one that made me laugh out loud. However, the latest version has been so much improved by overwriting that it has lost almost all its originality. It has also become more expensive. *Motel Hell* is a speculative screenplay, written by two young brothers. The plot involves a couple that owns a motel and also makes famously delicious smoked meats, sourced from their guests, whom they kidnap and plant in a secret garden, first cutting their vocal chords so that they can only hiss like geese. Here, they force-feed them until they can be smoked. If this sounds disgusting, it is also very amusing, inexpensive and without precedent. The accompanying artwork is headed 'Harvest Time Begins at Sundown' and features a tractor hauling out the unfortunates. I become a one-man promoter of this project, the only one that is both cheap and potentially commercial. It is approved. Initially, all goes smoothly. The producer is the writers' father and is well-known at the company. His career has lagged recently and consequently he's grateful to me for reviving it. My boss and I are invited to his house in Beverly Hills for caviar pie, astoundingly, a delicious concoction. Consultations with his sons go well. I insist that the first version be used and that the screenplay be filmed absolutely straight — under no circumstances for laughs. The cast can be unknown, thus saving costs, but the director should be experienced.

The trouble begins with the delay in finding a director. From my office in New York, it's harder to reach and meet the directors I have in mind, since most of them are in California. Among others, I try Joe Dante, famous for *Piranha*. He refuses. However, my chief handicap is that I'm inexperienced at this kind of thing and am up against a very cunning producer who doesn't care about the success of his sons' film, but only about moving the project forward so that he can get his fee. Before I realize it, the project is out of my hands and an old lag from the British Hammer Films stable (1960s B movies 'schlock-horror' like *The Mummy's Shroud*, *The Brides of Dracula*, etc.) has been hired to direct. This fellow engages ham actors, of the kind he is accustomed to. As anyone knows, to succeed, a joke must be told with a straight face, but he plays the story for laughs. When it's finished, I view the film at the L.A. studio. It's a disaster, without a single well-delivered line. I leave the screening room alone and in stupefied disappointment. This puts paid to my reputation, for what it may be worth.

I quote from a letter I wrote to an acquaintance later: 'I was an unwilling, protesting participant in the gradual but inexorable extinction of UA. To have been even a minor member of the management of a once-great company, and to observe with what blind obstinacy it was maintained on its doomed course, was a depressing experience, although it had its educational aspects.' Through good fortune, I'm able to recoup my option-money on *Tremor of Intent*. Someone has bought the rights with the intention of filming it under the unlikely title of *For Amber Waves of Grain*.

So, sooner than later, I'm facing the end of another chapter. I take a last limousine ride to the airport and return to L.A., where I rent a tiny studio flat in a new building at 1000 Westmount Drive. Until I find another job, I try to develop a few projects which have come my way. One is *Tomorrow and*

Tomorrow and Tomorrow, an original screenplay based in some future time when the population of the planet has become so great and the resources so inadequate that people must live only one day a week. For the rest of the time, they are confined to refrigerators, in suspended animation. As it happens, by some technical maladjustment, a 'Wednesday' boy meets a 'Tuesday' girl and the fun starts. Roy Disney, Walt's nephew, expresses an interest in this property and I visit him at Toluca Lake to discuss it. Of course my position is insecure, as I do not own the property. I am compelled to concede that I cannot advance it. I also hire a British writer to write a screenplay based on the book *Snowbound*, a true story of cocaine smuggling in Latin America. This is hopeless. The writer ends up in hospital when he drunkenly asks a black man in a bar why Nigerians are not called 'Niggerians'.

The building sports a rooftop pool, where many of the inhabitants meet on weekends. Among them are a Lebanese limousine owner, a bevy of real estate agents (read: desperate single women) and a pretty dental hygienist. The latter has the most beautiful hands and feet I have ever seen. She tells me they have often been used in advertisements. She's a nice person and lends me her car when I sell mine, prior to returning to Europe. Indeed, she's so appealing that I'm tempted to cancel my flight. But my life is going nowhere here and I'm fed up with the film industry in general. I hope she found the good man she deserved.

Chapter XIII

BE CAREFUL WHAT YOU WISH FOR, YOU MIGHT GET IT

1981

While I was running my ostensibly excellent job in New York into the ground, I used, sometimes, to run across a girl who worked in the literary department at the company. At the time, she struck me as attractive, but I was too concerned with my work to register her existence seriously. Yet she must have stayed on my mind because when, in 1981, I visited New York briefly, I called her. Perhaps in the hope of restarting my lagging career, I had made appointments to visit ex-colleagues. These led nowhere.

I don't recall the exact sequence of events, but Priscilla and I had dinner at my favourite Italian restaurant and ended up that evening at her studio flat, in her collapsible double bed. Needless to say, my body let me down as usual and I was moved, in my hopeless way, to say to her on the following morning, something like "I should know better than to mix pleasure with business." This upset her and made me feel even stupider than before. I sent her some flowers at work and we met again once or twice. Before I left, she allowed me to choose between two photos. One featured her when she had been modelling in Paris, in the other, she was using a sewing machine. I chose the latter, as it was more natural. I must still have it somewhere.

What I do remember and will never forget is that Priscilla was in all her particulars the ideal woman for me. She was bright and quick and about three years younger than I, slender, tall, had a lovely face, and possessed the irresistible combination of red hair and freckles. I had never supposed, in my wildest dreams, that I would actually ever meet such a person, or, if I did, that she might care for me. Furthermore, it turned out that she liked Blues too, having toured as an assistant with Freddie King. She played some records for me and I was able to add his talent to that of the other two Kings, with whose music I was familiar. What more could I ask for in a future companion?

Why I allowed this unique opportunity to slip away, I can only conjecture. I suppose it had to do with my subconscious conviction that I was not intended, did not deserve, to be happy; that any and all attempts I made at a successful, fulfilling private life must come to naught — if necessary, by terminating them myself to prove this thesis. In a practical sense, I reasoned my renunciation of this gift thus: we had had a trifling disagreement, so maybe we were not suited after all; I had paid several months' rent in advance on my apartment in L.A.; I preferred sunny California to New York. We spoke once on the phone thereafter and I received a Valentine's card from her in 1982.

In 1984, just before I was to be married in New York, I tried to call Priscilla, with what object exactly, I don't know. Maybe to save me from the union I was pledged to enter, about which I had premonitions. She had moved by then and seemed to be untraceable. Throughout my marriage, I tried intermittently to find her. I used to look through the phone books in the local library in Bend, Oregon, and write down likely numbers. Ridiculous as it may sound, I could not remember exactly how to spell her last name.

It only struck me later that such opportunities occur only once in a lifetime, if they occur at all; that I could have stayed in New York, with her or in a place of my own, that I could have looked for work there — all other aspects of life being secondary to this one.

Chapter XIV

MYKONOS AGAIN

1982

A sort of plan to live here and write. Mykonos, in confirmation of Jinx's nickname for it, has been degraded over the last twenty years. It's now distinctly Mickey Mouse: rental Jeeps and buzzing little motorbikes abound; charters decant drunks straight from Yorkshire onto the island's new airport; loud and ostentatiously garnished gays of every stripe throng the narrow streets. But it's still fairly cheap and, if one ignores the filth swarming around the stalls during the summer, apparently keen on gold frippery and, yes, fur coats, one could maybe make it work.

'Postcards from Mykonos, Cyclades'

<u>Mickey Mouse, Queen of the Sickladies</u>

Ickle grey mouse live in trash can
Beard grow like topsy
Try catch lizzer with grass loop
Sea make you sleep
But kamikaze mosquito
Whine like stuka in ear
Wake you up again
(quick turn on light roll times look for shadow on wall get up
Don't breathe SMASH BASTARD got him now how get off wall)

LIVED IT WRONG

Hotellady make nice eyes under fringe
And sometimes give free beer
But mean nothing

Heap weird folk like 6ft. man with dye blond hair
Wraparound punk-style sunglasses hula skirt
Sad old sagface French woman with fancy dress show
Underwear

Here come Englishman neck bent funny red like cooked
Lobster wear mud colour nylon t-shirt over pot belly
Over mud colour jeans over plastic sandals

Went in small boat bouncy bouncy over windy waves
To visit leper colony with pack lunch but lepers
Out on social call stop delos way back steal
Marble for headstone bring chisel write epitaph
Here lies decomposer

Must go now continue search for truth
(where he hidin'? hm? Nm? Schnarfl schnurfl
Under here? Hm?)

Or maybe not, after all:

<u>Down to the beach</u>

Down to the beach
To meditate
No peace there can I find
For all about
The festive folk
Expose their parts of shame

Happy frolicsome trippers
Piddling in the sea
Carefree subaqueous perversions

On the surface
The coppertone layer's

MYKONOS AGAIN

Oily bubbles gleam
Every wave sweeps
Relentlessly to shore
Discharges of tar

Convoys of cruise ships
Lined up in serried ranks
Discharge human pollutants

The eternal north wind blows
Eternal smells from open loos
And mainland smog and plastic bags
Pursue an aimless odyssey

In fact

Where once Ulysses trod
Do coke and sprite abound
Where brave men fought and died
Shrill shrieks and titters sound
Nature's triumphs infested by
The myriad tinsel toys
Of tiny minds at play

Now rise up Minotaur and Cyclops too
And gobble and trample
Rage and rend
And sacrifice this gaudy rabble
To purify the land

Although my father accepted an honorary citizenship of Mykonos at a function in September 1993, my parents never returned there for a holiday after the hordes ruined the island. There may be a parallel between Sixties and Eighties Mykonos, broken by the colonels' rule (1967-74), and post-Franco Spain (Franco died in 1975), in terms of the degradation of their respective societies. Among subtler subterranean causes, the lure of relative lawlessness, after military rule, meant a simultaneous sell-out of local culture and striving after commercial gain. Out of loyalty to the ousted Greek royal family, my father had refused to visit the island during the dictatorship, but he was 'stunned after an absence of seven years, to find Mykonos overrun by *"naked Beatniks of all sexes"*. He wrote to the mayor, explaining why he would no longer be holidaying in the fallen idyll, and his letter found its way into the Athenian national newspaper *Kathimerini*. He spoke of the *"locusts"* invading Greece and of Mykonos in particular becoming *"an island of ill fame"*. In less than a decade, Menuhin lamented, *"your noble Mykonos, where the visitors came for its own uniqueness and its proximity to the sacred island of Delos, has acquired the reputation of a place for all and every kind of decadence"*, a decadence which was *"costing you the best kind of foreigner"'* (*High Sixties: The Summers of Riot and Love*, Roger Hutchinson).

On Mykonos, I look up Danielle, now middle-aged and embittered. Exile suits those who profit early from it, who adapt and make the foreign place their own. Others repent early enough to resume their lives successfully in their native countries. The rest end up as so much flotsam or jetsam. Jinx, for instance, thrived in Greece, but when the time came and the adventure palled, she decided that she belonged in America and she lived out her life in Florida.

I also grow a beard, the first and last of my life. Despising as I do 'beardoids', or any kind of facial hair or adornment, as well as bow-tie wearers and a host of other decorated types, I would never wear a beard anywhere else. But in this temporary domicile, where masquerade is conformity, the experiment is permissible. In three weeks, it's fully grown. I then shave off bits of it over the next three weeks, from handlebar, to toothbrush, taking photographs as I go.

In the restaurant on the beach, a hundred metres below the house, a couple of English girls are helping out, probably escapees from dreary Britain. One is slender with a gazelle's grace. After a few tentative conversations, we agree to meet for dinner. For some reason, I am late. I race along one of Mykonos's alleys and trip over a paving stone, easy enough to do. After dinner, this girl amazingly consents to share my room (two single beds). Nothing of any kind happens until the morning, when I awake in great pain and with a swollen ankle. In panic at the thought that I may have broken something in this far-off place and may die of my injury, I limp off with scarcely an explanation. At a local surgery, I receive competent treatment for what is clearly just a twisted ankle, but my craven and hurried departure puts an end to this promising fling. I must have been an exception in her life anyway, as I later gather that she is lesbian. A sort of deviation then, in the intimate life of a deviant. Otherwise, my life on Mykonos is without incident and without improvement. Eventually, I pack up again and return to Gstaad, sadder but hardly wiser.

The Rehearsal

I know him well,
he's a huge appetite
for travel, for amusement, for life
which he suppresses
because it isn't seemly
because it isn't meant
because he isn't any good at it.
A man should know his limitations
he says.
Protected by prejudice
persuaded that he missed the bus
at birth
when already two whiskies
under par
he believes strongly
in a destiny
of disappointment.
When the voice cries out
powerfully within him
when his instinct
cringingly reasserts itself

tells him
WHAT HE WANTS
what to do
he won't do it.
A few years ago, the voice
was already
less insistent
now it's only
a disapproving murmur
it's almost extinguished.
But he's learning
he'll be all right
next time around.

Chapter XV

GSTAAD, AN OVERVIEW AND RETROSPECTIVE

In popular mythology, garrets are to writers what foxholes are to foot soldiers; places of reclusive confinement and suffering, from which each is expected to go into action, whether mental or physical. Many years ago, when I was earnestly preparing myself for a writer's life of solitude and alcoholic excess, I decided on impulse to spurn the comforts of Gstaad. I asked Nesta to find me a garret. In Switzerland, a truly run-down garret is hard to find. There are any number of grim concrete tower blocks near airports, reserved for foreign workers and seekers after political asylum, but genuine garrets have long since been converted into picturesque attic studios, pine-panelled and pile-carpeted and fetching a pretty price.

However, Nesta found one near Vevey, belonging to the widow of the Ukrainian conductor Igor Markevitch. On the appointed date, I climbed three flights of stairs (hardly enough) and knocked on the door. It was not a very thick door and through it, while I waited, I heard considerable scuffling and whispering. Eventually, the door was opened by the lady herself, her hair not entirely in place. On the sofa by the window behind her, was a much younger man, also slightly dishevelled. I gathered that it was not the remains of a rather unappetising-looking snack on a coffee-table that they had been rushing to conceal. My impression of having interrupted their sport made me feel unwelcome. I tried to take in my surroundings as rapidly as possible so as to be able to leave them alone again to get on with it.

The place appeared to be suitably decrepit and gloomy. While the walls were not actually running with damp, there were some stains and cracks that a real estate agent would not have hesitated to describe as 'characterful'. The single room was cramped, low-ceilinged and only partially illuminated by a window. A low-wattage bulb dangled at head height nearby. So far, so good: all was as it should be to provide the writer with an atmosphere conducive to cirrhosis and suicide.

The merry widow offered me food, I declined with a shudder. Perfunctorily, I enquired about the rest of the apartment. She raised a curtain to disclose a hotplate and basin with a single tap. I deduced cold water only; the standard in low-cost Vaudois accommodation. She told me that there were bathing facilities on a lower landing. I acknowledged this information uncritically, nodding and keeping my face averted from the young man who was showing every sign of restlessness. The time had come to enquire about the rent.

The woman clasped her hands, glanced at her companion and smiled at me. It was not a good smile. For one thing, she had food between her teeth which were themselves, I judged, of Eastern European origin or substitution, if her husband's name was anything to go by. I waited. She delivered herself of a figure so unexpectedly high that it made me smile too. Clearly, they had expected a dupe. I was tempted even so; there was unlikely to be a more depressing place within a hundred kilometres. Yet to have accepted her ridiculous conditions would surely have been to exaggerate the wretched circumstances in which a serious writer has to live; one need not be a masochist to find inspiration. I apologized for the intrusion and drove back up the mountain to Gstaad.

Imagine a place where farmers chase herds of cows — bells clanging, often at a gallop — through the main street at mid-morning, parting pedestrians and drivers to either side like debris in a flash flood, while dung accumulates in front of

Hermès and Cartier. This apparent incompatibility between aboriginal rudeness and modish frippery is one of Gstaad's essential features. Swiss agriculture is subsidized, and industry and tourism easily surpass it in economic importance, but in the Alps, the active farming community provides an irreplaceable framework which sustains all other enterprise.

The national good sense that awards farmers the space and support to persevere in their hard-working lives, also directed local legislators to decree that all construction should conform to the indigenous architectural style of the traditional chalet, and be built of or at least clad in wood. No matter how much Gstaad has grown, this far-sighted resolution has allowed it to preserve its original village air. So when the frolicsome tide recedes at the end of every season and the intrinsically unblemished nature of the place reasserts itself, writers and others sensitive to atmosphere may venture forth without fear of being oppressed by uncouth jubilation.

Alone amid heavy snows in winter but within sight of the supermarket, I conjured remoteness, and completed the first draft of a novel without being distracted by rumours of ubiquitously frenzied cheer. Spring arrived, and a daily walk to the same well-situated bench served to change the view and stimulate the imagination sufficiently to make revisions. Despite the mediocre quality of my work, I was satisfied that it was possible to write in civilized surroundings.

Even now, one can rely on being undisturbed quite close to Gstaad, for although its environs are occasionally overwhelmed by groups of dedicated walkers, the transience of tours and the grandiosity of other visitors keeps them from risking abandonment or demotion respectively, beyond the areas and attractions designated for recreation. The remoter mountain paths are almost as free of human encumbrance as they were in the Fifties.

Although it doesn't matter where a writer lives of course, there is something antithetical about trying to write in a resort, a place solemnly dedicated to hedonism and frivolity. Of the writers Gstaad has attracted, the most prominent are probably Richard Scarry, a writer of children's books, and William F. Buckley, the television intellectual. Buckley is a seasonal visitor, whose boob-tube notoriety allows him to perpetrate the occasional cocktail thriller, an imitative work which depends for recognition on its chatter value within the circle of the author's own acquaintance, rather than on its reception in the market place. (No matter the attractions of Buckley's studiedly dilapidated personage and interesting teeth, it's unclear how he finds enough fans among our relatively disillusioned society to fill the ranks of his indispensable claque, but maybe he brings them with him.)

By now, every parvenu has heard of Gstaad and pants with ambition to pack his Louis Vuitton suitcase (about as exclusive as a Luncheon Voucher) and come here. As one who has seen the place change over 40 years from a sleepy alpine village beloved of hikers in summer to a smoggy, noisy resort, crowded with international poseurs in winter — a sort of Rodeo Drive at 3000 feet — I can tell you that it is at once not as idyllic as you may imagine and not quite as ruined as some similar places. Now that the media have intensified their coverage of the environment, even the locals are gradually becoming aware that the seam is almost exhausted. There is the ghost of a chance that they will moderate their attachment to growth.

Who put Gstaad on the international map? Certainly not J.K. Galbraith, who modestly made that claim in an article in *The New Yorker* several years ago (not all 'intellectuals' are averse to self-promotion). When my parents first settled here, in 1954, in the dismal Les Frênes, near the great grey barrack of the Palace Hotel, the region possessed one chairlift. Ski school was a couple of hundred yards from the house, on a slope then completely bare but now crammed with the most expensive properties in the valley. It was quite easy, in those days, to avoid hobnobbing with resident celebrities, as there weren't any. One or two distinguished but retiring persons were known to come and go and even to inhabit the village, but none more exciting than the very famous, totally unknown poetaster, Stephen Spender (lately awarded a knighthood in recognition of his being a Sir-vivor of a group of rather more interesting writers of the Thirties). Hardly enough to fetch a tabloid up from nearby Bern.

Gstaad's other main recommendation, if you can call it that, was that it was home to several girls' finishing schools. In those days, in the absence of Roman Polanski and others, the girls were often finished by the school gardener, a position vied for by many a green-thumbed yokel. It's a sign of our sophisticated times that none of these institutions exist anymore, girls now being finished before they've had a chance to get an education; even, if some reports are true, before they can get out of the house. As recounted, I myself transitorily attended a grim little coeducational establishment, run by two elderly lesbians in a backwater at some distance from the village, from which the cries of homesick children did not carry. This too has closed and been sold, but they say it's haunted.

On hearing that I had attended this school, a man I met years later remarked "Oh, yes, I remember Chalet Flora, I was at Montesano School. We used to go for walks past your school and say, 'That's where the witch lives.' We were glad we didn't have to go to school there." I compare this recollection with my mother's answer, when I asked her why she sent me to this school. My mother's memory is that she and my father were lucky that they accepted me, despite hearing that I might be absent during term time.

Shortly after my father rented a more congenial chalet in 1956, he was asked to initiate a music festival to beef up the summer season. While Gstaad's inhabitants were naturally attuned to the lonesome hoot of the alphorn (the spiritual equivalent of the bagpipes) and the good fellowship of a yodeling chorus (a men's harmony club had been founded in the 1880s), and Bartok himself had hung out briefly in a chalet which now bears a commemorative plaque, institutionalized classical music was new to the region. When the neighbouring village of Saanen's frescoed 15th century church was proposed as venue for the concerts, there was dark muttering about profanity and two decades passed before clapping was tolerated, but my father's love of the unpressured colleagueship of chamber music and his characteristic generosity in making up deficits out of his own pocket, kept the enterprise running until the festival achieved its own distinction. It's now in its 62nd year.

With the arrival of some film stars and industrial playboys in the Sixties, and some judicious promotion by hotel owners, Gstaad's allure and prosperity swelled to monstrous proportions. While one or two decent souls have not forgotten to what and to whom they owe their good fortune, quite a few of the locals have allowed their new-found wealth to go to their heads. It's rumoured that one family of troglodytes, their tiny stunted bodies inflated beyond measure, came out of their kitsch emporium one Sunday morning on their way to praise Mammon and were immediately wafted skywards on the updrafts of hot air from the village, carried away into the upper reaches of the stratosphere and never seen again. That said, it's a great place for ballooning.

So what kinds of people are Gstaad's habitués? In the hardware store, the blond wife of a Belgian bank director examines a copper casserole with brooding dissatisfaction. She has two charming children, a couple of chalets and a castle, and to keep herself busy, she buys art for her husband's offices. "They really don't pay me enough," she once grumbled to me, "It must be because I'm a woman." Tall, slender and sulky, this feminist is an escapee from the pages of Mills & Boon. Paintings she would never be allowed to buy, because her disturbed persona would be incapable of understanding their enigmatic power, evolve over years in the nearby studio of the reclusive painter, Balthus.

Beside great talent and great wealth there exists in Gstaad of course great pretension. How could it not? The impecunious condition of an Austrian woman, for example, one of countless countesses (the Continental practice of awarding the title to all offspring results in a nobility as numerous and undistinguished as rabbits in a warren), has affected her outlook so radically that it is consensually agreed that she should be muzzled in public. Envious to the point of seizure over the perceived advantages of others, she bustles about the village like a peevish chicken — her incongruously large buttocks in green sweats fighting each other like the proverbial pigs in a blanket — attitudinizing frantically about her holdings (she lives in a humble apartment in a neighbouring village) and her noble friends (usually deceased unbeknownst to her).

So what is Gstaad good for? It's good for the earthy strength of early May, when the snow has receded sufficiently to permit the first walks, and the detritus of winter — broken ski sticks, discarded Kleenex, lost purses, muddy smartphones — has been pilfered or cleared away; when the feeble sun tempts out the first alpine flowers.

It's good for the piercing blue sky of a perfect August day, when the heart yearns to share its exhilaration.

It's good for quiet November mornings, when the peaks of the Diablerets range are backlit in ochre under a steel-grey sky, hillsides are wreathed in mist, larches stand out yellow against the darkness of firs, and the faint smell of wood smoke and the chorus of cow bells diffuse the unmistakable aura of a dying year.

As is the case in similar cases, Gstaad's goodnesses derive much from what was and little from what has come to be. To appreciate them one must possess at once the determination to overlook the vulgarity of stickers proclaiming 'Gstaad My Love', and a susceptibility to atmosphere without which the truly exceptional qualities of the place might remain invisible.

Autumn 1982

I sit at the pantry table, typing on my Hermes 3000. I'm all alone in the house. The only sound is the sudden berserk racket of an invasive marten which disports itself between roof and ceiling, along the corridor behind me. By the sounds it makes, it might be chasing a ball, but more likely playing with its prey.

I greet it loudly and it stops for a moment, then continues with renewed vitality. I like it. It's company, but not intrusive or demanding, as a person would be. Snow is falling, deadening what little noise there is; the perfect atmosphere in which to concentrate. Writing is interrupted only by shopping or a walk. Unfortunately, the house has been rented and I have to move out.

Chapter XVI

MISGUIDED NOVEL, MISGUIDED PROPOSAL

1983
Munich

I have found a room in the apartment of an impoverished countess, in a smart part of town. Actually, it's the living room and main bedroom, whose walls are covered with her ancestors' pictures. I feel guilty for displacing this elderly woman from about two thirds of her home. However, she needs the money, else she wouldn't do it. She's away quite a lot, but when she's back she sometimes makes a *Leberknödelsuppe* for me. It's delicious. There should be a learned cooking tome devoted only to dumplings. They're an ancient Central European speciality, traditional food of their kind.

Being me, I manage to make as little of Munich as possible. Among even less memorable events, I remember a minor car accident, a near-fainting fit on the Maximilianstrasse, due to the sudden low pressure for which the town is famous, and my timorous rejection of the forward approaches of a local woman during *Fasching*, the Bavarian carnival season during which women temporarily assume the assertive role.

In Gstaad again, I receive a long letter from Eva. She reveals that she and Bob have broken up after seven years together. She has been working at the Design Centre as a food photographer's assistant. She wonders if she could come over to visit me. Of course I agree. Eva and I do quite well together. She is in any case half-European, due to her parentage, and speaks German and Italian fairly fluently. So we spend a couple of pleasant months together. Most surprisingly, my body decides that it can function normally, *mirabile dictu*. It may be principally this unexpected bonus or breakthrough that encourages me, when she has returned to her parents in Seattle, to propose to her. How serious can a proposal of marriage be, when it's made by telephone?

I have had plenty of time to reflect on why I made this terrible mistake. It can be attributed to a number of causes, including Eva's attractiveness and our sexual compatibility, and her willingness to cope with my moods. We had declared our love for each other. She had been sending me regular letters, with a lipsticked imprint on the envelopes. Of course, none of these factors need have culminated in marriage. But I suppose I must have felt that I had no other choice; that no one else would accept me, and I shouldn't therefore let her get away. Another explanation is that I may have felt that I was doing my duty: accomplishing what someone hoped and expected of me, as I had been taught to do, failing which I risked letting her down. That this fulfilment of another's wishes lay in a direction more consequential than running an errand was immaterial, my impulse was inborn and coercive. In fact, it was just self-deception. I had no business proposing marriage to anyone. I was far too immature to enter into such a formal commitment. I had been smitten by Priscilla. So I knew what it was to feel love. While I admired Eva's talents, I didn't really love her. If in doubt, don't do it, should obviously have been my motto. However, in the Eighties, marriage still seemed like one of the major goals in life and I was already thirty-six. When I told Bob about my plans, he warned "She's very emotional."

The book is finished. It's far too long, but it tells a story, from beginning to end. I send it to the German publisher who has published my father's books. He returns it, saying that he would anyway not take an English-language novel before it had been accepted by an English-language publisher, but with the remark that he's glad to have met another story teller, and the recommendation that I send it to Weidenfeld and Nicholson, which I do, promptly. The editor at Weidenfeld, also a family acquaintance, rejects the book, but suggests another publisher: Hutchinson, a very respectable company. Hutchinson's reader, a woman of German extraction, invariably dressed in black leather and a member of a suicide covenant, is exactly the right person to evaluate my efforts. Based on her criticism, I modify the book and it is accepted.

April

I knew instinctively, when *The Sunday Times* announced its intention to publish 'The Hitler Diaries', that these could not have been genuine. It should have been obvious to any alleged expert such as Hugh Trevor Roper, who authenticated these diaries, that it was not in Hitler's nature to keep such a personal and private record. Besides which, he was a speechmaker and talker, not a writer (apart from *Mein Kampf*, of course, written with Rudolf Hess's assistance in prison, nine years before he came to power).

Summer

The sun is shining, the sky is an unblemished blue, the birds twitter, all is at peace; the doorbell rings, it's the mailman with an Express letter from my father, followed by another of the same.

I sit on the garden wall and read them. My father resembles his father in that, when upset, he discharges his opinions and judgements in an angry stream, his handwriting almost illegible. His thoughts are apparently unconsidered; certainly uncurbed. My grandfather would froth at the mouth, metaphorically speaking, when he spoke about the ultra-Zionist pioneers who first conquered Palestine, under and just after the British Mandate, the adherents of the Irgun and Stern Gang, for instance, and described them as 'dirty gutter Jews'. A child in pre-Mandate Palestine, he remembered the Arabs he had known then, particularly his dentist, as benevolent and pacific, and held the extremist Jewish pioneers to be responsible for fomenting hatred between Arabs and Jews. However, he could be just as vituperative about American politicians. No conversation about WWII was complete without mention of 'that sonofabitch Truman'. His anger translated into his prose, where five adjectives would do the work of one. His obsession with the wrongheadedness of Zionism found expression in his book *The Decadence of Judaism in Our Time*, which made him many Arab friends, and a few Jewish enemies. As T.E. Lawrence is supposed to have observed, Semites have no half-shades in their register of vision, and are only at ease when they think in extremes.

His son is scarcely more poised. To the public, he is the personification of peace and mildness, practitioner of yoga and advocate of reconciliation and harmony. At home it's another thing. He never comes right out and says it, but we are to conform to the environment he has generated. He is intolerant of deviation: what is good for him is good for us all. He is allergic to negativity: everything is for the best in the best of all possible worlds. How he has come to this conclusion is anyone's guess. He has seen and experienced his share of horror and disappointment.

June 9th, 1983

Dear Daddy,

Nobody should have to write a letter like this to his father, but I can't leave your spate of letters unanswered out of cowardice. As I see it, I have four choices: a) not answering at all, and leaving you to stew in your own juice; b) screaming down the telephone as I would have a few years ago; c) writing that your conduct is forgivable in one not governed by the ordinary rules of correct behaviour, which I don't believe; d) writing in moderate tones, addressing merely the facts as I see them.

Your act of reading my ms, wrapped and sealed and addressed to me, despite my refusal to let you do so (precisely because I knew how you would react to it), is offensive and unethical in the most obvious sense, and quite shockingly incongruous in someone widely respected for his high moral standards.

To follow your action by presuming to recommend to me what I should write (something of 'real worth'), and by condescending to me by praising my 'positive factors' and my 'basic integrity' (a quality which I had long thought you possessed in a high degree) is rankly hypocritical.

You counsel me to 'learn the ways of the world'. Consider please the fact that I am the only Menuhin to have known the contemporary world on a regular, nine-to-five basis. I have gone to work in all weathers, often unwell, usually by public transport, in three major western cities — in other words, I have lived as most people have to live. I have had to deal with boredom, frustration, bias, intimidation, mediocrity, etc., as you have never and will never know them, as no other Menuhin has known them. I have experienced some of the seamiest sides of humanity, and some of its ordinary best. In our family, I am uniquely able to speak of such things.

Your criticism (as opposed to your opinion) of my book is irrelevant, because you are not qualified to judge anything so worldly. Given that you are unfamiliar with life as it is lived by most people, and have been fortunate enough to preserve your lofty humanitarian ideals intact above the petty rigours that affect the common throng, you might pause to be grateful for this privilege, instead of preaching out of ignorance.

I know that your literary preference is for non-fictional, often theoretical works, when you have the time to read at all. Apart from the classics which you were fed at a young and untried age, you probably have not read more than a dozen works of fiction during the last forty years. On what information do you base your dismissal of a large part of my book as 'cliché'?

The chief impression your irate and mostly illegible notes make on me is that they closely resemble the impulsive and ill-considered reactions of your father to articles of which he disapproved and which he had annotated for your mother — angry and incoherent.

There's no doubting that all writing is to some extent cathartic, just as there's no doubting that many people might benefit from analysis. I don't like to pay for advice. I prefer to fight my battles with myself by myself.

If the tone of this letter is not as respectful as you might like it to be, it is because you have destroyed, by your own wilful act, a large part of the respect I had for you, as well as the trust I had in you.

With love, nevertheless,

An omitted 'D/addendum' says:

Over the years, you have been encouraged to believe — by an unprotesting and increasingly undiscriminating world — that your opinions, on a wide range of topics unconnected with music, were interesting and pertinent. There are occasions when your opinions are neither interesting nor pertinent, and this is a case in point. My book stands or falls (and it may well fall) on its ability to entertain — a quality which, in contemporary literature, you know nothing about.

I understand that your response is due to your presumption that any book written by your offspring should not only please you, but be measured among the great philosophical pronouncements of the age. By leaving my book within your reach, I unwittingly led you into a temptation which your surprisingly frail ethical sense was not equal to withstanding.

In any case, Nesta, my closest friend and confidant, persuades me not to send the letter at all. I have always regretted not sending it, if only because it is a good letter and makes a number of relevant points.

About six months later, my father makes his last attempt to stop, or at least censor my novel. He calls me from wherever he is and asks me to delete certain passages. For the first time, I realize that he may be trying to control the damage that he anticipates may be done to his own reputation. I accuse him of this, but receive no clear response.

It may well have been the opinion of his secretary, a South African Jewess, which my father parrots to me; even she who has been asked to read it on his behalf, having opened the sealed package. Her own husband, a gentile novelist of some repute, eventually divorces her. This woman's efficiency has doubtless been of great use to my father, but her coarsely ambitious nature is betrayed by her vulgar manner and presence which are, respectively, a disagreeable habit of staring people down in the course of normal conversation, unsuitably modish clothing, and a reek of perfume so powerful that it is necessary to throw open the windows urgently in her wake.

I remember receiving the news that my parents had decided to sell the Highgate House while we were driving somewhere together in California. This bombshell was blithely tossed by my mother, over her shoulder, as I was sitting in the back seat. Of course my parents had every right to sell their house, but their decision to do so was incomprehensible and senseless. It was true that my father had a longer commute to work at the Albert or Festival Hall, or to Heathrow, from Highgate, than he would have from Chester Square, but every other claimed gain was nugatory. My father could always fill time by going over his scores or taking a nap in the car. Maybe he had finally given in to my mother's grousing about the distance of Highgate from Central London and thought to put an end to this particular complaint. If so, he should have known better after thirty-six years of marriage. My mother's whingeing was her way of life. My father was just swapping whingeries. Instead of responding with something like 'the world has moved on since 1930' to her irrelevant nostalgic whine about hopping on a bus in Belgravia, his reaction was always something like 'Oh, my poor darling'. My mother was already then long past hopping on buses or indeed walking anywhere. He exchanged his uniquely attractive home of twenty-five years, with its dignity, its peace, its garden, the pure air, the view of the Heath and the new wing he had constructed, for a narrow, vertical, gardenless block, which shuddered every time a bus or truck went by. However, Mrs. Thatcher lived almost next door, so presumably my mother assumed she was in good company. The London Property Planner for May 1983 announced that 'Diana Menuhin, talented designer-wife of violinist YM has been busy furnishing their new home 65 Chester Square. ... *they* have long cherished the idea of returning to live in Belgravia where Diana was born' (my italics).

When my mother had shown me the Chester Square house (of which perhaps only the stone staircase had any distinction), before my parents moved, she had asked rhetorically, if she had not been so clever to have bought it at a good price. As I had no idea of the price, nor of the relative values of houses in general, I couldn't respond to this boast. In any case, her question was implausible. Since her marriage to my father, my mother had had no more idea of the price of houses than she had of the price of a bag of oranges. She had also shown me two small rooms on the fourth floor, where she said my brother and I could stay. As it turned out, not only did these two rooms become respectively my father's office and bedroom (he no longer shared a bedroom with my mother), but my father added a music studio to the house, making a fifth floor. So although the house had now become larger, there was no place for my brother or me, nor even a guest room. Any clearer demonstration of my parents' self-centredness would be hard to imagine. (Recently, I came across a collection of obsolete house-keys. They include the keys to my London flat, to Alma, the house on Mykonos, the house in Oregon, even to 4975 S. Albion, Littleton, Colo.; none to my parents' houses in The Grove or Chester Square.)

Chapter XVII

MARRIAGE

Eva and I were married in New York — convenient to both sets of parents — in a judge's chambers near Wall Street. My half-sister, for whom I have the highest regard, as I hope I've made clear in these pages, was to confide to Eva a few months later that she would do well out of a divorce in New York. More recently (April 6, 2016), she gave an interview to *The Times* in which she was confusingly described as 'glamorous' and was quoted as follows: '"I have no time for Gerard," says his step-sister Zamira.' This was a hurtful revelation, but I'll get over it.

Eva and I.

My father did his best to make this non-event successful. He rented space at the Plaza, across the street from the Sherry Netherland, where my parents always stayed, hired an all-girl jazz band (the highlight of the occasion) and a photographer. My mother didn't voice her disapproval at my choice of wife, but she wore a tightly-fitting beige scarf, which, next to her pale complexion, gave the impression that she was undergoing chemotherapy, or possibly was in mourning. Maybe this was intentional; a wake might indeed have been more cheerful. Apart from Jinx, there was no one I could think of inviting. Eva asked her sister. The rest of the guests consisted of my parents' acquaintances from nearby. Some who could not come sent presents instead. There was a nice-looking pair of silver fruit-spoons. The professional photographer managed to avoid taking a single good photograph. Maybe he sensed that the incident was not worth immortalizing.

1985

The novel (*Elmer*) is due to be published. Having been accepted with a certain amount of hyperbole, promises of publicity and even the mention of a prize, the book is submerged by the takeover of Hutchinson by Random House, which gradually swallows nearly all the established British publishers. As a result, the publicity person who had been so enthusiastic about the book leaves too. I do a few interviews for newspapers and radio, but I sense that the company's heart is no longer in the project. Perhaps most damagingly, due to my lawyer's oversight, my contract contains no mention of a paperback issue. As my initial intention had been to write a light summer entertainment, by implication a paperback for sale at airport news stalls, which might very likely be left at the beach, the publication of two thousand hardbacks does not bode well.

In fact, the novel was a mistake. It was far too juvenile to survive the glare of public exposure. I now think of it with embarrassment as a bad book. While I like the characters I created and still find a few of the plot twists and descriptive passages acceptable, the story and its resolution are unsuccessful. Anyway, the number of second-hand copies on the internet seems to include all those printed.

Married life becomes oppressive, after the novelty wears off. I had assumed that Eva would want to find a job at which she could use her undoubted visual talents or, at least, to begin with, would work at painting or drawing. I had intended to write. Both thus occupied with our own creative interests, I thought we could get along. But Eva doesn't seem willing to take the risks that independent artists must take, or to suffer the inevitable rejections along the way, in order to forge a career. She cooks marvellously, and reads cookbooks like others read thrillers. She looks after house and garden, but otherwise seems to need attention and entertainment, neither of which I feel equal to giving all the time. I feel guilty for my inadequacy and irritated at her power to distract me. My ability to concentrate, never strong at the best of times, breaks down completely. I sense her constant proximity. Increasingly, her presence in a room seems to take up all the space, almost to suck the air out of it. In the kitchen, I am always having to get out of her way; wherever I stand is exactly where she needs to go. She is quite a big woman. Her feet are large too, so large and broad that they tend to deform her shoes. Seeing these shoes in the hall is a daily reproach and a suggestion that they alone, had I paid better attention, would have dissuaded me from proposing to her.

Over the next ten years, the domestic climate deteriorates progressively. I know that Eva would like children, but she is usually very good about not pressing the point. I'm not confident that I could be a good father and our regular bickering makes it likely that our child might be born to divorced parents. Eva is, as Bob had warned me, very emotional. During one loud exchange on this subject, she tears her blouse and disappears behind a slammed door. We yell at each other a lot. She takes out her anger on objects, smashing pots in the garden. She also drives our car too fast, relying on the brakes. I try to support her interests, such as I suppose them to be, by introducing her to the few people I know who could be helpful. I write a short story for children for her to illustrate, but it doesn't inspire her. Probably, she senses that I don't love her. The latent subject of a divorce emerges in her bitter taunt "I'm not going to pull your chestnuts out of the fire," meaning that she's not going to divorce me.

In such an atmosphere, it's hard to keep my mind on worthier themes. A talent that I will go to my grave believing I possess is the ability to solve non-technical problems by means of untried solutions, and to come up with new concepts and proposals. My nature is to serve a cause. While I prefer not to be out of pocket, monetary reward is secondary to the fulfilment which comes from being instrumental in solving a problem. With goodwill, a solution to any and all problems can be found. If the majority but realized it, most problems share the same ultimate origin. Out of my early instincts grew my knowledge about the planet's single permeating predicament and my consequent will to serve the greatest cause: the cause of truth.

My aims are not always so lofty. I'm having trouble resisting the urge to send Klaus Barbie, on trial in Lyon, an encouraging cable reading 'You're a doll'. I've also developed the habit of writing to the *International Herald Tribune*. In order to spare my father, but also to make acceptance more likely, I invent a stable of correspondents, who contribute opinions on subjects as varied as French cooking, politics and literature. Over the years, about a dozen of these letters were published. Here is one about the Falklands affair: 'The way to return the Falkland Islands to their rightful owners with a minimum of bloodshed is to organize a great airlift of stereo equipment to enable the islanders to play at full volume and continuously "Don't Cry for me Argentina" (from *Evita*) until the invaders flee screaming. Believe me' (*IHT* April 10–11, 1982).

MARRIAGE

Or, less frivolously:

'If it has not been clear before, it certainly is now that the European Community is almost bankrupt: the Common Market, the dream of a handful of utopians, doesn't work. The concept of Europe that is embodied in the EC charter is false. Europe is a geographic region extending from the Atlantic Ocean to the Ural Mountains. The peoples who inhabit this area are not a homogeneous mass, to be formed into economic blocs, whether in the European Community or in the Soviet-led Comecon grouping; they are the inhabitants of nations and regions with distinct traits and traditions. It is extravagantly foolish to try to replace the results of centuries of practical necessity by imposing quotas and subsidies, themselves determined by the productive capacities of other artificially defined economic blocs. Apart from the dehumanizing effect of this kind of thinking, the superfluous amounts of goods thus created are in themselves an indictment of the system. Burdened by bureaucracy and supported by a complicated and arbitrary system of incentives and restraints, the European Community is a grotesque invention, a monkey on Europe's back' (*IHT* February 25–26, 1984). I had not then understood the intention behind the construct.

1989

Eva and I have built a small house on a ten-acre lot in Central Oregon. Oregon and Washington are the most civilized states in the Union, environmentally aware, low-key and full of natural beauty. Another magnet is that Eva's parents have retired to a community in nearby Sisters, about half an hour from Bend, the main town in the region. The lot is the last on otherwise unbuilt, mile-long, aptly-named Fryrear Ranch Road, a straight dirt path, ploughed through the flat brush, whose red dust announces visitors at a distance. The house itself is very modest, consisting of a two floor, board-covered structure in 'reverse' plan — the living room and kitchen are upstairs —

with a wonderful view over the brush and juniper-filled surroundings as far as Mount Hood. Only these ancient, stunted hardwood trees grow in the sandy soil, home also to rattlesnake and deer. The vegetation changes abruptly after Sisters, where tall Ponderosa Pines shoot up from the foothills of the Cascades Range and the climate is much wetter. At night, the hooting of the owls is all we can hear; in daytime, the stillness is even greater: out on the deck, I can hear my own breathing.

No house has the value of the one one builds oneself. The slightly worn earth tones of the furniture from Alma suit it well. The floor in the kitchen and eating area is of burnt umber Mexican tiles and a rough beige carpet runs throughout the rest. There is a wood-burning Scandinavian stove, which conducts the heat by pipes all over the house. It's very efficient. We have dug our own well, whose water is tested absolutely pure. We spend the winters in Oregon. Alas, I am no more successful at finding work or at writing here than I have been in Europe. I try my hand at a few articles for the local newspaper, but I'm obviously not a natural reporter. I travel the two hours to Portland several times to take part in a course for job applicants — a considerable concession for one who despises such aids as being useless traps for the desperate, which this is.

Chapter XVIII

ALBANIA

1989

As a consequence of not being able to concentrate enough to write, I seek something new with which to occupy myself and, above all, to free myself of my self-imposed shackles. I submit applications and go to interviews, but I am apparently such an odd fish and my experience is so difficult to classify that I am always rejected. As I cannot find work in any established structure, I must invent something to do.

Based on reports in the *International Herald Tribune* of exploration for oil in the Adriatic, off the coast of Montenegro, it occurs to me that Communist Albania most likely possesses offshore oil too. On a visit to London, I check the Albania file at the Petroleum Institute. There are only three pages in it. No one knows anything on the subject. At my father's urging, I drive to St. Gallen to consult a retired Swiss National Councillor, an acquaintance of his. This helpful man issues me with a letter to the Albanian authorities. I compose a list of ten proposals I intend to present to them.

However, getting into Albania is still as difficult as it has been since the war. Although the current potentate, Ramiz Alia, having reputedly acceded to his position by shooting a rival across the politburo conference table, is supposed to be slightly more accommodating than his notorious predecessor Enver Hoxha, the country is still firmly closed to nearly all foreign individuals, especially of course to Americans — representatives of the 'Great Satan' (how appropriate that formerly ridiculous epithet seems now).

So the only apparent way of entering Albania and gaining the necessary first foothold there is as a tourist, tourism being a welcome source of foreign currency. A British organization has long been the main organizer of tours to Albania. I join the next group, which consists of about thirty middle-aged Britons. Before disembarking, in accordance with the printed warning on the official immigration form, we dutifully declare that we are not importing bibles or refrigerators. Under Hoxha, the visitor had to walk through a symbolic pool of disinfectant.

Landing on Tirana's single runway is like driving over a corrugated metal roof. The single building is cramped and crowded, although flights seem infrequent, our plane being the only one present. The lavatories have shoe icons over the doors to distinguish the sexes. A bus takes us to the Hotel Tirana, the tourist hotel on the main square, a conventional glass block. It is the only contemporary building. In this square is a rather good statue of Skanderbeg, the 15th century national hero, on horseback. Skanderbeg reputedly repulsed several Turkish invasions.

Visible through the bus windows on the drive are numerous pillboxes, dotted about the fields (where mainly women toil), their shapes reminiscent of Japanese warriors' helmets. These defences are intended to protect the country against American or Russian invaders. The single-lane road carries a busy traffic of horses and carts.

The Khrushchev era brought about a cooling of relations between the USSR and Albania, as a result of which Albania turned to China for support. Unfortunately, China's machinery was not as efficient as Russia's, which often came from the DDR and was therefore of Germanic efficiency. Most famous among Albanian manufacture was the Little Red Tractor, which was so heavy that it simply bogged down.

ALBANIA

Our scheduled itinerary takes us south in our bus to Sarandë and to Gjirokastër. In Sarandë, I contract food poisoning, probably from the trout we have been fed on the previous evening. So I stay in my hotel room which looks onto the Adriatic, towards Corfu, missing the trip to the Roman ruins at Butrint. Feeling better, I go for a walk along the waterfront, taking some photos of dark blue speedboats, which I learn later I should not have done, as I might have been arrested as a spy. The boats are for chasing any escapee or fisherman tempted by Italy's proximity, only 70 kilometres away. I end up at a bakery, drawn by the smell. The woman behind the counter is friendly, despite our inability to communicate. I settle on a dark loaf and am waving away the change, as a small gesture, when the woman's expression changes as if a blind has suddenly come down over her face. She stares sullenly over my shoulder. I turn. A chunky woman in a dark blue skirt and jacket has entered the shop behind me. I take the few coins and make my exit, taking care not to look at the newcomer, who must be a policewoman of sorts. Back at the hotel, I tear into the loaf, it's good.

When we get back to Tirana, I find a message from the Albanian Trade Agency. Would I meet their representative in the hotel lobby that afternoon? We meet in a large, empty front room. This is the first time I experience the standard two-man communist delegation. Only a high-ranking official can be trusted to be alone with a foreigner. The so-called interpreter asks me the questions the other puts to him, then he stares and takes the occasional note. Later, I hear that the interpreter is unnecessary, as the senior of the two officials usually speaks the required language. They are there to check up on each other and perhaps to intimidate the foreigner. I hand over my list of ten points and they promise to examine it.

On subsequent visits, I stay at the Dajti, the best hotel in Tirana, some used to say, the best in the Balkans. Like all the most prestigious buildings in Albania, the Dajti was conceived by Italian architects in the Twenties. The hotel's concierge is first and foremost a professional of his kind, typical of concierges to be found in any reputable hotel in Europe. I meet my interlocutors in the offices of the Trade Agency, an anonymous block in a side street. I present proposals for improving the airport, and the Albanians show me their brewery and their telephone manufacture. (I have a working Albanian telephone — red, of course.) The brewery has been provided by the DDR and is still working efficiently after all these years. But they need new bottle sizes. I persuade a Bavarian company to send over some samples, with the understanding that the Albanians will order those that suit them. Instead, they keep the samples and simply copy them, cutting the German company out of the loop.

My impressions of daily life in Tirana are mixed. The populace appear to be resigned to the obviously ubiquitous grinding poverty. It doesn't help my conscience that my guides and I are invariably served two meat dishes at every restaurant we visit, as well as red wine, some of which is good. However, the towns I wander around are clean and safe. There seems to be no litter anywhere and the streets are regularly swept by gypsies with long brooms. Apart from the few modern buildings and the main mosque in Tirana, most dwellings are either bungalows or unfinished-looking raw brick blocks, the only exceptions being the elegant Italianate government offices along the main boulevard.

On one visit, I make the mistake of using the pavement outside one of these administrative buildings and am swiftly shooed onto the street by one of the armed soldiers on permanent duty outside. Once, with time to spare, I follow a path through some woods to the local 'zoo', a miserable collection of cages, in which a few aged and distempered animals suffer. Albania's most famous author, Ismail Kadare, exiled to France, is apparently unrecognized in a Tirana bookshop, whose only volumes consisted of Hoxha's equivalent to Mao's *Little Red Book*. On another occasion, having been advised by the Dajti's excellent concierge, I buy an Albanian flag as a gift for Larry Hagman. I am not by nature anyone's fan, but Hagman's marvellously evil impersonations in *Dallas* have often brought a grateful grin to my face. He kindly acknowledges this gift with a photograph.

In November 1989, I bring with me a geologist and a lawyer from Shell, Germany. We visit the rather decrepit Chinese oil refinery at Fier. While I would never spend a night outside the capital during the winter months, we do some sightseeing for the sake of those who have never seen the country before. They are probably taken aback by the primitive conditions. In one hotel, the lack of heating forces me to sleep in my clothes, with my overcoat spread over the bed. Back at the Dajti, the two groups pour over maps and research documents. Many years later, I chance to read that Shell has opened an office in Tirana, upon which I ask the company if they would send a donation to the school for restoration in the Czech Republic which I support — which they do. In 2003, the largest Albanian offshore oil field, the Durresi Bloc, is instituted.

The nearest I come to a breakthrough in Albania is when the local authorities agree to buy a used packaging line for tomato paste and orange juice. As these are two of the country's regular products and obviously in demand everywhere, I have approached Tetra Pak with the suggestion that they could set up a plant in Albania to supply Western Europe cheaply, as well as the Balkans. However, the Albanians want to pay for the used packaging line they have selected with their product, and the commodity brokers I contact are concerned about quality. The project hangs fire and in December 1990, in line with the rest of Communist Eastern Europe, the regime falls. As a result, my Albanian contacts become worthless.

A few months later, I receive an inquiry from one of the Albanian diplomats I have regularly consulted, as to whether I would be interested in going into business with him in Switzerland. Sensing that this might be more trouble than it would be worth, I decline. Later, I wonder if, in fact, this partnership might not have been quite lucrative — if also possibly illegal.

* * *

March 15, 1990

Our son's birth in the middle of the afternoon, at the local hospital in Bend, Oregon, is fortunately not a drawn-out affair. Eva's best friend and I are both present and I try to be useful by pressing cold washcloths to Eva's neck. Afterwards, the little creature lies with her in her room, a striped woolen cap on his head. So, after seven years of marriage, when our relationship is over, our child is born. I take full responsibility for the six wasted years, during which we could have enjoyed his company. My mother's response on learning that we have called him 'Maxwell' is "Oh, you didn't!" She had proposed 'Adam', which neither of us liked. Apparently oblivious to Maxwell Parrish or others, she can only remind me of Maxwell House Coffee and, as usual, is incapable of self-restraint. (She confides to my brother that she is uninterested in the birth of our child: "What does your father need an eighth — actually seventh — grandchild for?") From the moment of his birth, Max has been a constant joy, never causing his parents an instant of worry. In contrast to his father's tortured temperament, he's astoundingly normal. He's open, makes friends easily, couldn't care less about fashion of any kind, and gets on with life in a healthy straightforward manner.

Maxwell and I.

Chapter XIX

MY MOTHER AGAIN

1992

This is a very sad account and it would be heartless of anyone to laugh. 'Love is duty', blurted my mother loudly from the torpidity of too many vodkas. It was her response to the speech my father had made in praise of her on her 80th birthday. He had gone to great trouble and expense to celebrate the occasion, by renting a room at Claridges and inviting fifty illustrious acquaintances. Among the guests were the ex-King and Queen of Greece and the Queen of Spain and her sister, various lords and lordesses, and the Australian female impersonator with the rude wife.

This dinner had taken months to arrange. My half-sister had busied herself with the invitations and the menu. Naturally, none of the distinguished guests would have accepted to attend had it not been for my father. My poor mother, if she existed at all in the minds of others, did so despite herself. Among my mother's fantasies was that she had rescued my father from near-extinction after his divorce and single-handedly returned him to greatness. My father would nod along benignly whenever she recounted this. No wonder the poor old loony had been able to construct such an enormous edifice of her fancies. A swift crack to the chops would have set her straight. On the other hand, if my father had been a subtler man, one could have credited him with realizing that his wife's manner added to his saintly image, as all who met her pitied the great man for suffering this demented bore, and admired him for bearing his burden so bravely.

My parents.

Tony Palmer, director of an insightful documentary about my father, laid open the pervasive malaise that afflicted the family. His fascinating film, to which I made a modest contribution, stirred up considerable comment. My mother, evidently confusing herself with Garbo, complained about her appearance in the film, saying that 'film directors used to be gentlemen and photographed older women flatteringly, without harsh light'. In fact, it was her demeanour, not her physical appearance, which struck viewers so forcibly. Many people mentioned how she continually interrupted my father, how overbearing she was, how she treated him like a foolish child. One female viewer even wondered, in a letter to Palmer, 'if Lady Menuhin thinks she is quite all right'.

This of course was the crux of the matter. My mother was very far from quite all right. For years, it was on the tip of my consistently-bitten tongue to tell her that she had a permanent reservation at The Priory, the gentlepersons' lunatic asylum which had sheltered her schizoid brother for his entire adult life. There was no doubt in my mind that, without the constant care and pandering my mother received, the men in white coats would have come for her long ago. Metaphorically swaddled in cotton wool for forty-eight years, she did not even know how to call a taxi. When she needed basic information, she asked any handy person for it and then promptly forgot it until the next time.

My mother's sister, Griselda, a few years younger than she, also betrayed an unstable mind, but again, her income allowed her to satisfy her delusions without contradiction from actuality. In order to bolster their egos and retain their social status, both women indulged in beneficent routines. For years, Griselda was a prison visitor at an all-female prison. This enabled her to regale her dinner guests with lurid tales of lesbian sex and violence. When she became too old to condescend to prisoners, she continued to lapse into the jargon she claimed to have heard in jail, which, with age, grew increasingly unbecoming. She probably credited herself with being bohemian, but what was artistic and merely risqué in a forty-year-old became grotesque in a widow of seventy. Had she retired from the stage or any other public arena or even achieved anything at all during her active life, such words as 'shit' or 'bugger', or her admonition to my lawyer to 'go and piss on himself' might have been amusing, but in a white-haired, bent-backed old woman with intellectual pretensions, they were merely demeaning.

My mother also loved to display her artistic credentials. Although she had more right to these than her sister, having once been a *prima ballerina*, her ever-readiness to show a leg was exquisitely cringe-worthy. Seated perhaps on a sofa next to her hostess, she would suddenly give a little shriek, *à propos de rien du tout*, and raise one leg stiffly in the air. Usually those present knew what to do and applauded or exclaimed politely, but there had been occasions when no one understood why this elderly woman, merely on being notified by her husband that it was time to leave, had suddenly had a seizure.

My mother's gracious habits often took the form of pressing unsuitable and often unclean clothes, as presents, on employees or relatives, who could not refuse them. My ex-sister-in-law once received a dirty nightdress. Perhaps these donations were an expiation of the guilt my mother felt at spending a fortune on clothes which she sometimes wore only once. Being permanently in a frenzy of anxiety about everything from my father's faithfulness to the condition of her hangers and towels, she had to distract herself somehow. Instead of finding some worthy pastime like a charity, perhaps connected with the ballet, when left to her own devices, she merely went shopping.

Seeing me on one occasion in a new overcoat, she asked me accusingly how many coats I had. In the basement where my mother kept her coats on two sturdy racks and in a cupboard, I had counted fifty-seven of them. And what had this paragon of taste bought? PVC mackintoshes, pastel-hued capes, epauletted trench coats, Emma Peel gear and other trendy trash, all presumably having fallen under her avaricious eye during some frantic time-filling forage at John Lewis's sales. When I once remonstrated with her that it surely would have been better to own half a dozen well-made classical suits by a Parisian couturier which could be let in or out according to fashion, she argued that if she did not appear regularly in new clothes, people might think that my father was slipping. Ever since I became aware of her, my mother entertained the strangest delusions about herself. In this age of regular psychoanalytical relief, few people remain ignorant of the manifestations of mental disorders. Yet no one, to my knowledge, ever proposed that my mother should be seen to.

Inevitably, the children of parents who spend next to no time at home develop a detached, analytical view of them — when they are not cursing them for their parental indifference. One of the most fitting lines I know is 'Be quiet, accursed progenitors', Hamm's exhortation in *Endgame* (Beckett) to his parents, before clamping down the lids of the garbage cans they live in. Larkin's conclusions were never truer than in the case of my brother and myself. We suffered the intellectual equivalent of child abuse. My brother, after a decade or more of psychoanalysis, once advised me to treat our father and mother as if they were just people who happened to be our parents, but from whom no parental comportment could be expected.

At some point during his analysis, my brother announced to our mother that he could not decide who was his mother, she, his biological mother, or Frau Blaser, the constant companion of his childhood. He decided that he could no longer call our parents by the usual endearments and settled after long trial and consultation with them, on 'Father' and 'Mum'. What difference this made to the relationship, I cannot imagine, but it evidently made him more comfortable.

Frau Blaser, Jeremy and I.

LIVED IT WRONG

<u>Die Erlkönigin</u>

Stranger halt! Tell me straight —
Did you see a figure far
That dragged itself through wind and rain?
Did it wear a red kerchief
Bound tightly 'round its head?
Did its shoulders limply droop
Burdened by worldly cares?
And did its arms hang down
Weighted by plastic bags?
Why then, stranger, know this,
'Twas my mother,
Homeward bound from the sales.

Stranger stay! Tell me more —
Did the figure pant and groan
As you were drawing nigh?
Did you offer (kindly fool)
To help her with her load?
Did she lengthily bewail
Her hellish existence?
Did she declaim
One leg thrust out like this
Pelvis forward, hands on hips?
'Twas her, for sure
Showing her old pro's stance.

Stranger wait! Tell me all —
Did she speak of ballet days
Dids't hear the ritual moan?
How her roommate got the role
By sleeping with the star?
Did she mention Diaghilev
Who died too soon for her?
Karsavina, Tchischinskaya,
Gerard and Jeremy
Who is the ungrateful wretch

MY MOTHER AGAIN

Who hath betrayed her last?
Black Fairy done it all.

Stranger! Don't go yet —
Did she offer right away
To decorate your house?
Did she give her opinion
On stylish dress and speech?
Did she modestly reveal
How in intimate discourse
Nehru, Charles and Kissinger
Had welcomed her advice?
How fortunate you were,
Her ladyship talks to none
Who are not standing still.

Stranger, I sympathize;
I see the sweat upon your brow
I note your wilted look
I would not add to your distress
But I must hear it all —
When you had almost reached your goal
Did not a man, expression pained
Come bounding out a door?
Did he not wring his hands and grieve?
Why then, stranger, know this,
'Twas my father
Re-shouldering his cross.

Gstaad, ca. 1984

Chapter XX
DALLYING

June, 1992

My loveless life has made me so unhappy that I fall for the woman who rents the house next door. She's Polish and lives alone with her two young children. She drives a black BMW with tinted windows and one of those low licence numbers one can buy if one needs to. When I go by, I catch a glimpse of her on her balcony. She is rather fetching, blond with a good figure. Some excuse allows us to meet and for the first time I hear her peculiar French and English and observe her eccentric life. Wiktoria tells me that she is trying to sell her share of the company she ran in Poland with her estranged husband, and to start a new life in Switzerland. She gives me her business card, on which a dozen enterprises are listed, none having anything to do with the other. It appears that they have been very successful at profiting from the opportunities the political transformation has brought to Poland. An educated woman from a middle class background, Wiktoria's looks and intelligence have attracted a Communist Party member. Marriage to him means swift promotion from qualified welder at her father's heating company to company director. She shows me a photo of a plane with her name on it. She describes her husband as a rough diamond, whose manner she must smooth over whenever he alienates the authorities, which, in Poland, often consist of the Catholic Church. According to her, his antics have finally affected their relations and she refuses to bail him out any longer. She has told him 'The ambulance has gone'.

Speaking of ambulances, in her absence at some party at the Palace Hotel, Wiktoria's daughter rings the doorbell to announce that her seven-year-old brother has run his miniature car with the real engine into the barbed wire fence at the bottom of the property. I rush him, bleeding into a towel, to the hospital in the next village, where a nasty wound in his stomach requires stitches. After some anxious telephoning, his mother turns up and I can thankfully leave the rest to her. This brings us closer.

We meet for a drink at a hotel in neighbouring Schönried. Wiktoria smokes narrow, black cigarettes. She has grey eyes and an inviting mouth. On the drive back, I sense her eyes on me. "What are you looking at?" "I'm looking at you." Our affair ensues because I'm desperate for affection and endures because it gives me something to hope for. I don't know what she gets out of it, maybe just my flattering attention. Whatever it is, it's futile. Wherever we are, she never seems to have the time to relax, but answers disjointedly and deviously to my questions. Among her favourite expressions are 'incredible', as in 'you're incredible', possibly meant as a compliment, and an all-purpose modifier: 'whatsoever'. I'm not sure how much I believe of what she tells me, but I prefer to disregard the possibility that she's making it up. Wiktoria claims to feel a 'spark' between us, and, despite constant disappointment and frustration, I feel I'm in love with her.

A Spark or Whatsoever

Having been refused a photograph
How reliable is my memory?
Your hair is associated with your gesture of
Combing your hand through it, drawing it over to one side
Shaking it out
(Yesterday, was it trimmed for travel?)
It's a certainty that your eyes are grey
That your nose is yours
That your lower lip is enchanting
(Did you know that you sometimes speak

DALLYING

out of the side of your mouth?)
But I can't seem to see your eyebrows

Was that a nightshirt?
The blue one, I mean
White shorts, black shorts —
In short
I've catalogued your entire wardrobe
(what I've seen of it)
But if you would just sit next to me again in that
Sensational little green dress
And meet my eyes as directly as you have once or twice
I would be oblivious of day or night

Why did I ask you not to annotate my book?
I would have been charmed to find
Scribbles in the margins
Exclamation marks and underlinings
(to be discussed at leisure)
At least you left the pages disordered
And a faint whiff of cigarette smoke
Thank you for that
Else I'd not know you'd touched it
Let it breathe, you said, let some air into it
I've lived compressed for so long
Like a diver on restricted air
I've forgotten how
Remind me

I bring luck, you said
I know you bring inspiration
Best of all
You make me
Smile   July 15, 1992

Our trysts consist of lunches at local restaurants, to which we drive in her new red sports car, while I crouch below the dashboard in a cap, so as to remain unrecognized by the locals.

The proximity of our homes is more of a risk than an advantage. Wiktoria comes over for an hour one evening when my wife is at her gym, or, as I learn later, enjoying the company of a local gigolo. Neither of us is relaxed and, when she leaves, I spend an anxious half-hour effacing the traces of her visit.

There's a kind of lipstick that, no matter how hard you scrub at it with fingers and soap or with a washcloth, won't come off entirely. It has an adhesive quality, and tends to gleam too. It tinges the lips a deeper shade and can be felt when they're compressed. Lipstick is only one problem. Perfume is another; so are cigarettes (although they're such a risk that you might as well give up if someone smokes in a non-smoker's house), and what about a long hair of the wrong colour or type? Or a fallen ear clip? And what about lipsticked glasses and glasses period, when one alone and that for water is the rule? Practice, habit make perfect, I guess, before they make sloppy, anyway. This comical to-and-froing; how much time do I have? Is that really a strong whiff here — but surely we didn't pass this way — or is it on me, on my hair? Must I wash my hair? — I've already washed my face and neck. (Down on hands and knees searching with a flashlight for hairs.) Open all doors and windows in the critical area for a start. Or try a candle, burn some paper in the fireplace. Pour wine back into bottles, wash jug. Should I shower; no, will simply go to bed and turn off the light.

The one time we happen to philander in a ground-floor bedroom at her house and I cautiously exit over the windowsill, I emerge on the street just as the wife is driving by. Better opportunities are available away from Gstaad — available but scarcely more rewarding. We meet in Zurich (where she's taking a banking course) and in Düsseldorf (something to do with modelling) — to no avail.

If I yell loud enough (not that I ever would), I used to think, she could hear me, in her house just 7 minutes' walk away. If I wait for dark, lights will spring on in the windows, in her bedroom. During my sleepless hours, I will check if she's awake too, absorbing statistics, informing herself about the dispersed distribution by age of the mentally handicapped in hospitals. (I can easily see the relevance of this statistic to international banking, where the ratio must be even higher.) On my occasional weekend visits from Brussels, she never seems to be there — 'I will always be going away.' I'm living a romance for two in my head:

<u>Out of Season</u>

Why did I mention the sea?
Where the oleander blooms pink and cypresses rustle in the breeze
I won't see you
Where leaves have begun to fall and the days are drawing in
I won't see you either
While I approach
You abscond
To African shores
Where if tradition holds, while salt stiffens your hair and sand gets between your toes, you could succumb to temptation
Say it won't happen
These are the lazy empty hours I hoped to share with you
Next to you
Amid rumpled sheets
Carelessly, lovingly dragging my fingernails
Across your brown back
While you doze
Going out only to splash one another in the green surf
or to wander endless beaches
The tide washing away two pairs of meandering footprints
Grey and brown eyes, fondly absorbed in each other
In daylight and dark
Abandoned to instinct
      Quinto do Lago, Portugal, September 1, 1992

This is wishful thinking. Instinctive reactions are entirely absent from our relations because we're rarely together. If I could work the spreadsheet/database of this software, I would be able graphically to describe the mood swings her communications evoke in me. The chart goes something like this: message received (line climbs); affectionate mention (soars); puzzling remark (slight correction); unexpected news with negative connotations and no way of learning more (plunge). No doubt this emotional roller coaster has something to do with real life. After all these passionless years, I'm grateful for that. I just wish the peaks and troughs were not so far apart and regular communication not so complex.

August 11, 1992

Mrs. Thatcher visits my parents for tea. I give her an opinion I have written about the situation in Yugoslavia (to my everlasting shame, I have, out of ignorance, taken the NATO side, the position the press is promoting). Mrs. Thatcher is pleased. Maybe this meeting helps later when I apply successfully to her foundation for support for the Czech school.

Chapter XXI

BRUSSELS

October 1992

In order to make the connections I need to test my theory that training in architectural restoration offers all kinds of advantages, including long-term employment, I have landed myself in Brussels, at a peculiar operation called the European Foundation Centre. It purports — as far as I can make out — to be a connection between important international foundations and the European Commission. It occupies a building in central Brussels, just off the Avenue Louise. Every day, over thirteen months, I catch the tram from my flat to these offices, never once paying the fare. Once, I am caught, but I plead ignorance of the law in broken French, not normally an acceptable excuse. The tram runs between the four-lane traffic on the Avenue Louise, which is straight for three kilometres. The rails are not straight. So the tram sways at high speed the length of the avenue. I don't see why I should pay for such atrociously poor public transport, in such a backward country.

It's not just that Belgian society is corrupt from top to bottom; it's that Belgians have such outmoded interests. They are stuck in a post-war time warp. For instance, although they set great store by cars, they are extremely bad drivers. That is so because, until 1977, it was possible in Belgium to purchase and hold a driver's license without passing a driving test, so Belgians could buy a car and drive it straight out of the showroom, without actually knowing how to drive. In Brussels, collisions between trams and cars are not unusual. Wherever they are in

Europe, their red licence plates are a warning to other drivers. Their priorities are as confused as their driving habits. One may walk the streets of Brussels and observe the phenomenon whereby a doorstep and the pavement in front of it has been scrubbed, yet the intervening space is infested with dog shit. It is in fact impossible to walk in Brussels without keeping one's eyes on the ground, lest one walk into a pile of this. The modern Belgian, however sophisticated, is enamoured of American cars, fur coats, hunting and other Fifties values. Due to the unnatural nature of his cobbled-together country, linguistic differences have created an insurmountable cultural divide. The Flemish hate the Walloons and vice versa. This makes getting directions difficult, if you address a passer-by in the wrong language. They are also keen to cheat you, but not bright enough to do it successfully.

Of course, this fractured and corrupt country provides the ideal environment in which to plant the EU's pretentious, would-be-intimidating palaces. In a cohesive society, their interfering commissioners or better said commissionaires would have been lynched long ago.

My tribute to Brussels and to Belgians: <u>'Why Tintin left Brussels'</u>, or <u>'Dog Shit Days'</u>.

Exceptionally among European cities, Brussels is inhabited by cars, not people. After four months here, I hope I know my place as a mere human. For instance, I'm always grateful to the car that leaves me six inches to squeeze into my building. After all, the poor creature has had enough trouble fighting to find room for itself between those little concrete mud and dog shit catchment areas with those woody things stuck in them that started life as trees. A car's life is tough in such a crowded city.

In case it sounds like I'm over-sympathetic to the plight of cars, let me say that it's not all plain sailing here for people either. However, don't take my quibbles to heart. I find living in Brussels, among the free-spirited Belgians, an adventure, a real thrill. Probably most foreigners don't feel this way, judging by the grim expressions they carry around all day, but I'm thrilled and I'll tell you why. For one thing, every step you take here is a risk. I was brought up to carry myself well and to look straight ahead when I walk, but if you try that in Brussels, either you trip up over the uneven pavement, or you tread in one of the city's 700,000 pieces of dog shit. How do I arrive at that number? Well, if Brussels has 1,000,000 inhabitants and at least 10% of them own doggies and are too free-spirited to curb them, that makes roughly 7 pieces of doggy doo-doo a week per dog, multiplied by 100,000, smack in the middle of the pavement. (There are always more or less that number because while people pay taxes to keep the place clean, these very same people allow their dogs to crap on the pavement all over again.) I guess this is the single fact of life in Brussels I find most rewarding because it makes you concentrate. I've heard some foreigners complain and say, why don't they fine the bastards, it's not civilized. Spoilsports, that's what they are. The Bruxellois are too free-spirited to mind the dog shit. It also keeps doctors in pocket money when the babies who have swallowed some dog poo that daddy has brought in on his shoes have to be dosed with antibiotics. Hey, that's what makes the world go around, right?

Belgian politicians have just discovered conservation. They dreamt up a garbage separation scheme all their own. It works like this: coloured plastic sacks are distributed; you put cans and paper into the blue plastic sack and biodegradable stuff into the yellow plastic sack. When the garbage collectors come around, they stack the blue sacks on one side of the truck and the yellow sacks on the other. Then they run the crusher as usual. The garbage doesn't get confused because there's a gang of sorters at the other end, see? They also had some revolutionary plan to recycle bottles, but the bottling industry soon put a stop to that.

Another entertaining aspect of Brussels is teasing information out of people who are paid to inform you, like at the train station. This can be quite a game as they've been trained to test your patience by withholding information. The train I wanted to take to Basel didn't exist, I was told. Humour me, I said, you'll find it on your computer screen. (Just to prove that being right doesn't count for much in Brussels, he booked me a middle seat, instead of the window I had requested. What a scream!)

Yesterday, I asked a waiter how to get to the Avenue Cinema. He didn't answer, but advised me not to go to such an antiquated cinema, and to try Kinepolis instead. It was an interesting response and raises all sorts of questions about what people here consider to be entertainment.

A major department store did have some information about a particular perfume I wanted: it was not to be had anywhere, it had been withdrawn from the market entirely — except as it turned out, from the innumerable Paris XL perfume stores, as I discovered.

Or take this, see if it doesn't tickle your funny bone. Before getting my answering machine and printer mended, I asked for an estimate. With typical unsuccessful cunning, they told me both were in such bad shape that repairing them would cost the same as replacing them, a total of BF 17,000. When I had stopped laughing, I took both back to Switzerland to be checked. Cost? The equivalent of BF 3,000. It's all good clean fun.

One of the best times I had was hanging out at Zaventem, the national airport, trying to get my suitcase back after a trip to Moscow. Sabena had decided to strike, leaving all checked luggage to be delivered individually. This was a moderate laugh riot, but I confess that it put a dent in my disposition and I now fly Swissair to Geneva.

For an all-round cheerful experience of travel, I recommend the atmosphere of the mainline train stations. At the Gare du Midi, two benches in a boarded-up area under the main tracks appear to constitute the waiting room. There are no policemen to prevent you from associating with the continually trolling bums. Nor will railway employees impose unwanted assistance or refreshment. The stained corridors, dilapidated furnishings and dimly-lit, divertingly filthy subterranean platforms of the Gare Centrale are reminiscent of London's notorious Northern

Line Underground on a bad day. It's reassuring to know that, in Belgium, not only is the age of the train long past, but that this mode of transport is not fit for free spirits, but only for the destitute.

Which brings me to driving, I don't. I use public transport. When I gaze out of the tram window of a morning, at the traffic jam stretching the entire length of the Avenue Louise, and think of all those free spirits at the wheels of their shiny late-model cars, I have to smile. The Belgian's *joie de vivre* is most noticeable when he's driving. Waiting for the tram one morning, I watched two of these devil-may-care characters brake to a stop and then start up again, and slowly crash head-on into each other. They must have been doing all of 5 mph. I understand that there's an unwritten law that if you give way more than five times, you should go home and hang up your car keys.

What's good for a giggle is when your tram rams a car. It happens quite frequently. Belgian drivers like to zip in front of the trams, as if they're running the bulls in Pamplona. What they maybe don't realize is that whereas the bulls can dodge a bit, the trams have to stay on the rails. So the car gets gored, and everybody has to get off the tram and walk to work, because there won't be any more trams before the police come to assess the damage and the line's unblocked.

The post office here has to be seen to be believed. The one I use on the Chaussée de Charleroi recently featured a hand-scrawled notice saying that it was closed for a week because it had been burgled. In thirty years of a sheltered existence in London, Paris, Los Angeles, New York, etc., I had never known a post office to be closed during normal working hours, especially not for a week; nor had I ever heard of one that had been burgled. But it didn't seem to bother anyone much. When I first went into a Brussels post office, they almost had to carry me out of it, I was laughing so hard. I couldn't believe the clerks were actually licking the stamps (they were huge stamps too, with pictures of Belgian wildlife, the kind Belgian hunters like to shoot, covered a quarter of the envelope). Then the girl had to answer the phone, the plumber was calling. If, by some whim, they don't lick your stamps, they shove them back at you with your letters, but they don't provide one of those little sponges. The only thing to do is, spit on the stamp. That way, you don't have to lick it and maybe catch a disease. I tell you, it's a laugh a minute living here, it's a privilege.

On alternate weekends, I fly to Geneva and take the train to Gstaad, to visit my son. On one of these visits, I chance upon a locked cupboard in the master bedroom. A matching key from another cupboard opens the door, to reveal a pile of unpaid bills from the grocery store at which I maintain an account. There are several thousands of francs worth.

In Brussels, my days are not improved by the sight of children's toy shops or clothes stores, a constant reminder of my little son. On the other hand, women's modes remind me of Wiktoria and confirm my conclusion that the best-kept secret of the fashion world is that fashions are immaterial: an attractive woman can wear anything and look good in it; a plain woman may strive all she can to be stylish, to no avail.

My flat is tolerably comfortable, but I catch my landlady purloining my property. When I point out to her that something I spot in her flat is mine, she offers no explanation or apology, but simply hands it back to me.

Belgians have a reputation for their food, but they're gourmands not gourmets. The vaunted Belgian cuisine consists mainly of mussels and French fries. The population is commensurately refined, in looks as in behaviour. One day on the tram, I watch in fascination a man who unconcernedly but diligently picks his nose uninterruptedly until he gets off at his stop.

During my time at the European Foundation Centre, I have had to put up with uncomprehending remarks about how it's very worthy of me to want to support culture. But my timing is good: Eastern Europe is in a ferment of reawakening and Western governments are keen to profit from this by supporting causes that will allow them to influence political developments. On a visit to Prague, I have the opportunity of presenting my vision to Dasha Havel, President Havel's sister-in-law. She, in turn, introduces me to Havel's publisher who heads a group of Czech restorers with similar objectives to mine.

March, 1993
Prague

Into a lodging house, start to look for contacts. Meet this group of restorers. For the symbolic price of one Czech crown, they have rented the library in the town of Litomyšl, about two hours east of Prague, where they plan to start a school for architectural restoration. It turns out to be a handsome baroque building. They also have the backing of the mayor. I am convinced of their serious intentions and offer to find the funds for the school, in return for 5%. I become the school's External Relations Manager.

April, 1993

Wiktoria's invitation to visit her in Gdynia results in one bafflement after another. At Warsaw airport, she meets me with her arm in a sling. A chauffeured Mercedes conveys us in near silence, as she prefers to be undemonstrative in front of the driver. She only confides that she has fallen down the stairs. Where is her (brutish) husband, I ask, drawing the obvious conclusion, but the response is that he has been imprisoned, on account of tax irregularities. The house, protected by a gate and guard box, is brand new and unfinished. The wide semi-circular staircase, in the dim characterless hall, must be the site of her recent accident — if accident it was. The enormous kitchen sports two American fridges filled with food. She plies me with sausage and cheese, while she picks distractedly at her plate. My room is bare of furniture and decoration. She comes in to kiss me goodnight, but declines to stay, ostensibly because her mother-in-law is also in the house. What then is the purpose of this solicitation?

On the next day, the two women visit her husband in his prison. I wait for them outside, staring up at the rows of barred windows in the brick wall, wondering which is his and if he's staring down at me.

<u>Shards</u>

To think I believed you fell
my little Baltic welder
(boiler mender, model, math wiz, Lear pilot)
the Wall may be down
but your society's not yet civil
A former Party-man embezzling state funds
as if by right three years after
deserves a slight correction
He's out in a fortnight
and may need to prove he's still a man
by breaking your other arm
I'm not important, you say, I'm just passing through
and light another cigarette
(If he doesn't kill you they will)
No one can change me —
All right, let's keep it light
I can see down your robe
Don't close it, Ms. Prim; I've seen it all, remember?
(just never for long enough)

A succession of one-night flops, weeks apart
snatched from a half-life
when at any unexpected moment
over bad Chinese food (in Dusseldorf, was it)
or over the plate of cold meat and cheese
which was all you would eat (and left half of)
by the alpine lake (what lake, I didn't notice)
I became tearful
Here I go again, I said, sorry to use the napkin
only it's been so long since I felt anything
it seems I can't help it
Would you like to come up to my room for a drink
you said correctly later

BRUSSELS

For the first time I saw the constellation of seven freckles
below your left shoulder blade and a scar
My husband did that, broke down the door
You were passive, I uncertain
flattered because you never slept in the afternoon
you said, meaning perhaps that you felt safe
But you woke in time to make business calls
giving fluent instructions
When you speak your language you don't pause for breath
it always sounds like you're making love

Another hotel, another uneventful night
Because you had not prepared for your exam
you knelt by the bedside in your t-shirt
drawing pie charts in your statistics notebook
(some women take cooking courses)
Just my idea of a romantic weekend
Actually I liked it, we were like a familiar couple
Last for breakfast on the wasp-infested river terrace
honey and geraniums, sweetness and colour
must I renounce them again?

Expectation is the best part
not knowing when your flight has landed
if you're on it
then — there you are, pushing your cart out of the customs
 area
facing straight ahead but
a secretive smile shows you've seen me
(replay that bit)
just the shoulder bag and briefcase as usual
once only the briefcase
contracts, bank statements and a toothbrush
Welcome to Zurich, you say, as if it's yours

Again the tacky luxury of an airport hotel room
overheated, overpriced, overlooking the car park
(first class salesmen stay here, masturbating to porno rentals)

LIVED IT WRONG

We hang up our clothes in unison down to our underwear
while CNN blares self-important inanities
Mutuality masking insuperable awkwardness
Why won't you let me shower with you, wash your hair —
do you really want me?
You return, towel-wrapped and damp
I lie back in anxious anticipation, while you
borrow my nail scissors
Domesticated strangers
Is this a pretence or are you really so detached?
You're on the second quarter of white plonk from the mini-bar
mineral water, me
(what I need is a quart — of scotch)
Unwrapped and damp now
compliant but not consensual
each of us still wrapped in isolation
I can't have you so
I'm going to lose you

In the morning
a final hug —
Why are you so gentle with me?
(Perhaps you prefer abuse)
Then, alone on the platform
watching a car with blacked-out windows
pull inscrutably away

Brussels, June, 1993

Most foolishly, I enter this free verse pseudonymously in a poetry competition in Oregon, where it wins second prize. My father-in-law, who habitually forwards our mail, for some reason opens this notification, whereupon I am exposed to Eva's wrath. She moves into an apartment in a neighbouring village.

Chapter XXII

TRAINING IN ARCHITECTURAL RESTORATION

December, 1993

My assumed task to find funds for the Czech school is just what I need to take my mind off my impending divorce. With no regrets at all, I leave Brussels and move to Bern. A very modest flat on the fifth floor of a building in one of the capital's through-streets has been spruced up by a politician for his mistress, now apparently redundant. Under the sloping roof, I have a double bed, a work table on which to place my fax, another to eat at, a cosy bathroom under a skylight and even a fireplace. There is no lift, but a communal washer and drier in the basement. The first trams go by at 5:30 a.m. I find their rising and falling cadence reassuring. The flat costs CHF 730 a month. I throw myself into mailing and faxing my proposal for the school. Leaning against the wall opposite my desk is an H&M poster featuring my favourite model: Lauren Hutton, a portrait of determination.

May 1994

100,000 Guilders from the Prins Bernhard Foundation represents the first grant of what will amount altogether to about a quarter of a million dollars in cash and kind — including computers, art books, and a microscope — is transferred to the school. There, the trailer factory across the yard from the main building has been transformed into a two-floor studio, there is a laboratory and even the medieval brick tower at the end of the complex receives a new roof. The donations have come from several international foundations.

I drive the school's director on a round of visits to various German restoration centres and take him to Bush House in London, where he is interviewed by the BBC World Service.

In the meantime, the school's staff has been interviewing the first students, graduates of the ex-Communist state's excellent training system for young restorers. There are many applicants, but the school's entry exams are rigorous and only the most promising are accepted. I have made the rounds of the relevant ministries in Prague to raise awareness of the school in the brazen way which only a foreigner could. At first, the Ministry of Culture is unwilling to recognize the school because of its unofficial character, but as Communist habits dwindle, and the school demonstrates its quality, it overcomes this hurdle.

In the Council of Europe's publication about architectural restoration stands the following: 'The school could not have existed without the support of the Town Council and specially the Mayor, and the work of the External Relations Manager, Mr. Gerard Menuhin, who found the necessary funds and obtained recognition of the school by the State' (p. 69). At the official celebration of the school's opening, I am asked to cut the ribbon on national television and invited to scribble a message of goodwill under President Havel's on the office door: "You are the first students of this brave new venture. Good Luck!"

Fairly regularly, I take the train from Bern to Zurich airport and fly to Prague, where I am picked up by a member of the school's staff and driven to Litomyšl. Sometimes I stay in the Prague flat of one of the restorers, on the river across from the Staropramen beer brewery, whose beer I recommend. On a corner is Madeleine's French bistro, which brings variety to the diet of duck with red cabbage and potato dumplings.

I travel regularly to Hungary and Romania to investigate prospects and conditions in the field there. Unanimously voted onto the board of a thriving training centre in Saxony, I can introduce my own projects there. Although one of these projects

TRAINING IN ARCHITECTURAL RESTORATION

is carried out with support from the EU, the pilot-project by which I had hoped to demonstrate that architectural restoration can create permanent employment never materializes. The project involves the cooperation between a restoration centre and a local township, which would select young people on the basis of their aptitudes and the town's requirements, for training at the centre. Once training in whatever discipline is suitable is completed, these restorers would work on historical buildings, churches, cemeteries, cobbled streets, etc., in a schedule that would ensure regular employment in the restoration and maintenance of these sites and monuments. Thus local inhabitants would be ensured of permanent employment for which they could be proud, and not be tempted to move elsewhere; existing, dignified structures could be used instead of deteriorating, or being replaced by urban renewal eyesores; the town would be enhanced, and visitors would be attracted by cultural heritage. At a friendly interview at Saxony's employment ministry, I am given to understand that my proposal would contravene the state's job creation measures. The wondrous irony, whereby a project which sets out to prove that young people could achieve jobs for life is rejected because it does not fulfil an official scheme to create employment, leaves me flabbergasted.

Eventually, I am offered the directorship of the Czech school. Flattering as this is, I decline, as my ignorance of the Czech language would mean using a permanent interpreter, and the challenge of learning Czech seems insurmountable. After all, I am not a restorer, just an enthusiast with a theory. In 2017, I am invited to celebrate the 25th anniversary of the school.

In Bern, a circular informs me that a law has been passed which compels landlords to modify their rents: my flat becomes even cheaper. Only in Switzerland.

Chapter XXIII

DIVORCE, NEW INTERESTS, OLD RESENTMENTS AND A MINOR ACHIEVEMENT

1994

On Christmas Day, I ring Eva and my son to wish them well. Her response: "Fuck off!"

On New Year's Day, I ring Eva and my son to wish them well. Her response: "Fuck off!"

The Saanen community headquarters is in a rather charming, medieval building with a tower at one end. I have been here a few times, to inquire about civic matters. As regulations began to overwhelm Gstaad, a simple village whose streets were unnamed, the police began to enforce new parking rules. For a while, I paid no attention to these. I never parked anywhere for long, as my errands were invariably quickly accomplished and I assumed, if I happened to infringe by a few minutes, that my car would be recognized as a local one and locals would not be fined, as might visitors. I was wrong. When I protested the forty-franc fine to the local judge, he told me that the alternative to paying it would be to spend a night in the cells in the building. I replied that this might be interesting. But, he said, this would be entered in my record. So I paid the fine.

On 30 May, the atmosphere of the courtroom in the Saanen community building is reminiscent of Kafka's *The Trial*. At one end of the dim room sit three judges; at the other, the conflicting parties, with their lawyers. Eva and I do not look at each other and mutual hatred is in the air. This escalation of feeling is entirely due to the unrealistic expectations with which her lawyer has crammed her. On one of my weekend visits from Brussels, she has left on a counter — perhaps deliberately — a magazine promoting the success of a British divorce lawyer who has exacted on behalf of her female clients large amounts from their wealthy husbands. The article mentions Princess Diana, among others. Eva has no doubt been given this information by one of her idle acquaintances. I blame myself, in part, for the entirely inappropriate attitude with which life among Gstaad's parvenus has evidently imbued her. As a result of such gossip, Eva expects to prevent me from seeing my son unless my father supports her in the style to which she has become accustomed. However, when she has the nerve to declare this intention to my father, he turns her down flat, opining sensibly that our divorce does not concern him. Eva must therefore be satisfied with the lump sum which my lawyer advises me to offer her. Although it's certainly more money than she has ever had, she manages to run through it in record time, by renting a flat in London that she cannot afford and 'lending' several thousand pounds to the Italian gigolo with whom she is still linked.

I advise anyone contemplating marriage to consider the likelihood of divorce at the same time. Both encourage intrusions by the state, which is keen to keep track of the status of its citizens, with a view to taxing them and otherwise bending them to its dictates. Whereas marriage is a joyous affair, often accompanied by a carelessly expensive celebration, divorce is a grim one, often costing a good deal more, both in emotion and money. A private relationship, particularly one as intimate as marriage, is no business of any external agency. The law's incursion into such a relationship is therefore intensely humiliating. While both Eva and I wanted to be free of each other and I anticipated the inevitable exaction of financial support, I refused point-blank to reveal more than necessary about my affairs to the inquisitive judges.

At a lunch given at Clarence House by the Prince of Wales, to which my mother takes me (she and he correspond), there is

— besides Tom Stoppard, to whom I speak about the Litomyšl School as he is of Czech origin (at his request, I send him the prospectus) — a vaguely Indian-looking woman. Lili proves to be half Indian and half Iranian. She is available, but as time tells, without a serious thought and prone to fatuous effusiveness (the expression 'hilarious' plays a large part in her small vocabulary); not that I am endlessly serious, but there is a difference between mindless frivolity and an intelligent sense of fun. *Faute de mieux*, I see her in London and in Geneva and in Gstaad, without noticeable advantage. In Gstaad, where her parents and siblings usually meet for Christmas, I meet her lovely youngest sister, Nancy, who lives in Los Angeles. Unfortunately, although we meet briefly in California, she is not keen to join her relatives in Europe and I renounce what might otherwise have been a promising relationship. A few years later, I am invited by Lili to join her sister and her new husband at a village tearoom. Nancy looks run down; she has lost the effervescent glamour that used to characterize her. The presumed cause sits next to her: about the purest example of Israeli arrogance one could imagine. Poor girl, influenced by Los Angeles's superficiality and in her mid-thirties with no marriage in sight, she probably yielded to this offensively overbearing creature — without realising that she was betraying all that her Indian-Iranian heritage represents. In a minor way, this breathing anathema serves as an example of the universal defilement practiced as a way of life by his kind.

1995

However, at a reception at the British Film Fund for a film Lili has backed, I meet a very attractive Indian journalist. Knowing Sumi is, in more than one sense, an education. Not only does she correct my paragraphs, but she leaves me with an indelible insight into the workings of the Indian Brahmin caste. Her thoroughly modern outlook in no way displaces her rigid adherence to the traditions with which she has been raised. If her long, hand-written letters are evidence, she really cares for me.

Sumi's profession provides her with free entry to fringe theatres, which we attend all over London. This is often more interesting and inspiring than the West End equivalent. However, our relations are not helped by our geographic separation, nor by her living conditions. On my visits to see my son, I share the room she rents in North London, whose door she cannot lock. Cosy intimacy is thus diminished by the constant possibility of intrusion by her landlady, who manages to time her unnecessary visits to find us in bed. Bathroom and kitchen are also common to all tenants, so that seclusion is never guaranteed. We are freer to speak our minds when we are out of the house than inside it. How much these restrictions offend my habitually obsessive craving for privacy I cannot say, but they must contribute to the irritations which little by little defeat our affection for each other. During a trip to London after our breakup, I am prompted by a fortuitous meeting in the Tube to ask her for her new address. "No, no, no," comes the familiar staccato response. I am no longer appealing. Brahmins, she has told me, are stricter than Catholics when it comes to adherence to their beliefs. Insofar as we never have the opportunity to experience the full potential of our friendship, this is one loss which remains with me.

March 1996

A dinner for 350 guests, given by the Prince of Wales for my father, at Buckingham Palace. On the farther side of one of my neighbours sits Peter Ustinov. We have met a few times already, in Gstaad and Paris. Famous folk (as opposed to today's 'celebrities', or as I prefer to think of them 'celebrites', as in perfectly gleaming teeth) often visit my parents. Ustinov is the eternal entertainer, which means that he never relaxes or behaves like a normal person — in contrast, for instance, to David Niven, who drives over from Château-d'Œx in his VW Beetle and is charmingly low-key throughout the meal. My feelings towards Ustinov on this occasion are not particularly friendly, as I have received no reply to my letter of many months previous, asking him if he could help personally or by advice to support the Czech school for restoration. As this is a logical request in favour of an obviously practical cause, to which moreover several respectable foundations have contributed very generously, the very least I expect from this friend of my father's is a polite refusal. So I ask him why I have not heard from him. He claims that the volume of his correspondence has prevented an answer. A while later, I happen to see a televised documentary about him. His house in Bursins is shown, in which a table in his living room or study is literally invisible under a load of papers. So he is apparently incapable of keeping order, even with the aid of the secretary one presumes he must have.

November 1996

My father has generously booked me a flight on Concorde to join him, via New York, in Los Gatos, to attend the last hours of his mother, who at 100, has been hospitalized. Knowing my attachment to his parents, my father has asked me to dispose of the contents of their house. Alas, we are a few hours too late. When my father and I arrive at the hospital, my half-sister is already *in situ* or, better put, in possession of my grandmother's remains. On arrival at my grandparents' house, where she is staying, her first words on entering the house are "These belong to me," gesturing at a red-leather-bound multi-volume edition of the Jewish writer Sholem Aleichem's works. As no contemporary reader, let alone my shallow half-sister, would show the slightest interest in these, her covetousness is inexplicable. At the burial, only my grandmother's Italian factotum, and my father and I are present.

During my regular visits to my grandparents in the Seventies, my half-siblings were never mentioned. Although I had once tried to encourage my grandparents to welcome my half-brother, Krov, into their lives, they refused with the excuse that "It's too late for us to make new friends." Yet this exclusion apparently no longer applies to Zamira; in recent years, she has adeptly insinuated herself and her family into their bosom.

Since I had definitively returned to Europe in 1982, the coast had become clear, so to speak. However, my mania for genuineness moved me, unwisely, to communicate my estimation of my half-sister to my grandmother. This worthy, to whom I had as a child formed a lasting attachment in spite of geographical distance, deliberately left my letter where my half-sister could see it, with predictable results. (Any benefit my half-sister may have derived from this sudden mutation is unknown to me. Shamed be he who thinks evil of it.)

On the 7th of January, my parents and I had joined an assembly of my grandparents' friends at their house, to celebrate my grandmother's 100th birthday. During this festivity, my grandmother asked me to forgive her for her duplicity. What can a grandson say to his hundred-year-old grandmother under such circumstances? Although it contravened my credo of 'never forget, never forgive', I did so.

February 1997

My father and mother are in Prague for some event. Evidently spurred by curiosity, my father hires a car and driver to take us to Litomyšl. During a tour of the school, he is told that the new construction is nicknamed 'Gerard's building', after me. Judging by my father's pleased reaction, I assume that it takes this visual confirmation to convince him that his useless son has really achieved something.

My grandmother at 100, my parents, myself.

Chapter XXIV

SWITZERLAND, OVERVIEW AND RETROSPECTIVE

2002

Once upon a time, when the world was young, as long ago in fact as the late 1950s, there lived in Bern a man with a poodle named Vinaigrette. This man — let's call him Albert — knew he inhabited a country that, although small, was perfect.

Albert realized that his country was not powerful and that it did not have a world-class army, or an empire, but it ran well, like a cable car over oiled cogwheels. Its reputation was so high that one had merely to whisper the country's name for the whole world to know that it was first rate. Where God had made the world and found it good, the Swiss had made Switzerland what it was, and it was also good.

Look where you liked — sniff the mountain air, cast your eye over the postcard vistas of lake and alp, catch a train or plane, or simply walk down a swept street — all, all was unsurpassed, and quietly so. Not that excellence should need to be trumpeted about, or lead to complacence. God forbid. But now and then, when reading the newspapers, for instance, or travelling abroad, Albert, as a Swiss, was tempted just to smile a bit.

All these excellences, Albert took for granted. It would have been unthinkable, for instance, for his train to be late, for its windows to be dirty, for its conductor not to receive the respect that was his due, even if he earned less than Albert. The very idea of his environment being affected by graffiti, by litter, by shabby or flashy clothing, by beggars and drug addicts, by noise after 22.30, by cigarette-smoking fourteen-year-olds, by vandalism — in short, by any of the plagues we take for granted and pretend to shrug off today — would have been inconceivable to Albert.

Albert sold insurance. It was a solid, profitable business, as his countrymen bought more non-life and more life insurance than any other people on earth. He was proud of his company and its standards, which were a byword for reliability. As he walked along the Marktgasse, during his lunch hour, in his dark suit and unremarkable tie, Albert might cross paths with his country's president, similarly attired. But, although he recognized him, and although this distinguished executive appeared in public without bodyguards or any other sign of the importance of his office, Albert would not have dreamed of approaching him. Just as Albert sold insurance as conscientiously as he could, his president fulfilled his duty as a member of the Federal Council and representative of his people by formulating laws, which were in the main sensible. If one were not, Albert, and 99, 999 others like him, would feel obliged to sign a referendum demanding its revocation.

You could say that Albert, like most Swiss, felt responsible for his country. The Swiss did not, like the inhabitants of so many agitated and quasi-democratic states, carry pride in their country on their sleeves, but they knew its worth. If foreigners occasionally derided Switzerland, it was only because they envied its inherent substance and stability. The concept of 'Swiss' as a kind of brand name, or catchy advertising slogan, would never have occurred to Albert. Switzerland simply was, and it was superior.

Moving along a few decades or five, Albert, now in his eighties, experiences a personal revision: he is knocked down in the streets of his capital by a youth he has reprimanded for discarding a cigarette carton. Albert has, until then, never seen a Swiss youth littering. True, he has experienced all sorts of disillusionments over the past years. But these were minor, compared to the effect on him of the fates of two of Switzerland's proudest companies: Bally and Swissair. First, Bally, internationally synonymous with excellence among shoemakers, and where Albert bought his shoes every ten years, is sold to a Texas entrepreneur with no background in the field — Bally's executives having been too apathetic to rescue their company themselves. The new company, despite several ambitious public announcements, is unable to reconcile its core business of shoe production with the sale of modish frippery, a relatively recent deviation.

Until then, Albert might have been forgiven for believing that those who led his country's international companies would have a notion about how to develop them, and adapt them to changing circumstances. Far from it. He now discovers that these highly paid heroes outsource the problem to intermediaries, to consultants, the parasites of the business world.

It suffices, for instance, for a member of the board of Albert's bank (one of the country's largest) to have belonged to the sect of McKinsey & Co. — as sinister a group of theoreticians as can be found outside Scientology — for him to persuade his colleagues that to pay millions to this group would not only provide them with all the answers 'as practiced in the USA', but, almost as important, would afford them the protection of collective blame should things go wrong. The company opens its books and obediently complies with the business-babble foisted on it. Arbitrary dictates, supported by charts and graphs, prescribe a 33 1/3 reduction in staff across the board. That is their chief recommendation. No matter individual geographical circumstances, the company fires 33 1/3 of its employees. Naturally, the stock price rises as a result, in the short term. But the quality of service plunges. Why? Because all the older and therefore more experienced personnel have been fired, before pensionable age.

Then, the unthinkable occurs: Swissair, the country's pride and joy and flagship airline, in every respect a resplendent ambassador for Switzerland's qualities, goes bankrupt. In the mid-Nineties, Swissair had furtively embarked on a very un-Swiss venture, buying up half a dozen second and third rate airlines, with the ambitious — not to say presumptuous and reckless — goal of transforming them into an international alliance, to rival other consortiums. Swissair's managing board, consisting of twenty of the country's most successful bankers, businessmen and politicians, sat back tranquilly, smugly, while the company's chief executive squandered the so-called flying bank's three billion in cash reserves. Of course all this only comes to light in a gradually accelerating chaos and meltdown, which culminates in the grounding of the entire airline on 3 October 2001. Albert sits dumbfounded in front of his television. What has his country come to? Has it lost its senses? Has it forgotten its *raison d'être*, the quintessence of its philosophy: small is beautiful?

Not exactly. With the wisdom of eighty years of hindsight, Albert begins to think things through, to try to work out what has happened to his beloved country.

Switzerland, an island of non-conformity at the centre of the European Union (sometimes artfully known as 'Europe'), is not impervious to outside influence. Unlike a real island, unlike Britain, for example, Switzerland shares languages with its neighbours, and, to varying degrees, has also been affected by their cultures. Such influence has been historical and natural. A more potent and inorganic influence comes from the United States, through the media, through trade, through certain ethnic lobbying, through the ignorance of demagogic politicians. The country cannot remain politically or commercially uninfected by the growing European Union which surrounds it; it cannot resist the lure of the dynamic but transient and superficial world of advertising, of promotion, of the internet. The Swiss boat is rocked as it hasn't been rocked since the early 1930s. When things become less idyllic, political polarization, that indicator of latent instability, crawls out of the woodwork. So far, so clear.

Gradually, the world's most genuine and successful democracy, which is streets ahead of most others in communal administration, in environmental preservation, in civil defence, begins to falter and to look about it for direction, for solutions. And, again, despite its rawness, its gaucherie, its general ignorance and conviction that might makes right, it is the vigorous U.S. — the simplicity of black and white and good and evil empires — of all the available models, that seems to attract Swiss decision makers. In March 2002, the Swiss vote, by a slim margin, to join the United Nations, the non-exclusive club which is, of course, led by the U.S., although the U.S. itself is delinquent in its dues. Henceforward, Switzerland will be subsumed into the crowd of nations and their collective decisions, and will pay higher fees for this perceived advantage, without gaining a whit of influence. Thus, another strand in the rope which anchors the Swiss to their unique conditions, to reality and individuality, is parted. Although he despises populism, Albert is tempted to swap the Liberal Party, of which he has been a lifelong member, for the SVP, the Swiss People's Party, which represents 29% of the voters.

Grass-roots democracy or not, not all Swiss are equal. There is in Switzerland a two-tier society. However — and here's the difference — these two tiers do not consist of rich and poor. There are rich and poor in Switzerland, to be sure, but here the two levels consist of those who belong to the internationalized groups, such as top executives and some government leaders, on the one hand, and everyone else, on the other.

Until the late 1980s, this dualism was under control, balanced by parliamentarians and a population that had not quite lost their attachment to communal valucs. In 1986, Albert remembers, adherence to the U.N. was defeated by 76% of the vote.

Maybe it shouldn't surprise him how easily, how quickly, a person only a generation or two removed from animal husbandry or other soil-associated occupation, may turn his back on the values he and his ancestors have cherished, and face outwards, away from his country, over the heads of his compatriots. Such people become intoxicated when they begin to mix with the names and faces they were used to seeing only on television. To travel the world first class, to be slapped on the back by Pat and Mike in the corridors of power, and actually to call these folks 'Pat' and 'Mike' too; to vote at the United Nations, this is quite exhilarating for someone whose vote, perhaps, has even gone unexercised in his own homeland — for lack of enthusiasm, because of the numerous calls on it. Such people lose touch with their roots.

To Albert, it all seems to have occurred very suddenly. During the 1990s the country was overcome by a rash, an epidemic, of Anglicization. American slang infested the Swiss-German dialect. People previously called 'Heinrich' became 'Henry' or 'Harry'. Very popular among the young, were casual clothes, manufactured in Asia, exhibiting nonsensical sequences of English words. This linguistic invasion was supported by the school board of the city of Zurich, which determined that the first foreign language taught in schools should be English, instead of French. Demoting Switzerland's second language for reasons of expediency threatened the country's fabric. As Albert knew, you can insure fabric against tears, but not a country against disintegration. The internal linguistic divisions which trouble the country just under the surface would long since have erupted into civil strife, were the country as bankrupt and corrupt as, say, Belgium.

In any case, with this official encouragement, it naturally followed that bankers and busboys all proudly spouted expressions they had picked up from the entertainment media. Whereas the banker might use what the poster for a course called 'Wall Street English', the busboy preferred to pepper his speech with the 'f-word'. After the Swissair debacle, both habitually referred to any failure or collapse as 'grounding', thus joining other peoples with a smattering but no understanding of English, in reinventing their own language. Scarcely a sentence could be uttered without the inclusion of half-digested and often misused American colloquialisms. If the problem resided only in language, it might pass, just like any fad. But, to Albert, Switzerland's misfortune lies deeper; it is an identity crisis.

Worse still, with ironic timing, innumerable uses of the prefix 'Swiss' have sprung up. There is Swissport, the airport services (incomprehensibly, also 'Swisspor'), there is Swiss Backpackers (apparently another breed to your typical backpacker), etc., etc. — the Zurich telephone book alone lists 404 Swisssomethings. Just as Switzerland begins to flounder and to doubt itself, a younger, less firmly fixed, but also less modest and rigorous generation of Swiss decides to capitalize on their country's hitherto unblemished reputation for excellence. Being impatient products of the 'Just do it' culture; the culture which imagines that achievement is based, not on learnt skills, but on mere promotion, they bring about disasters in Switzerland's name. Many lives are lost and the company forced into bankruptcy, when Swissventure, a rafting company, allows its foreign clients to embark on a white-water trip despite weather warnings; the foreign client of another, similarly named unserious agency, smashes into the ground, tied to a bungee cord of excessive length.

At least the Swiss government ensures that Swiss citizens, usually well-informed participants in their communities, are protected from sleazy business practices which, throughout the European Union, favour commerce above public health — or does it? In a move which contradicts the country's tendency towards, and desire for, biologically produced food, additives which previously had been forbidden in Switzerland are to be admitted and experiments with genetically engineered crops, allowed.

At least the world's only functioning participatory, as opposed to representative, democracy is still flourishing — or is it? When in February, 2008 a majority of 53% of citizens decided, as a result of a referendum, to expel foreigners convicted of serious crimes, the government delegated the decision for discussion to the parliament. There, the matter languished until the deadline expired in July, 2015. So this inconvenient instance of the people's will was simply disregarded.

Albert reflects that the Sixties probably represented the zenith of individual expression. Subsequent mass movements of people and capital, the transmission of huge and incessant quantities of information, and the resulting problems caused by a shrunken and homogeneous world, were not balanced by a commensurate investment in sensible solutions. Information is not knowledge, and knowledge is not wisdom. Yes, better days his land had known. Albert has seen them and has no regrets. He is resigned and ready to leave.

And what of the poodle, Vinaigrette? I hear you say. As a Swiss doggie, he is better off than his French, Austrian or Italian counterparts. Protected by a license, by pedigree and diet, and insured six ways to Sunday — both for his own protection and that of others, lest he should momentarily lose his self-control — he pursues his life unaware that his entire country is going to the dogs.

* * *

25 January, 2003

While I was driving from Geneva airport up to Gstaad, my brother called to advise that our mother had died. Two days earlier, I had visited her at the nursing home where she had spent her last months. Although by then only intermittently aware of her surroundings, she made a loud sound of recognition on seeing me. So I sat on her bed and recited to her all my favourite nonsense poetry, which was all I could think of. My mother seemed to respond to such verse as:

> The shades of night were falling fast
> The rain was falling faster
> When through an alpine village passed
> An alpine village pastor

She had always appreciated poetry. Her funeral was held in London, at St. Paul's Church in Bedford Street.

Chapter XXV

ZURICH

June 2004

I have settled here, in a modern version of the local farmhouse, with typically low ceilings and an open plan. As the configuration is like that of a large flat, it suits a solitary inhabitant. My hope had been to find an early 20th century villa with personality to match, that marvellous air of solidity and permanence, and the vital grounds attached to it. Time and again, I was presented by estate agents with such houses, forlorn on land reduced to postage-stamp size, in the midst of modern developments. They had lost their *raison d'être*. Often, they had been turned into offices or flats. As it was closer, I began my search in French Switzerland, around and above the Lake of Geneva, but could not afford any of the few houses that met my criteria. Another factor which affects many of Switzerland's 'Mittelland' or flat parts is the presence of highways, which pollute the air and impose the permanent drone of traffic. As sound rises, this noise is often clearly audible in the hills nearby. At one stage of my search, I even spent the night in a chalet immediately above the highway between Lausanne and Montreux, from whose balconies both ends of the lake were visible. The situation was ideal but the incessant noise penetrated the wooden walls. In fact, I am by nature more attuned to the eastern or Germanic part of the country than to the west. While I appreciate certain aspects of francophone culture (the greater variety of cheese, for instance), I object to their manifestations (deplorable slang and advertising, Latin loudness). So I began to look around Zurich and ended up in this characterless but comfortable house. Better characterless than too much character of the wrong sort. It provided the perfect neutral background to house my things.

Actually, my life doesn't seem to be about much except things. Things I have inherited or saved from my father and my mother. I have a few objects of my own, but many of those I cared for most have been lost along the way. I'm comforted by the proximity of these relics. I like their familiar worn look. They're the perfect decoration. Because they've more or less always embellished my life, they must be right. If I write like this, it's because I'm rereading Joan Didion's *A Book of Common Prayer*. I've always appreciated her spare, blunt prose. Despite her rhetorical, self-conscious voice, she has real insights and a message to convey.

Didion's narrator recounts the life of a despairing woman who seems indifferent to her fate and powerless to forestall it. I'm not entirely convinced of the verisimilitude of this character. For instance, I've made things happen. Positive things, I mean, even for myself. Perhaps the problem is that they've never been enough, that I've given up, that they've never lasted long enough to seem like a permanent way of life; that they've never caught. Failure, giving up, is so much more comfortable, familiar, than the striving, the hope-against-hope, and the feigned optimism that goes with the slight possibility of success at something new. There, I know I'm not alone.

A couple of remarks about domesticity. There's a rule in my house which goes 'No shoes, no dogs, no ethnics'. The order is immaterial, but the principle is rigid. I have a corresponding ideology: 'Separation'. This means that all that makes contact with the floor is excommunicated from surfaces such as kitchen counters, tables, etc. (Pet owners rarely make the connection between their animals' feet and their carpets. A pet may be clean in the sense that it does not actually stink, but it carries into the house all that it has walked in.) Once a towel has touched the floor, it goes into the wash. Just as one would never walk barefoot in a hotel room, so one should always walk barefoot in one's own bedroom, so as to attract the minimum of nasties and not transfer them to the bed. Separation also applies to contact with people. Shaking hands is a dirty Western habit. Shake hands as little as possible. If forced to do so, wash your hands at the next opportunity.

I wish I knew someone who understood me; who liked me in spite of understanding me. I still think my ex-wife came closer to understanding me than any other woman since, or tried to.

My heart goes out to the smart, slim, pageboy coiffed, casually elegant American women I see in entertainment or on the news; earnestly dedicating their lives to their jobs, or even to their families. Rich or poor, talented or not, they personify unsentimental composure. But would they tolerate me? I think I knew one once, my first girlfriend. But she was too much older than I, or so I thought at the time, which comes to the same thing. And neither of us had any means. How do you hold even a loving relationship together on no money and against depression and the conviction of failure? How do you hold a relationship of any kind together against the suspicion of infidelity and hidden motives?

In fact, the mention of pageboy hairstyles reminds me that I almost succeeded in getting to know better a woman I had often watched on CNN and whom I found irresistible. She was moderating a discussion session during one of my visits to Davos. Under the table on the dais, I could see that she had kicked off her winter boots and replaced them with a cute pair of slippers. Afterwards, I joined the little crowd of listeners who wanted to speak with her. When I got her attention, I tried quickly to sum up the Czech restoration project and asked her if she had any advice. "Would you like to go somewhere and discuss this more privately?" she asked me. What self-defeating devil in me then caused me to say (truthfully) that I had to leave shortly to catch a flight to Hamburg, I'll never know, but she turned away. Probably, she didn't mean what I hoped she might have meant. By then she had left the channel, yet is not to be found among CNN's alumni. Maybe she had spoiled her chances by not belonging to CNN's reigning ethnicity, or got fed up with its blaring and monotonous inconsequentialities. Her colleagues are for the most part still present and have advanced their careers. For a successful and familiar face, on such a notorious medium, this was strange but, to me, it made her all the more interesting. I hope you're happy, Hillary.

On the subject of television, I have such unlikely, outlandish desires for a vocation. They run opposite to my most deeply-seated trait of ascetic reclusion. I mean, I wanted to host a radio show and that's only audible. About fifteen years ago, I compiled a tape in which Blues was interspersed with sarcastic commentary about current affairs. An ethnic acquaintance claimed to be impressed by it and, allegedly, passed it on to his colleagues at the national broadcaster. Neither they, nor any other station I approached, showed any interest in this project, although nothing of the kind existed in Switzerland.

No, what it is, is that I have all these opinions, and they're going to waste. They're about changing the world, but they're also about setting things and people straight. My scope for doing this, like most people's, is limited. So I wanted to enlarge it. I saw myself behind the radio mike, responding to callers in more or less of a provocative, original way, and praising and supporting those I approved of, whose views were interesting; and putting down those I found pretentious and false, and cheaply ambitious. Hey, quite a few people do this, and successfully too. Often, they have nothing going for them but a big mouth.

But I imagine they don't have something I have: my paralysing self-consciousness. This is what happens to me on camera: even if it starts out OK and I'm on a roll, all of a sudden, inevitably, the situation will catch up with me and I'll say to myself 'You're on camera', and then it's over. You have to love the camera and it has to love you. You have to love the glare of publicity. I don't. I'm a reaction, still, to the over-exposure and publicity I felt as a child whenever my father was around, and often when he wasn't, because of his name. I'll never get over that, so whom am I kidding?

ZURICH

If one can't find a new interest, maybe one can find a new companion. Recently, I have had relations with a *grande dame* and with a schoolgirl respectively, both of the same age or a few years younger than I. This is not a riddle: I speak about bearing. (I have never had any kind of connexion with either, the one having been out of my social and the other out of my psychological reach, when I was of an age to appreciate such women.) In the interval between these two companionships, but not apparently during them, I tried quite hard to enjoy life. I failed. I simply don't know how to have a good time, not even for ready money. So I returned to a solitary occupation: writing. Now my writing has got me into trouble with the only people who seem to count in this sad, delusional world: the middlemen, the influencers of opinion.

How to explain the enigma of being? Let's leave money out of the equation for now. Style is as good a way to start as any. Let's steal stealthily into the workshop of style, the birthplace of 'tolerance' and turn-ups, of antimacassars and 'anti-Semitism'. Of meaning and fashion. That's all that guides our world: transient trends. When does a trend become a belief? When naive 1930s Cambridge undergraduates became Comintern spies? Does it have to pass through a 'lifestyle' first? Why should bell-bottoms be less serious than theology? Because they'll be replaced at the end of the season, whereas the concept of God has lasted for many seasons? Is it all just a matter of perception? Do we just perceive religion and the stock market as significant and bell-bottoms as frivolous because of the time they respectively occupy? After all, fashion in thought as in dress is manipulated, just as the stock markets are manipulated, by those who produce the effects that influence our collective lives. Is it really less profound to say that one was born in the UK at the height of Carnaby Street than, say, in France in 1789? Well, yes, because being born in 1789 could have exposed one to harm. But if one accepts that the French Revolution was a manipulated event, as much as were, say, slanted pockets in the mid-Sixties, by the ultimate manufacturers of style, it becomes merely a matter of degree. Can you see them, at their lathes, churning out political correctness and other neologisms by the yard? Oy vey! There's one that has his beard tangled up in a fearfully messy derivative. It took me fifty-six years to discover who operates that workshop. Now I have it, I wish I didn't. These purveyors of perception are so unworthy of their power, so lacking themselves in style.

Now that these ideological wheeler-dealers have succeeded in kicking three out of four legs of our customs and heritage from under us, they have turned to undermining our very way of thought. Their media have substituted their lies for truth. Whoever voices a contrary opinion is accused of spreading 'fake news'. In other words, the middlemen are imposing their own way of thinking, which is based on expedience. Whereas most children have been brought up to tell the truth, these mediators of mendacity are congenital liars. They regard truth as an embarrassment, an impediment to the success of their mission, which is to control the entire world.

We have raised truth to an icon of our existence. How else could we function, in private as in public, in business as in leisure, without the measure of trust which truth in all transactions entails? Yet, our code of moral conduct must apparently now be revised to include the prospect that our reliance on truth is merely a fixation with an outdated ethic. This gross revolution in basic behavior will complete the shift to chaos and allow only the peddlers of data, of falsified statistics, to decide what matters.

Whereas in youth, when time seems eternal and even hangs occasionally on one's hands, and one's approach to the future may be scattershot, as time runs out, one's focus on life improves. In my youth, I was bored, unhappy and scared of my shadow. I settled on the film business, as it seemed to contain some attractions, although it would be hard to list these now. When I thankfully left its unstructured structure about fifteen years later, I saw a bit clearer and focused on something closer to my actual needs — on writing. Not yet being mature enough to express thoughts worth reading, I made a hash of my novels. Later, under the pressing need to escape my marriage, I discovered successively Albania and ancient buildings. I made an advantage of necessity and threw myself into support for this odd little isolated country, and then for architectural restoration as a way to create jobs. I concentrated hard on finding money for the Czech school, in order not to go mad for longing for my son and for revenge on his mother. Despite this vital distraction, spectres of suicide and homicide kept me awake at night.

When I was entirely free of my wife (but also deprived of participating in my son's development), my old longing for Scotland meshed with an equally old yearning to learn to paint. Glasgow hove into my consciousness. Helpful contacts introduced me to the city. I spent a few days getting a hang of the centre. I introduced myself at the university art school and at the prestigious Charles Rennie Mackintosh School. Equipped with the documentation and entry forms for the first and hopeful of receiving the same from the second, which I really wanted to attend, I returned to my leaden life in Switzerland. Here, the élan over what had seemed to be a worthwhile new venture dissipated over the next weeks. Doubts arose about the sense of uprooting myself once again. Had I not moved enough? Instead of remembering the true purpose of my quest and renting a flat, any flat, in Glasgow, with the option of falling back on Switzerland should things not work out, I had visited a promising flat for sale, on the top floor of a converted warehouse, and tempted myself with the prospect of exchanging one domicile for the other. When I received a call from the estate agents to say that the conversion was second rate and when the Mackintosh documents failed to arrive, I got cold feet. This seemed to be a sign that I was not intended to move to Glasgow.

However, I occasionally return to Scotland, chiefly to the Highlands. Recently, I was enjoying the solitary silence in the spacious grassy enclave of the Old High Church cemetery in Inverness. The generous gaps between the stones give the 19th century dead room to breathe, as it were. An unusually large and healthy holly tree bows over one memorial. Lifting my eyes from the weathered grey stones reveals the restful backdrop of Craig Phadrig Wood on the hill across the Ness. I'm grateful. Thus it comes as a bit of a jolt when a young woman with a scarred face, towing by one hand a small child, calls across the graves, presumably to ask for directions. Before I can advise her that I am a stranger, she tells me she has cervical cancer and asks for help in getting to some place for treatment. A clutter of contradictory reactions overcomes me. I assume she must be lying. She has robbed me of the peace I was enjoying just an instant before, so my habitual rejection of such importuning is increased by my indignation at being disturbed, even here, in one of the only places mercifully free of the Saturday throng. On the other hand, maybe she is telling the truth. After all, a cemetery is an unusual place to beg and does not offer the same opportunities as the busy pedestrian zones of the town. However, I tell her that I don't give money on principle. She seems to accept this right away, and moves on. This also speaks in her favour. During the coming days, I will castigate myself for not having given her at least a couple of pounds. Even if I would have been cheated by doing so, my conscience would now be clear. This is the effect the multitude of bussed-in gypsies has had on decent, generous citizens. They have hardened their hearts against all beggars, including those that may deserve a hand-out. My father would certainly have given her something.

Chapter XXVI
MY FATHER

How did Yehudi 'the Jew' Menuhin respond to his gradual awakening to the undisguised Jewish nature, when he discovered it? There is no evidence that he ever did discover it. Having grown up with only one driving impulse, music, in a non-religious household, a household which revolved largely around himself, he had been free to develop his utopian mission, by which conflicts between peoples could be overcome by music, his music, undisturbed by the mundanities of life. Unlike most musicians, whose ignorance of all beside their profession and perhaps a hobby or two is always evident, my father regularly read the news and engaged in public affairs of all kinds. He also tried to mediate between the two sides in Palestine, for which he must be honoured, however hopeless such efforts may be. Certainly, audiences all over the world were impressed and soothed by the unmistakably pure tones of his violin, and responded to the nobility and sincerity of his bearing, as well as to his legendary generosity in favour of a multiplicity of causes. His heritage comprises many unique recordings, a world famous, government supported music school, a programme for concerts in prisons and hospitals, a foundation for musically linked projects in schools (of which I was briefly head of the German chapter), and a wealth of good thoughts and sayings on general subjects. Above all, perhaps, 20 years after his death, his legacy of goodwill is still to be encountered, sometimes in unexpected places.

LIVED IT WRONG

While still young and naive and politically uninstructed, he co-sponsored *The Black Book* (1946), a Jewish compendium of horrors allegedly committed against Jews by Germans during WWII. (Originally begun as early as 1942, it was considered to be evidence at the Nuremberg trials.) Whether or not he did this at the prompting of his agent, it was a logical conformity. He would not then have criticized the treatment of Palestinians in the soon to be created state of Israel, however often he might have heard his father inveigh against it.

One of his most enduring habits was to ignore — to push under the carpet, as it were — anything that disturbed him. He must have been bothered by the enmity of New York Jews, when they, who had of course come through the war unscathed, attacked him for his defence of the great German conductor, Furtwängler, and for backing him for the post of conductor of the Chicago Symphony. Untroubled by facts, by the evidence that Furtwängler had protected many Jewish musicians in his orchestras during the war; they found this an appropriate or even useful excuse to attack my father. On the one hand, the Italian conductor, Toscanini, wanted the position, on the other, my father had adversaries in the New York Jewish musical world, notably a violinist called Stern, who, in the manner of a coarse careerist, considered Yehudi Menuhin his rival, and led this attack from somewhere in the rear, motivated by envy of my father's inspirational insights and general superiority. They bore him a grudge anyway because he had refused to join a musicians' union which planned to embargo foreign violinists from playing in the U.S. *The New York Times*, ever the primary medium for Jewish propaganda, reported on February 2, 1949 that my father's concert in Rome had been boycotted by Jews and had therefore been half-empty (as though a few Jews could have had that effect), when in fact it had been so packed that a delegation of Jewish students who came to ask my father for free (of course) seats had to stand. This lie was followed by a regular campaign of slander by the U.S. Jewish press, asserting that Menuhin had dared to play on some silly Jewish holiday — in the UK. Not only had my father changed the date of the concert, but he had renounced part of his fee to placate the organizers. Presumably, my father had earned this Jewish persecution merely because he had stood up for Furtwängler and turned over his fee to German orphans, when he played in Berlin after the war.

My mother's diary for 23 September 1949 records a dinnertable conversation in Berlin with a Rabbi Schwarzschild, during which he recounted 'his address in the synagogue in which he attacked the Jews for their anti-Semite-provoking behaviour'.

New York, described by my grandfather as a 'cesspool', and the enormous void between it and the West Coast that is America (rather like the space between two ears, I always think), couldn't compete with Europe's sophistication and rich variety. Probably, this experience, added to my mother's preferences, impelled my father to resettle in Europe, first in Switzerland and then in London, which he had visited frequently during the war and which is, after all, one of the great musical capitals of the world.

Over the next fifty years, my father became a fixture in British public life. The British system is in the habit of awarding honours not only in recognition of worthy deeds, but also to those who play the game. During the Sixties, it is probably fair to say, it was still the case that only those who had distinguished themselves were rewarded. These days, perhaps in nostalgic memory of Empire, awards like the MBE or KBE are distributed almost wholesale in the New Year's honours list, to all kinds of people, from amenable politicians and popular television personalities, even, lately, to hairdressers. These awards have therefore become superfluous if not downright ridiculous and, outside the UK, totally meaningless. As someone who had at least contributed significantly — through his music school, for instance — to the attributes of the nation, my father was granted a knighthood, then a life peerage. A more meaningful and universally understood award might have been the Nobel Peace Prize (however degraded by recent recipients), for which he was eminently better suited than many who have received it. However, to his credit of course, he had apparently not played the game compliantly or reliably enough to fulfil the required qualifications.

Travels alone with my father were infrequent, consisting mostly of several visits to Davos, for the self-important World Economic Forum, and his regular tours in Germany. Setting off on one of the latter, the conversation must have run along family lines, for I found it appropriate to ask my father how I had offended him in earlier times. I must have thought that it would help me to clear up any uncertainties I had on the subject. He thought about this awhile and then came up with an unexpected answer: the expensive and indulgent dinner I had ordered for my brother and myself, at the Plaza Athénée, in 1969, while we waited to be admitted to the embassy, after the guests there had finished their own meal. He had a point. The excellent menu at this hotel had presented us with the possibility of enjoying not only lobster Thermidor but also chocolate soufflé, both of which I requested. However, if this was truly the worst he could come up with, it was hardly wicked. He could have cited my habitual petulance, my disappointing performance at school, my hopeless adult life, and countless instances of my being 'horrible to Mummy'. How curious that this minor incident had stayed in his mind!

Now, in late February 1999, as we descended from Davos towards Zurich, in the chauffeured Audi which is the World Economic Foolery's appointed brand, my father unexpectedly embarked on some early reminiscences. He recalled his first love, Esther, with whom he had had an affectionate if tentative relationship, and spoke about his visits to her family at Tahoe. My knowledge of my father's early life was limited to what I had gleaned from remarks my mother had dropped and Robert Magidoff's biography, so I listened with curiosity. Any recollections of the past were unusual, where my father was concerned, especially those expressing remorse (on our visit to bury his mother in 1996, he surprised me by confiding that he regretted

MY FATHER

selling Alma, his property in Los Gatos). However, my memory does not provide me with any other details of this conversation.

At the W.E.F., I had persuaded my father, who was as ever concerned about my mother's health, to consult an American doctor then renowned for his current best-seller. This affable personality gave his recommendations and, in answer to my parting question about my father's own health, delivered the diagnosis that he would live at least another ten years. The question had been casually posed, as an afterthought, and the response, equally cursory. No serious diagnosis could have been given in the circumstances. However, in view of my father's imminent death, to an experienced physician, his already failing health should have been visible in his features. In fact, my father had been popping pills from the large black leather case which contained his travelling pharmacy with more than usual assiduity, and from his voice and bearing was suffering from some kind of bronchitis.

I wish I remembered more about this conversation with my father as it turned out to be the last we had in person. He deposited me at Zurich's main station and drove on to the airport. A few days later, he called to ask me to join him in Berlin. To my everlasting regret, I responded that I could see him in Freiburg, where he was due to play later and which was closer to Switzerland. He thereupon said, in an unusually plaintive voice, that he would miss me. He had never said as much and it triggered my guilt. A few days after this, my brother called to say that our father was very ill and in a hospital in Berlin. While I was contemplating flying up there, my brother called again to say that he had died. The news came as a great shock, both to the family and to everyone who had known my father. He had been assumed to be the acme of health and vitality, even at 81. So he died alone in hospital, attended only by his agent and the aforementioned ambitious secretary. I will never forgive myself for not accepting his invitation. Most probably, my presence would not have changed anything, but he would at least have had the company of a member of his own family. On the other hand, given the nature of the companion he had, as described above, I have a lingering, if minor doubt about her commitment to my father's health.

My father's body was flown back to the UK, where he lay, in his coffin, on the floor of the dining room, at 65 Chester Square. There, each of us children had the opportunity to commune alone with him, before saying our final farewells. He had on the handmade but rather old tweed jacket with the reinforced cuffs, which he had worn as far back as I could remember. It hangs in a cupboard in my cellar. As I leant over to kiss him, I felt the bristles on his cheek for the first time in my life. So they do continue to grow after death, was my first thought. I was accustomed to my father's clean-shaven face, smelling of eau de Cologne. His appearance had always been exceedingly soigné; so much so that I used to feel slightly soiled by comparison, whenever we exchanged the glancing embraces that passed for affection in our family. My father was buried in the grounds of the music school he had established and which remains, after his recordings, his greatest legacy.

Chapter XXVII

FOUNDATIONS AND SUBSTRUCTURES

A memorial service for my father was held at Westminster Abbey on June 3, 1999. 'The turnout for one of the century's outstanding musicians, humanitarians and idealists stopped central London traffic and filled all the 2,200 seats crammed into the abbey for the occasion' (*The Guardian*, June 4, 1999).

At this event, my older half-brother and I read aloud a prayer our father had written. I had originally divided this prayer into three equal parts, to which it lent itself well. However, my younger brother refused to read his part, for reasons known only to him. Certainly, reading aloud before such an eminent and numerous audience required a modicum of courage, but the occasion and the obligation to honour our father should have overcome any faintheartedness. On the way out, the Prince of Wales kindly congratulated me with the words 'Well done', for which I was grateful.

After this ceremony, a few of those who had been present in the Abbey congregated at some venue I now forget. Among them was the German ex-minister Rita Süssmuth, whom my father had known. She asked me if I would assume the position of president of the German branch of my father's foundation, based in Düsseldorf. Although I had gained a certain contempt for the employees of foundations during my work to support architectural restoration, I readily agreed, considering this to be a worthy assignment in the perpetuation of one of my father's many useful legacies. The foundation was concerned with a project to foster musical appreciation in primary schools, through dance or the fashioning of simple musical instruments, for instance. Accordingly, I attended meetings of the foundation's board in Düsseldorf twice a year, and visited schools participating in the project. Usually, these visits were encouraging experiences, which proved the value of the project, as enthusiastic young children are always invigorating.

On one occasion, I was shown a row of very imaginative and amusing fantastical animals drawn by a class. As one of our board members was a well-known television starlet, with her own studio, I asked her if she would explore the possibility of introducing these obviously imaginative children to the craft of animation, with a view to setting them on a course which could lead to a career. This handsome dyed blonde, however, was unable or unwilling to grasp my patient explanation. Soon thereafter, she married a loathsome lawyer, whose ethnicity had saved him from conviction for drug offenses and human trafficking for purposes of prostitution.

In 2004, I finally succumbed to my long-held ambition to communicate with the *National-Zeitung*, a patriotic German newspaper to which my grandfather had contributed a regular column during the Sixties. As a result, I began myself to publish such a column under my proposed title '*Menuhin und wie er die Welt sieht*' ('Menuhin and how he sees the world'). These articles were well received by readers of the newspaper, but a few months later they came to the attention of my colleagues at the foundation, who reacted with commendable German knee-jerk alacrity and fervour, and, without bothering with the usual courtesies, directed me by registered letter to resign my position immediately, or take the consequences. As I did not respond within the dictated time, I was fired.

One day, about a year after I moved into this house and soon after I began to contribute articles to the newspaper, I found myself lying on a stretcher in an ambulance on the way to a hospital. My last memory was of the forest in which I had been taking my daily walk. After my right ear had been sewed on again, the surgeon explained that I had been found by a local hunter, unconscious next to a log against which I had apparently fallen. This surgeon (a professor and the senior specialist at this hospital) described the origin of my injuries as dubious. While my ear had nearly been torn off in my fall, there were wounds which could not be explained by such an accident. Was I sure that no third person was involved? I could not respond to this, except to say that I thought I had been alone.

This unpleasant experience could not necessarily be linked to an incident in London, when, without any warning, I had fallen unconscious on a platform of the Underground, and again had to be transported to the nearest hospital with concussion. To associate either of these events with a death threat issued on some imbecilic, semi-literate Israeli internet site at around the same time would certainly be mistaken.

2008

On a brisk morning in November, I almost stopped breathing. I was reading on the sofa when I suddenly found that I couldn't inhale. I rushed outside to gasp a few breaths, but this hardly helped; as soon as I was inside again, the same thing happened. Panicked at the thought that my life was over, I managed to call my doctor, luckily only about five minutes' drive away. Two nurses appeared shortly and administered a cortisone shot, which helped immediately. In hospital I was told that I had a double pulmonary embolism. The medical verdict was that my condition was due to my having moved insufficiently during two consecutive days of travel.

Four days previously, at the suggestion of Horst Mahler, a German lawyer I knew slightly, I had agreed to visit his friend, Sylvia Stolz, also a lawyer, imprisoned for three years in Heidelberg jail for speaking her mind. It seemed the right thing to do. I had cleared the interview with the *National-Zeitung* and looked forward to seeing the unfortunate woman's plight described in print and online. Accordingly, I had checked into a peculiar hostel in the town. It operated an anonymous system, whereby the guest inserted his dues into a contraption next to the locked entrance and received a numbered key in return. Accepting the key also activated the front door. The room or cubicle had a shower and the bed was clean. No other human was in evidence.

On the next morning, I crossed the street to find my legal acquaintance where he had spent the night, in his camper. We took a taxi to the prison. There, procedure required visitors to deposit their phones at the reinforced, glass-protected front desk, and to leave their coats in a locker in the claustrophobic waiting room on an upper floor. Eventually, we were called, crossed a passage and entered a room with a table, chairs and a high window, next to which sat a wardress on an elevated platform. The lady lawyer entered and flung herself without more ado at her friend. I did my best to look away and ignore this desperate demonstration of emotion. The wardress seemed to show a glimmer of sympathy.

Ms. Stolz took a chair on the far side of the table and I and my companion, opposite her. I presented my list of questions, which she answered in her high, childlike voice. The interview cannot have lasted more than half an hour. Outside again, we accepted indifferently the absence of our taxi, which we had requested to await our return. This allowed us to converse privately during the time it took us to walk the mile or so to the station. There, our ways parted.

An essential coda to this encounter concerns Horst Mahler, perhaps Germany's most prominent political prisoner. He has been languishing in prison in Brandenburg for years now, convicted like Frau Stolz for saying and writing what is, in Germany, literally indefensible. He is 83 years old and has lost both legs to diabetes and poor health care. Despite his age and infirmity, the German state does not dare set free such an indomitable patriot and fighter for truth. Recently, I wrote to Gerhard Schröder, former chancellor and Mahler's colleague when they were both Leftist lawyers, now enjoying position and riches, to ask him to intercede on Mahler's behalf and allow him to spend his last days with his relatives. Schröder didn't bother to reply.

2009

A word has just come to me: laundromatisation. I feel it must mean something, don't you? Why else would it have turned up? Google is a blank on the subject. Reducing the word by a few letters provides an address for a Laundromat in Satellite Beach, Florida. But that doesn't explain the 'laundromatisation' of everything, if you know what I mean. The Laundromat (cf. 'launderette' UK), a coin-operated, self-service experience, is synonymous with many activities in which other humans no longer play a role — like brainwashing via self-abuse of the mind. Pretty soon, all our interactions will involve machines, as a result of which we should not feel demeaned or insulted if, on the day of reckoning, we are removed by machines more intelligent than ourselves. But I am no science fiction writer, so I had better abstain from such predictions.

November, 2012

In Paris, to visit my son and his girlfriend. We look up some of my old haunts. The centre of the city is now liable to be confused with any other metropolis: it has lost its essential cultural ambiance and is only identifiable by its famous sights. The Arc de Triomphe, the Eiffel Tower, etc., are visible at distance, over a sea of humanity, composed preponderantly of tourists and groups of aggressive North Africans — trippers and troublemakers — who block the streets and the perspective, even if this lately consists not of *boulangeries* and *brasseries*, but of McDonalds and Starbucks. In the Tuileries, a cherished park since my childhood, I dodge pairs of American joggers with headphones, obliviously going about their goal-oriented careers, just as they would in Central Park. One didn't like the Parisians, but it was their city. No longer. Like Florence, Paris has lost its soul. Never again.

The result of having stopped contributing to the *National-Zeitung* was that I had nothing to do. Naturally, I had thought about writing something else, anything else. Ideally, a subject for a novel should have suggested itself. Apart from innumerable short pieces and false starts, I've written two novels, one published, one rejected. Both these attempts at fiction have been based in part on myself and my experiences. The central challenge in writing a novel is that you have to invent believable characters which interest the reader. To achieve this semblance of real life, you have to sympathize with people and their predicaments. Unfortunately, I cannot identify with most people and am quite uninterested in their fate. This was always the case, even before they degraded themselves to the extent that their motivations became completely incomprehensible (queuing all night to buy the latest smartphone; eating more Frankfurters than anyone else so as to earn an entry in the *Guinness Book of Records*). If you don't care for people, you can't write about them. So I was reduced to writing a kind of autobiography. It is of necessity somewhat higgledy-piggledy, but the reader may be entertained by the factual accounts as much as by the flights of fancy and opinion it contains. They also are anchored in reality.

While writing it, along the way, as it were, I described, cursorily, my unpaid engagement at the *National-Zeitung*. I had abandoned the paper in 2008, after the owner refused to publish the Stolz interview. I realized then that the *National-Zeitung* was only a somewhat more conservative organ than the mainstream press, with the difference that it covers subjects deliberately ignored in other media. At this point in my autobiographical venture, I discovered that the purpose which had caused me to approach the newspaper in the first place remained as pressing and unfulfilled as ever. So I shelved the autobiography and began to research my subject instead, starting with the simple question '*Why won't the world come to rest?*' As a result, what had been merely a section of a book grew and became a book on its own. In October 2015, it was published under the title *Tell the Truth and Shame the Devil* (unaccountably, at least nine other books appeared under the same title at around the same time). Recently, the book was translated into German, Russian and French, in that order. More recently, in February 2018, the German publisher, a retired ship's captain, was raided by the police, all his electronic equipment confiscated, and the book censored. Contrary to Article 5 of the German Basic Law or '*Grundgesetz*', which asserts 'There is no censorship', the Federal Republic runs an agency which indexes literature allegedly harmful to youth ('*jugendgefährdend*'). (The German Basic Law has substituted since 1949 for the promised but never drafted constitution, but informed commentators believe that even this code may have been nullified in the wake of the so-called 2+4 Agreement of 1990, rendering the BRD, in effect, a lawless land, or rather one run exclusively in consonance with the whims of the Allied occupiers.) Accordingly, the publisher inserted an online warning to potential buyers advising them of this, but bravely continued to issue the book. Most recently, on 2 February, 2019, he was again raided and shut down completely. On 26 March 2019, he passed away and was buried at sea.

Of course, the source of such a grave misdemeanour could not expect to remain unaffected by this censure. I myself was intruded upon by the Swiss police in November 2016, at 8 in the morning, pursuant to a request for 'legal aid' from their German colleagues. There were five of them, including the public prosecutor. It appeared that some quite unremarkable but virtuous German citizen had taken it on himself to charge me with a contravention of Article 130, in Switzerland, Article 261bis. (I learnt later that this principled person had performed the same service previously, presumably at the behest of, and with a reward from, the traditional enemy of truth. As a German saying has it: '*Der grösste Lump im ganzen Land, das ist und bleibt der Denunziant.*' — 'The greatest scoundrel in the entire country is and remains the informer.') This German law, which has been described as exceptional by several German experts, is designed to smother all dissent by making it illegal to speak or write positively about National Socialism, or to disbelieve some tiresome, hugely publicized event that reputedly equates, or indeed surpasses in memory, the importance of the discovery of fire, or, more in keeping with its implausibility — the official account of the New York towers implosion of 2001. As it happened, I was reading a report by the admirable French dissenter Robert Faurisson at the time. The policeman in charge, seated at my computer, presumably understood the significance of this, although, being German-speaking, he was not necessarily fluent in French. Later, this fellow very decently asked me to forgive his holstered gun. I responded that I wasn't bothered by what I took to be part of his regular equipment. While these public servants were going through the papers on my desk and perusing the books in my bookshelves, I sat in an easy chair and contemplated my position. It was a new experience for me, about whose outcome I was unclear. Eventually, I got up and informed them that I was going to shave. This seemed acceptable. They must have spent at least a couple of hours in the house, departing with my computer, every copy of the book including my own, and an (inferior) French translation.

In the normal order of things, I had to engage a lawyer. His costs were added to the five-figure fine that he advised me to accept, conjoined with the imposition of a two-year gag order, infringement of which was punishable by an outrageously high financial penalty. By agreeing to this, I became officially a felon convicted of 'racism', and as a result, am unable to find a job or rent an apartment. The alternative would have meant the expense of defence before a court, possibly resulting in a guilty verdict or even a prison sentence. The confiscated books were incinerated. A futile action, one would have thought, as both the English and the German publications had been available for months and for free on the internet. All this fuss just because I had expressed my (well-founded and fully-confirmed) thoughts.

Although the literary era is well over, the boots of Orwellian neo-cretinism are still desperate to stamp out any hint of political protest in printed matter. Books may be despised and unread these days (except of course for sensational trash), as the effort and concentration required to digest them are beyond most minds under fifty. Yet this near total cultural vacuity hasn't prevented a few of these text-challenged folk from declaring their consternation, not only over a book they haven't for the most part read, but over its author, who is commonly supposed to be a descendant and therefore an adherent of the Jewish — I almost said 'faith' — formation.

After this episode, I was faced with the autobiography again, but unsure what to do with it. Should I, after all, try something else? To be totally frivolous, how about an *auto*-biography? I could list — with photographs and nostalgic descriptions — all the cars I have owned: about 23. At seventy, one may buy what will probably be one's last car and one's last bed. I drive less than 10,000 miles/15,000 km per year, so my present car will certainly last me until they take my licence away, and I hear that a good mattress should last about 15 years. Actually, I bought my last bed — the one in which one can raise the mattress in three sections by means of motors built into the frame — when I was fifty, with the thought that it could be the one I died in. It turns out that that was premature. But now I'm genuinely getting old. My body began to show unmistakable signs of age several years ago. Overall, my appearance is closer to eighty than seventy. So, joy to the world.

Chapter XXVIII
MUSINGS

No autobiography is complete without a dose of the author's personal philosophy. So here goes.

The human race has failed and is doomed collectively to a condition more dire than any it has experienced hitherto, with the obvious exception of those who have brought it there.

Occasionally, I wonder what the world would have been like had a certain ethnicity, or in the majority of cases as is commonly accepted, a claimed ethnicity, and its rapacious followers, not intruded in its development. By this I mean that the average human, with all his inborn defects, but also his inborn abilities and interests, would quite likely have succeeded in creating a balanced environment for himself, in which the important human constituents counted most.

Deriving first from personal responsibility and common sense, he would have respected himself, as a responsible individual but also a member of a community, who lived among others and therefore was at all times potentially responsible towards (not for) them.

He would have respected the natural environment in all its forms, as he would have respected cultural diversity in all its forms. Different cultures would have been able to survive within their inherited territorial boundaries, independent of national borders.

Perhaps in solitary communion with nature, he would have accepted his role as a humble being among other beings, and yet have experienced the spiritual exaltation which comes from this bond.

He would have striven for a fulfilling existence through the realization of his internal drives, rather than by externalizing his modish persona, by buying unnecessary objects he couldn't afford, as a distraction from the burden of being alive. He would not have degraded himself by debasing his body, his health, his appearance through bad food and absurd fashion.

Collectively, he would have ensured sufficient natural food, clean water and air for all. He would have developed an educational system which catered to individual needs, resulting in a fulfilled individual, who could form a life in tune with his interests.

He would have reproduced with forethought, according to his inherited culture.

Goods and services needed by any community would have been traded either by barter or by means of some commonly accepted, portable symbol of worth, which could not have been accumulated against interest. The exclusion of money and interest as we know it today, would remind us of its actual value as nothing more than a handy medium of exchange.

Governments would have been discarded as futile baggage; no responsible society needs to be governed. As a result, politicians and politics as a profession would also become redundant. In place of government would have been a transparent management of all commonly used resources and services, working in tandem with, but not in thrall to an independent central bank.

It follows that the robbery from an ensnared population called 'income taxes' and all other taxes allegedly required to support a government and its cumbersome, self-serving legislation would have been abolished.

Finally, having concluded a fulfilled life, the individual would accept that he is a biological element of the planet, destined to die and to join other biological elements, without rebellion and without superstitious need of support from organized religion or any similar substitute.

This is not a utopian projection. It would have been perfectly feasible, if humanity had been allowed to develop organically.

Would organic development have averted religious belief? Religious belief is the consequence of superstition. The human race, particularly in its contemporary degraded state, cannot come to terms with its mortality and has succumbed to delusion. This reveals itself in an abundance of more or less peculiar and artificial concepts of God, or church, including sects. A higher, more rational but unattainable belief, could only exist if humankind would learn to believe in itself and free itself from its fear of death. Meanwhile many believers as a matter of course have renounced their belief in God and instead have adopted consumerism as a distraction from mortality.

Instead of regarding himself as a spiritual as well as a biological being, which, like all natural beings, joins nature at the end of its life, Man ascribes to himself a special importance, even an afterlife or a rebirth after death. This useless battle against biological inevitability ensures eternally the dominance of superstition and the doom of humanity. Man is clever, but he is not wise. Through his intellectual capacity, he is able to discover much which for animals is impossible. So Man tries to rule nature. He does not live with and among nature, but over it. That is his greatest failing. If Man were humble, he would notice that his mental superiority does not make him happy, if he does not employ it wisely. If Man would observe nature, he would learn how self-sufficient the smallest insect is, how it does not take for itself more than it needs, and lives mostly without damaging the environment irreparably. As long as Man has not developed the efficiency and biological logic of a spider, he will remain a victim of those who profit from his superstition.

Chapter XXIX

ENDING UP

As a child and even later, I think, I must have been looking for something that wasn't there: unconditional love. My parents' love for their children was absolutely conditional. Neither of them had experienced the straightforward, simple affection that should exist between parents and children (or maybe I'm making that up; maybe that's idealised, fictional). My father's parents may have doted on him, but one wonders if their attachment wasn't at least a bit mixed with awe at this cuckoo's egg that had been laid in their nest. By contrast, my mother's mother appears to have been more than usually cold, even for an English parent. My father developed in a hothouse of over-attention; my mother under near neglect. Neither had the patience or interest to watch over their more typical children. What advice I received from my parents was theoretical, outdated or unfitting, and therefore useless. Consequently, I had to look to my own development. Feeling my way forward in life afforded me not a few knocks, shocks and bad experiences — although the latter were also a result of my solitary dejection, of sensing that I was unnecessary or at least inconsequential. Wisdom can only come with age and experience. Decisions made in a vacuum and while still callow must be mistaken, unless luck intervenes. Mine were invariably wrong. My reasoning, such as it was, was reflexive, emotional, self-defeating.

From the perspective of a seventy-year-old, one essentially minor detail stands out as having perhaps been instrumental in setting me on the wrong path: the late loss of my virginity. Preposterous as it may sound, it is nothing less than indispensable — at least to men — to experience sexual intercourse at the earliest age commensurate with psychological readiness, in order later maturely to meet the challenges that life may impose. While the impediment of male virginity may be more serious than its female equivalent, both must be assumed to inhibit clear-sightedness about and among one's fellow creatures in general, and are therefore hindrances to self-fulfilment. Once one has got the first relationships out of the way — with luck without too much bad feeling — one is much better placed to choose a lasting partner, for the best reasons. One almost sympathises with the earlier practice among some upper-class British parents who sent their sons to prostitutes. If the woman is kind, the experience may in no way be regrettable.

In any case, I lost mine at twenty-three, far too late. The repeated breaks in my upbringing, whereby I changed boarding schools, languages, continents, and had to relearn basics in four different countries, under different conditions and educational systems, also trying to make new friends each time, meant that the continuity and stability essential to every child's upbringing was entirely lost to me. There was simply no consistent central *point d'appui*, no homing base to which I could return for advice and support. While of course experiencing the same urges as any child, I had no concept of how to further them. Women scared me; I had had few chances to know them, to familiarize myself with their presence, since my early schooling in California. What few opportunities I had to meet women were frustrated by other circumstances and my own growing inhibitions. As already said, there was nothing natural about my childhood. So the climbing of this metaphorical mountain assumed huge importance and when fulfilment eventually lured, with an older woman, a warm-hearted American who really cared for me, she became my priority. For her, above all else, above the retention of my American citizenship and the lure of Northern California as it existed in my memory, I returned to the U.S., giving up my job, my career and all my European links. It seemed a brave venture at the time.

I see now that it was a colossal mistake. To hell with my citizenship: I would have stayed in Europe, continued to take jobs in films perhaps, or started to write seriously. To hell with a university: the boys who left public school with me would not have dreamt of further education. Only in semi-literate America is a degree from a so-called university vital to respectable employment. Not only did my classmates find work, but the universities that existed in the UK in the mid-Sixties were out of all our reaches: they were genuinely places of higher learning, their reputations unsullied by inferior or modish studies. They were therefore not accessible to those without some claim to erudition.

Who knows, I might even have improved my outlook on life in general and not ended up as I have, with a conviction of doom. Probably, I would be ignorant of the true course of history and the driving forces behind it, but, if not blissful, I could have been content in my ignorance. I would not now be struggling with the conundrum whether to continue to speak out and risk my life further, or to accept that no one can change anything. I live with fear, as it is.

Plenty of children suffer the same as or worse than I, but they don't necessarily develop an insight into the workings of history; this was therefore a concomitant gain which balanced my impairment. The defensive detachment that I perforce developed from not having a close relationship with my parents, or, with very few exceptions, with anyone else, helped me to gain the necessary perspective to observe the world objectively. For instance, to understand how a single gang can operate, soullessly, inhumanly, century after century, in pursuit of its plan to subvert the entire planet, no matter the cost to others. Certainly, you don't need to be inhuman to be like them, but it helps. Anyone can be calculating and indifferent to suffering, but to be able to seize this essential difference that allows them, collectively and exclusively, to function as they do, to create suffering and to profit from it, you might need partly to share their cold-blooded isolation.

Maybe you would need to span the divide between humanity and inhumanity; between real human kindness and mawkish Hollywood sentimentality. This faculty, coupled with at least some grasp of the alien impulse that drives them, horrifying as it is, enables me to understand them. It may also have spurred my sense of Adolf Hitler as an intuitive and inspired person, and allowed me to deduce that their most useful and abominable lie depends for its survival on the Jewish-owned media's compulsion to diabolize him. It followed that he was not as portrayed and, in turn, that most of the history I had learnt was also false.

While we're on the subject of the great leader, gentle reader — gentle indoctrinated reader — let me assure you that there is nothing more convincing of AH's rationality than his own voice. Contrary to political correctness and to 74 years of defamation, Hitler didn't normally shout or scream; his manner is usually measured and his sense of humour, unmistakable. It's my habit to listen to his speeches, of which I have a drawer-full on compact discs, while I'm cooking or baking. German is not as modish as French and successive generations of supposed Anglo-Saxons, because they can't make head or tail of German, have adopted the juvenility of mocking it. Of course, this reluctance to gain at least some familiarity with the language of a country only just over 300 kilometres distant is also a consequence of history being written by the victors.

While my disengagement from the commonalty provided me with an analytic capability, I wish I hadn't had to develop this insulation as a kind of protection from my own parents, but I suppose it was a reaction to what I came to view as their betrayal of my trust in them. I was unable to form an attachment to my parents, or they to me. Consequently, I was unable to form attachments to others. That accounts for my decision to marry someone I didn't love and for my unfeeling marriage, and my rejection of, or fear of the risk of involvement with, anyone I cared for. Yet I cannot forgive myself for the mistakes I have made, nor absolve myself of the guilt I feel towards those I have disappointed. Not all of these last were particularly worthy of my consideration, but I need not have encouraged friendships of which I eventually showed myself to be unworthy. Did they feel betrayed when I drifted away — is disloyalty an inherited trait?

Relationships, like friendships, are modes of life that one acquires by practice. One has to learn them when young. I never learnt them. I probably didn't fit my allotted role. I was certainly a disappointing child. I let both my parents down, never achieving what they doubtless expected of me. Maybe they discussed my failures openly; maybe they lamented them privately. However, they brought my failure upon themselves, were the originators of it, by thrusting obstructions in my path. They were both in their individual ways extremely selfish and self-centred. My mother was probably dysfunctional like her siblings, and my father was totally concentrated on his interests and aspirations. His own self-disciplined, utterly undeviating and goal-oriented upbringing gave him no insight into or sympathy for the ordinary development and the self-doubts of normal children. Neither did it apparently occur to him that he had not been expelled at an early age from familial surroundings, as I had, and thrust into an adverse environment. Both my parents profited from knowing that I would probably come to no great harm at boarding school, at least physically, while learning my lessons, and they were thus freed from the distraction of the more difficult of their children.

'Yehudi Menuhin: The genius who put the fight for justice before his family' (*The Times*, April 6, 2016). My father was remarkably uninvolved in my development; he never showed any interest in my progress. Entirely ignorant of formal schooling, he left decisions about my education to my mother. I expect children bored him — unless they were musically gifted, as was my brother (now, a gifted pianist). However, he was an inveterate letter-writer, whether about politics to *The Times*, or about his uncooperative son. Recently, I came across a letter my father had written to the headmaster of my prep school in 1960, when I was 11. In it, he explains why, as a result of my disinclination to learn, I would be tutored at home. This decision 'seems to make sense for more reasons than one: his own nature in the first place, which is in all respects singular, both figuratively and literally, and has been starved since he was six of a continuous and unbroken contact with his own family, which before its next transition into adolescence should fill out these gaps in his personal experience with his parents and his home'.

This clinically disengaged view of my early years, recounted as if my estrangement from my roots were the result of an act of God rather than of my parents' own will, or as if I were a laboratory experiment that had temporarily gone wrong, demonstrates my parents' relations with their children. Neither of them could spare the time for us. Unless I fitted in with them, or at least showed unremitting sympathy for my mother's grievances and emulated my father's optimism, I was out of favour. But children are not innately hypocritical or intentionally obstructive. They do not mean to disappoint. Hypocrisy and rebelliousness are also learnt traits.

Children have a right to their parents' time and support. Parents have the advantage of seniority, of their years of experience of life. They should instinctively feel sympathy and understanding for their own children. Instead, they often institute a kind of intellectual abuse of them, which starts with their own intolerance and provokes in their children a vicious cycle of misery-obstreperousness-misery, which, in turn, provokes more intolerance.

Why did my parents have children at all? What was the point? My father had had two already, although his first son did not see him for about ten years, and my mother was far too self-absorbed to take her focus off herself. By the time I was seven and had experienced the initial desertion, I had probably already developed troublesome tendencies and had become a nuisance. ("Why did you engender me? / We [I] didn't know it'd be you." Beckett, *Endgame*) It was therefore not only English custom, not only my mother's English background, which landed me at an early age in a boarding school.

Another letter, this time addressed to my housemaster at Eton and dated January 1962, when I was 13, states 'The sad thing is that he is actually very happy at Eton...' In fact, I was hideously unhappy at Eton, at least during the first four years. So my father must have been describing some other person, or rather, modifying circumstances to suit his delusions. Like his own parents, an unbeliever, my father then goes on to write 'It seems to me that if he were only old enough to have the kind of religious conversion which brings all the simple but basic qualities of humility and faith, his problems would be resolved forthwith.' Almost 60 years later, I have still not emulated St. Francis: I am absolutely faithless, while appropriately humble.

My mother's addendum to my father's letter in the following year, again to my housemaster, contains the following illuminating remark: 'I am so sad and disturbed. ... I feel rather sorry for him where I used to feel anger.' Where previously, the researcher had been angered when the guinea pig showed an unexpectedly rebellious disposition, now she was only saddened by this baffling phenomenon.

My most outstanding trait is perhaps being able to make the least of every opportunity. The *Pogo* quote 'We have met the enemy and he is us', whatever it may say about society in general when it refuses to face up to vital changes, accurately describes my association with myself. Since my earliest experiences of disappointment or mortification, I have always lived at odds with myself, detached from myself, at one remove from reality. Often, I cannot relate unequivocally to my being, to my body, to my own space in my environment, wherever that happens to be. There resides in me the doubt that I am entirely real. Being recognized is sometimes an unpleasant jolt, as I am convinced that I am not only utterly ineffectual, but practically invisible as well. This dichotomy of almost-being versus being is rooted in my childhood, when I believe I felt more than most children that I was the victim of arbitrary decisions, decisions contrary to my welfare. So it was natural for me to seek solace in books. It occurred to me only recently how much the refuge books offered me as a child derived from my wretchedness then. Apart from the classics, like *The Wind in the Willows* and *Alice in Wonderland*, I was spellbound by the *Narnia* series, but also by earlier children's reading such as the E. Nesbit tales in which I was completely absorbed. My life was so saturated with depression that these fictions became a vital escape from it. Of course the lack of balance or of accord with a normal boyhood that ensued from this distraction meant that I never kept up with my contemporaries in their progress to adulthood. It seemed to me that I always evolved a few steps too late to benefit from conditions for which they were already equipped. While they were daily dealing, more or less successfully, with some unavoidable fact of life, I was still hiding in my room behind *Five Children and It*.

This attachment to imagination was most obvious later, during my quests for employment, when I had almost to tear away the cobwebs of unreality before I could face up to the practical demands which would be made of me, in positions which I was ostensibly seeking. In fact, my motivation during interviews was never wholehearted and this may have been apparent to prospective employers. If I managed to get a job, my self-consciousness and general awkwardness around people prevented me from joining the crowd at work; my hopeless shyness around women prevented me from declaring my interest in them. My most familiar memories are not of joy or contentment, but of embarrassment and humiliation. I suppose I'm not a bad-looking sort of person, but I have always found my reflection to be a challenge. My body is just my shell, a carapace. It carries my mind and it often lets me down; I've already said too much about it. Some damn fool of a doctor told me just the other day that I should love my body. He was not the right person to tell me this, as he had managed to disfigure this very body through his clumsy intervention to correct a hernia, as well as being a rather impersonal little Swiss surgeon into the bargain, striving, I daresay, to fulfil some semblance of the Hippocratic Oath. Otherwise, I might have taken his advice seriously.

On reflection, how disjointed my development has been! And yet, with regard to joints, my right knee still clicks sometimes. Walking down the long, empty, carpeted corridors in Grosvenor House in 1965, Mariam found amusing the clicking sound this knee repeatedly made. So there has been some continuity in my life after all. Continuity without progress. The late or very late realization about how I ought to have reacted to certain situations or opportunities over fifty years ago still haunts me. I keep asking myself: have I caught up now? Am I now able to judge adequately what may happen to me — am I in sync with my time?

I would be glad to get a handle on whom I have become. For most people, one supposes, life is about becoming. Goals present themselves anew throughout active life. Ranging from shopping, through personal improvement, simply to staying alive, these goals provide incentive. Is it usual to lose one's goals at a certain time of life? The naiveté of youth, when all seems possible, eventually gives way to the cynicism of old age, when nothing seems worth the trouble. So, are they driven out of one by age and weakness? Take staying alive. I'm getting tired of fighting gravity. Recently, it occurred to me that I would prefer to contract some terminal disease, whereupon I could resign myself to dying within a given time, providing I could die at home — rather than to experience repeatedly an enervating new emergency which forces me to spend a few more days in hospital, as a dupe of the sick people business.

I have tried to join the world — against my deepest misgivings. I have achieved none of the things I wanted to achieve. Not to get too biblical, but I have done those things I ought not to have done, and left undone those I ought to have done. In a last reference to my mother, whose inviting suggestion it was to us on Millie's day off to finish 'left over scraps' so as not to waste food, I could conclude that this account consists of unwasted scraps, patched together from a wasted life.

* * *

A word to critics in the form of a postscript: don't bother. I sympathize with those for whom an individual is inconceivable and who must therefore strive to categorize me. I also take for granted your brief to disparage my book for a variety of reasons, not least because my attempts to tell the truth are hated by those who pay you to lie. Furthermore, if you have not experienced my privileges, as well, of course, as my privations, and the fluctuations between them, you are incapable of assessing my autobiography. That goes for most of my contemporaries. So, by all means quote a passage out of context in order to ridicule me. That's the only way you can fulfil your mission. This book stands or falls by one criterion: entertainment.

> **DISCLAIMER**
> If the publisher applauds the courage of the author in his struggle for historical truth, he does not necessarily share various other opinions expressed in this work.

January 2020
Reconquista Press
www.reconquistapress.com

www.ingramcontent.com/pod-product-compliance
Lightning Source LLC
Chambersburg PA
CBHW071221080526
44587CB00013BA/1457